SALLY'S
BAKING
101

"Everything we've come to love about Sally's baking is tucked between these covers—sharp instructions, oodles of tips, lots of smart advice, many how-tos, beautiful images, and, best of all, recipes we'll make now and always. Sally has a gift for creating recipes that bakers trust and that families and friends crave. There's so much to learn and so much to love here."

—DORIE GREENSPAN, *New York Times* bestselling author and author of *Dorie's Anytime Cakes*

"You'd be hard-pressed to find a more reliable source of baking recipes—recipes for home cooks with real kitchens—than Sally; this is the kind of cookbook we'll keep forever."

—DEB PERELMAN, *New York Times* bestselling author of *Smitten Kitchen Keepers*

"*Sally's Baking 101* is destined to be an American classic! Sally always delivers on deliciousness, and her friendly baking guidance will guarantee success. This book will be a trusted kitchen companion for all bakers, from beginners to those with a lifetime of experience."

—ZOË FRANÇOIS, *New York Times* bestselling author of *Zoë Bakes Cookies*

"Sally McKenney's new cookbook solidifies her as our undisputed queen of baking. Her expertise shines on every page. Her Chewy Chocolate Chip Cookies are so spot-on you'll never need another recipe—EVAH! At the end of the day, *Sally's Baking 101* is the baking book to end all baking books. We mere mortals are just lucky to be in Sally's presence, soaking up all the sweet wisdom she's serving."

—JOCELYN DELK ADAMS, television host and award-winning author of *Grandbaby Cakes* and *Everyday Grand*

"Sally brings her signature style to this book for recipes that are reliable, fun, and always delicious. Sally is right by your side, guiding you every step of the way. Bakers of all levels will be inspired to make everything from craveable cookies to picture-perfect cupcakes to savory crowd-pleasing snacks—and best of all, they'll have a great time doing it!"

—ERIN JEANNE McDOWELL, author of *The Book on Pie* and host of *Happy Baking*

"Perfect for every baker from beginner to experienced, *Sally's Baking 101* makes baking approachable and fun. Filled with beautiful photographs for every recipe, and detailed step-by-step instructions, you'll find yourself making these recipes on repeat!"

—HOLLY NILSSON, creator of Spend with Pennies and author of *Spend with Pennies: Everyday Comfort*

"*Sally's Baking 101* is everything you love about her blog in cookbook form—an essential for any home baker. Every recipe I tried was a hit, easy to follow, and turned out perfectly thanks to her step-by-step guidance. From Maple Brown Sugar Cookies to Sky-High Chocolate Mousse Pie, the hardest part is choosing what to bake first! With stunning photos and foolproof recipes, this book will be a staple in my kitchen. Sally is a legend, and this book proves why."

—MATTHEW JAMES DUFFY, baking professor and chef, creator of Sourdough Duffy, and author of *Bread Etc.*

"Everybody knows that if you want a baking recipe that turns out right, accompanied with beautiful pictures, Sally's Baking Addiction is the place to go. And now she's pulled all the most important information out for us and put it in her beautiful new book! I have no doubt *Sally's Baking 101* is going to become the ultimate baking resource in households all around the world, including mine."

—NAGI MAEHASHI, cookbook author and creator of RecipeTin Eats

"*Sally's Baking 101* will quickly become your favorite cookbook! Sally's meticulously tested recipes, thoughtful instructions, and expert advice will eliminate any baking anxiety to practically guarantee perfect results from your home kitchen. The mouthwatering photos are just the icing on top. I've dog-eared nearly every recipe!"

—TESSA ARIAS, cookbook author and creator of Handle the Heat

SALLY'S BAKING 101

FOOLPROOF RECIPES FROM EASY TO ADVANCED

SALLY McKENNEY

Recipes co-written with Beth Walk

Photographs by Sally McKenney

Clarkson Potter/Publishers

NEW YORK

To my encouraging and endlessly
supportive husband, Kevin.
And to our children, who fill my heart
more than baking ever could.

Contents

Introduction

"Mommy, do you have a taste test?" my daughters would ask with bright, hopeful eyes every afternoon when they got home from school.

For the past three years I've been working on this book, the answer was usually yes. If something looked good to them, they were thrilled to try a bite of my latest creation.

Though my recipe development career has spanned more than a decade, I've never had the volume of kitchen work that this cookbook demanded. And while it was at times overwhelming . . .

. . . like when my oven broke right before a deadline and I had to bake pies at my neighbors' house and then—extremely carefully—carry them back home to photograph them (thanks, Mel & Tom!) . . .

. . . or when I spilled cake batter on my keyboard and my computer began typing random cAPiTaL LeTTeRs in my manuscript . . .

. . . it was mostly exciting, as I welcome creative challenges with open (and flour-speckled) arms!

My name is Sally, and back in 2011, I decided to share a baking recipe online. When I was growing up watching my grandmother and mother in the kitchen, I learned firsthand the power of from-scratch baking. They taught me that there's comfort in the kitchen, and when life gets loud, hectic, or confusing, just pull out the flour and bake something that brings you joy. When I was on my own in my mid-twenties and uncertain that my office job in finance was the right path for me, I turned to the kitchen. I opened a blog account, took a photo of peanut butter blondies with my iPhone, typed how to make them, and pressed the publish button without much thought. And certainly no idea that the recipe would eventually be seen by millions of people!

That was the stepping stone to the—rather untraditional—career I have today. Four readers (my parents and siblings!) turned into hundreds, then thousands, and now, millions. I've upgraded my blog to a professional website, fine-tuned my recipe writing, and massively improved both my photography and baking skills after developing and shooting thousands of recipes for my site and three previous books. I now have a wonderfully talented and dedicated team that helps me operate my business and test recipes. I didn't know it on that December day nearly fourteen years ago, but I was on my way to building a business from scratch.

My recipes are approachable for everyone, because I focus on the fundamentals and take the time to explain how and why the recipes work. Baking is a science, and I understand the importance of publishing a recipe that's not only well tested but written with attention to detail. I take that responsibility seriously, even if it takes me ten tries to get the perfect Strawberry Cake (page 89), so that it will take you only one!

For this cookbook, I mixed dozens of either sweet or savory new baking recipes with a sprinkle of beloved classics from my website. You'll see the latter labeled as Fan Favorites because they each have hundreds of positive reviews.

I rate all of the recipes by skill level, so you know what to expect before starting:

Beginner: Recipes that have simple steps and require minimal technique.

Intermediate: Recipes that need more precision and/or specialty baking tools.

Advanced: Recipes that use more advanced techniques and tools, and make for an exciting yet challenging baking project.

Regardless of your skill level, I encourage you to read through the Baking Basics in the beginning of this book. I cover some key principles and tips, and recommend essential ingredients and tools for stocking your home kitchen. The extra few minutes you spend reading this section will set you up for success and help you feel confident before you begin.

This book asks you to spend time in the kitchen, and I want it to be fun and fulfilling—either quality "me time" or time spent with your loved ones. Baking isn't just a means to an end, it's a rewarding journey. And a fresh batch of cookies is a welcome bonus! I hope the recipes on these pages earn a permanent spot in your baking repertoire, and become part of your family's traditions, celebrations, and memories . . . just as they have for me. Remember to enjoy the process . . . and the taste test!

Sally

Baking Basics

Principles

Be Prepared

THIS IS KEY: Read through the recipe completely before you begin, and measure out any ingredients that are needed right away. Starting the baking process this way leaves very little room for error.

Know How to Measure Ingredients

The difference between a recipe's success and failure could be the way you measure your ingredients. Use a food scale if you have one. Metric weights are most accurate. Cup measurements are standard where I live, so that is why I test and write my recipes in both cup and metric measurements.

Flour and Other Dry Ingredients: Flour is the most commonly mismeasured ingredient. Whether you're using bread flour, cake flour, all-purpose flour, or any other type of flour, if you're not weighing the

ingredients, then use the "spoon and level" method. Spoon the flour into the measuring cup, letting it pile high. Do not pack the flour down or tap the measuring cup, as either will cause the flour to settle in the cup. After you've spooned the flour into the cup, use the top edge of a knife blade to level off the top. And never use the measuring cup to scoop the flour out of the container, since that compacts the flour and you will end up with more than you need (and a rather dry baked good). Same goes for sugar and powdered sugar, cocoa powder, and other dry ingredients.

Brown Sugar: This is the exception to the previous rule. Unless otherwise noted, brown sugar should be packed into the measuring cup.

Liquids: Liquids such as milk, water, and oil should be measured at eye level in clear liquid measuring cups.

Semi-liquids: This means ingredients such as sour cream, yogurt, peanut butter, applesauce, and mashed banana. Spoon and level these into dry measuring cups, or weigh them on a food scale. They are too thick to be accurately measured in liquid measuring cups.

Butter: Butter in the United States typically is sold in sticks, with measurement lines on the wrapper marking 8 tablespoon portions. This makes measuring very convenient—simply slice off however much you need for a recipe. If your butter isn't in tablespoon-marked stick form, weigh it. If a recipe calls for melted butter, measure the butter in its solid state, then melt it.

Room-Temperature Ingredients

Baking recipes often call for room-temperature eggs or dairy ingredients such as milk or yogurt. There's a reason for this: Room-temperature ingredients emulsify quicker and easier, reducing the risk of overmixing, which could ruin a baked good's texture. For eggs, you can either leave them on the counter for an hour, or place cold eggs in a bowl of lukewarm water for 10 to 15 minutes. For other cold ingredients such as sour cream or milk, microwave them in 10-second increments, stirring after each, to bring up to room temperature.

Prep the Butter

The temperature of butter can dramatically affect the texture of baked goods, so it's important to have it ready exactly as the recipe states.

Room-temperature butter is about 65°F (18°C). It's cool to the touch. Your finger should make an indent without sinking down into the butter. The butter should not be shiny or greasy. To get that perfect temperature, take the butter out of the refrigerator 1 to 2 hours before you need to use it in your recipe.

Cold butter is butter that has been well chilled in the refrigerator so that it does not melt during mixing. This helps create flaky layers in such recipes as pie crust, biscuits, and scones.

Melted butter should be liquefied and slightly cooled to lukewarm. If melted butter is too hot, it can begin cooking the eggs in your batter. Melted butter can also be browned (see Tips & Tricks/Browning Butter, page 20).

Know Your Oven

All ovens are different (and even temperamental!), so the better you know yours, the more prepared you'll be.

Understand the type of oven: The recipes in this book (and on my website) have all been developed with and for conventional ovens. If you use a convection oven, reduce the oven temperature by 25°F; you may need to reduce the baking time as well.

Use an oven thermometer: Unless you regularly calibrate your oven, when you set your oven to 350°F (177°C), it might not really be 350°F (177°C) inside. To avoid a potential baking disaster, use an oven thermometer. Place it in the center of your oven and adjust the temperature on the oven's knob or digital panel controller so the thermometer reads the intended temperature.

Adjust the oven racks and baking pans: Unless otherwise indicated, the recipes in this book should be baked on the center rack. If you're baking two batches of cookies (or muffins, etc.) at once, bake them on the center and lower oven racks, and switch the pans' positions halfway through baking.

Use the oven light to check on your baked goods halfway through the baking time. If baked goods are browning on one side more than the other, rotate the pans 180 degrees. If baked goods are browning too quickly on top, tent a piece of aluminum foil over them.

Just keep it shut: Your oven, that is! It's very tempting to open the oven door to peek at your cake, but doing so interrupts the baking process. Instead, use the oven light. And when you're testing the doneness of a baked good with a toothpick, do so quickly and immediately shut the oven door if it needs more time.

Don't Double

In most cases, I don't recommend doubling baking recipes. When the quantity of batter or dough increases, so does the risk of under- or overmixing, resulting in a dense cake, unevenly textured bread, or overspread cookies. Also, some ingredients, particularly baking soda, baking powder, and yeast, shouldn't be doubled exactly; you typically need a bit less. Because baking is so dependent on precision, I find that it's best to make two separate batches of the recipe as written.

Ingredients

Flour

The type of flour specified depends on what you're baking. The protein content of flour, a function of the variety of wheat from which it is milled, affects its gluten-forming potential and hence the structure of the finished product. To ensure success, use the type of flour that a recipe calls for, and always choose unbleached when you can. I have not tested the recipes in this book with gluten-free flour alternatives.

All-purpose: This type of flour has a middle-of-the-road protein content, so it's perfect for just about any baked good.

Bread: Bread flour has a higher protein content than all-purpose flour, which means it can develop more gluten. This is desirable in many yeasted bread recipes, contributing to a stronger, more well-developed structure and chewier texture.

Cake: Cake flour has a lower protein content than all-purpose flour, which means there is less gluten formation, resulting in a softer, fluffier texture. I use it in many cake and cupcake recipes.

Whole-wheat: All-purpose flour is ground from only part of the wheat kernel while whole-wheat flour uses the entire kernel, including the bran and germ. Like bread flour, its protein content is high although the bran and germ inhibit gluten formation, which can make baked goods dense. I use it when I'm looking for a heartier texture.

Butter

Butter is commonly used in baking because of its unmatched flavor and the texture it provides. But not all butter is the same: American-style butter has 80% butterfat content, while most European-style butter is 82% or higher. Regardless of which style you choose, use unsalted butter, as the amount of salt added to salted butter can vary by brand. And with unsalted butter, you can more accurately regulate the amount of salt in the recipe.

Sugar

Sugar does so much more than sweeten; it serves an important function in creaming butter, plus it locks in moisture, aerates batters, tenderizes doughs, and caramelizes, allowing baked goods to develop a deeper color and more complex flavor. When you see "sugar" in this book, it refers to white granulated sugar, unless specified as one of these:

Brown Sugar: This is granulated sugar that contains molasses. In this book, when "brown sugar" is called for, you can use either light or dark brown sugar, unless specified. Dark brown sugar contains slightly more molasses, but in most cases, it makes little difference in the final baked good.

Powdered Sugar: Also known as confectioners' sugar, icing sugar, or 10x sugar, this is finely ground sugar and, depending on the manufacturer, it can contain a starch to prevent clumping. Still, it can be lumpy, so when this could affect the result, my recipes will instruct that it be sifted.

Coarse Sugar: This is sugar that isn't cut as fine as granulated sugar and adds wonderful crunch and sparkle when used as a topping on baked goods. You can use a brand such as Sugar in the Raw or something called "white sanding/sparkling sugar," found in the baking aisle with the sprinkles.

Eggs

Be sure to use large eggs in the recipes in this book. Substituting other sizes can throw off the intended result.

Salt

Salt is a crucial flavor enhancer and is used in pretty much every recipe in this book. Unless otherwise indicated, "salt" in this book means table salt. On occasion, you'll see flaky sea salt as a garnish on top of baked goods. This not only adds flavor but also a slight crunch.

Cream Cheese

For all the cream cheese in this book, use full-fat blocks or bricks, not the spreadable kind in the tub. Unless, of course, you are topping your bagels (see Hot 'n' Fresh Bagels, page 193)!

Sour Cream

Full-fat sour cream adds unparalleled moisture and richness plus a very slight tang to otherwise sweet

baked goods. It's also an acidic ingredient that reacts with baking soda to aid in leavening. In some cases, you can substitute plain 2% Greek yogurt.

Milk
Unless whole milk is specified, you can use any kind of milk, dairy or nondairy. Avoid using nonfat milk.

Buttermilk
Buttermilk, like sour cream, aids in leavening and adds pleasant tangy flavor and lots of delicious moisture. You can use either whole or low-fat buttermilk in these recipes. If you don't have it on hand, you can make a reasonable substitute (see below). However, if a recipe calls for more than 1 cup (240g/ml) of buttermilk, use the real thing, otherwise you will sacrifice flavor and texture.

> **DIY Buttermilk:** For 1 cup (240g/ml) buttermilk, add 2 teaspoons white vinegar or lemon juice to a liquid measuring cup and add enough whole milk to reach 1 cup (240g/ml). Stir and let it sit for 5 minutes before using.

Leavening Agents
Baking powder and baking soda are chemical leaveners, but they react differently depending on the acidity in a recipe and therefore are not interchangeable. Yeast is a biological leavener; it's a living organism that feeds on sugars and starches in dough. The recipes in this book use dry yeast (as opposed to fresh cake yeast). There are two basic types: active dry yeast and instant yeast. Unless specifically indicated, they are interchangeable with no other differences in the recipe except the rise time, which is shorter with instant yeast. To learn more about working with yeast, see Baking with Yeast Cheat Sheet, page 242.

Unsweetened Cocoa Powder
There are two basic types of cocoa: natural and Dutch-process. Natural has a more bitter and naturally acidic flavor profile. Because of its acidity, it is often used in recipes leavened by baking soda. Dutch-process is darker in color and has a much deeper chocolate flavor without the acidity, and is often used in recipes without chemical leavening or with baking powder. Because of their different roles in leavening, the two types of cocoa are not always interchangeable.

Chocolate
For recipes in this book (and on my website) that call for chocolate, use chocolate sold in bars or blocks. Baker's and Ghirardelli are my top choices because they are widely available and usually a good price for their quality. Both brands are sold in 4-ounce (113g) bars in the baking aisle. Unless a recipe specifically calls for chocolate chips, avoid using them as a substitute for chopped chocolate bars.

Vanilla
Though used in small quantities, vanilla extract is the unmistakable kiss of flavor in most baked goods, including "non-vanilla" recipes such as chocolate. For the best possible flavor, use pure vanilla, not imitation. Vanilla bean paste is a syrupy, slightly sweet flavor enhancer that combines both vanilla extract and vanilla bean seeds. Because vanilla is used in small quantities, you can usually substitute one type for the other. If a recipe calls for a vanilla bean, purchase soft, plump vanilla beans. To remove the seeds, use a small, sharp knife to slit open the pod from tip to tip, then scrape out the seeds with the dull side of the knife.

Tools

With a solid recipe and the proper ingredients, you're on track for baking success. The final step is to stock your kitchen with the right baking tools. These are my recommendations for essential equipment; select a few recipes and begin slowly building your supplies stock.

Pans

Bundt pan (10- to 12-cup capacity)

Cast-iron skillet (10-inch)

Glass pie dish (9-inch), at least 1½ to 2 inches deep

Half sheet pans (13 × 18-inch), also known as baking sheets, the term used throughout the book, at least 2

Large roasting pan (for cheesecake water baths)

Loaf pan (9 × 5-inch)

Metal baking pan (9 × 13-inch)

Metal baking pan (9-inch square)

Round cake pan (8-inch), 2 or 3

Round cake pan (9-inch), 2 or 3

Springform pan (9-inch)

Standard 12-cup muffin pan, 2

Tart pan (9-inch), with removable bottom

Measuring & Mixing

Dry measuring cup set

Food scale

Large mixing bowl with pour spout

Liquid measuring cups (assorted sizes, preferably heat-safe glass)

Measuring spoon set

Measuring tape

Mixing bowls (assorted sizes, preferably heat-safe glass)

Appliances

Food processor

Hand mixer

Stand mixer (with paddle, whisk, and dough hook)

Hand Tools

Bench scraper

Box grater

Citrus juicer

Citrus zester

Cookie scoops (small, medium, and large)

Egg separator

Fine-mesh sieve

Instant-read thermometer

Pastry bags and piping tips (the Wilton #1M open star tip is a great choice)

Pastry blender

Pastry brush

Pizza cutter or pastry wheel

Rolling pin

Silicone spatulas, 2 or 3

Silicone whisk

Small icing spatulas (1 straight, 1 offset)

Sturdy wire whisk

For Baking

Cooling racks, 2

Oven thermometer

Parchment paper

Silicone baking mats, 1 or 2

Helpful Extras

10 × 15-inch baking pan: This is a great size for cake rolls, including Tiramisu Cake Roll (page 105).

Ceramic pie weights: Needed for blind-baking pie crust, but if you don't have them, use dried beans instead. One pound is enough for one 9-inch pie.

Donut baking pan: For baked donuts, including Baked Chocolate Cake Donuts (page 205).

12-inch pizza pan: If you don't have one, you can bake pizzas on a half sheet pan.

8-ounce ramekins: A nice size to have for prepping ingredients and for baking individual items such as Maple Brown Sugar Oatmeal Brûlée (page 197).

Tips & Tricks

Testing Baked Goods for Doneness

Your eyes, and not the oven timer, are the best tools for determining when a baked good is done. The following three indicators are helpful for cakes, muffins, cupcakes, and quick breads. For other baked goods, use the indicators described in the recipe.

1. The visual test: The top should appear set and slightly domed, and the edges should be very slightly pulling away from the sides of the pan.

2. The bounce-back test: Using your finger, gently press down on the top of the baked good (careful, it's hot!). If it bounces back completely, it's done. If your finger left an indentation, the baked good needs more time.

3. The toothpick test: Insert a toothpick in the center of the baked good. The toothpick should come out clean, or with just a few moist crumbs. If there's wet batter on it, the baked good needs more time.

Using a Double Boiler
(and What to Do if You Don't Have One)

A double boiler is a two-piece pot that uses steam from simmering water to gently heat food. It's especially useful for melting chocolate and keeping it fluid. It's also handy for gently cooking eggs, a step in Sky-High Chocolate Mousse Pie (page 153) and Swiss Meringue Buttercream (page 107). To use, bring 1 to 2 inches of water in the lower pot to a simmer. Set the upper pot over the simmering water and add the ingredients to it. The steam will indirectly heat the food. If you don't have a double boiler, use a regular small pot for the water and a heat-safe bowl for the top. Make sure the bowl you choose sits comfortably over the pot and that it doesn't touch the simmering water below.

Melting Chocolate

You can use a double boiler (either method), following the directions above, and place the chopped chocolate in the upper pot, over the simmering water. Stir the chocolate constantly until melted and smooth. Or you can use a microwave: Place the chocolate in a microwave-safe bowl and cook at 50% power in 20-second increments, stirring well after each, until melted and smooth.

Browning Butter

Brown butter is melted butter with an enhanced flavor brought on by gently cooking until the milk solids caramelize.

1. Cut the butter into small pieces and place it in a light-colored skillet or saucepan over medium heat. Why light-colored? It helps you see when the butter has browned. (If you only have dark cookware, in step 2, spoon some butter into a glass bowl to check if it has browned.)

2. Stir or whisk the butter constantly as it melts. After 5 to 8 minutes, the butter will begin browning. Lightly browned specks will begin to form at the bottom of the pan, and the butter will have a nutty aroma. Once browned, immediately remove from heat and pour it into a heat-safe glass bowl or liquid measuring cup, including all the browned solids at the bottom of the pan. (They're where most of the flavor comes from!)

3. Use as indicated in the recipe.

Toasting Nuts

If you have the time, toasting nuts before adding to a dough or batter enhances their flavor. Spread the nuts on a lined baking sheet and bake in a 300°F (149°C) oven for 6 to 8 minutes or until fragrant. Give the pan a shake halfway through for even browning. Cool completely before using.

Sifting Ingredients

Sifting an ingredient with a fine-mesh sieve or a sifter aerates it and rids any lumps. It is important, however, to note where the word "sifted" appears in the ingredients list: If a recipe calls for "1 cup flour, sifted," measure the flour first, and then sift it. If a recipe calls for "1 cup sifted flour," sift the flour *first* and then measure it.

Creaming Butter and Sugar

In many baking recipes, butter is called for at room temperature and is then beaten with sugar in a process called "creaming." When thoroughly creamed, the butter traps air. While your batter or dough bakes, that trapped air expands from the oven's heat and encourages your baked good to rise, resulting in a soft, fluffy baked good.

What Is an Egg Wash?

An egg wash is a simple mixture of an egg combined with milk or water that's applied to certain doughs and pastries with a pastry brush. It can help a topping or filling stick, such as the oats on Oatmeal Wheat Sandwich Bread (page 263) or the filling in Cinnamon Raisin Swirl Bread (page 267). And it is commonly used for aesthetic purposes, giving your dough a beautiful golden sheen. Sometimes I skip the egg yolk and use only the egg white, which gives baked goods more of a clear sheen instead of golden.

Freezing Baked Goods

Cool baked goods completely before wrapping and freezing. Most baked goods can be frozen for up to 3 months, unless otherwise noted. I recommend labeling them with a use-by date.

Breads, Quick Breads, and Loaf Cakes
Wrap tightly in plastic wrap, followed by a layer of foil. Thaw the wrapped loaf at room temperature or in the refrigerator and bring to room temperature before serving.

Individual Rolls, Biscuits, Scones, and Bagels
Place in a freezer-safe container or bag, with parchment paper between layers. Thaw at room temperature, then warm in the oven or microwave, if desired. (Or use the toaster for bagels.)

Cookies, Brownies, and Bars
Place cookies, brownies, or bars in a freezer-safe container or bag, with parchment paper between layers. If they are iced or topped with chocolate, wait for the topping to set before freezing. Thaw in the refrigerator, then bring to room temperature before serving, if desired.

Cakes
For best taste and texture, freeze cakes before frosting. Wrap the cake tightly in plastic wrap. Place the wrapped cake(s) in a freezer-safe container or wrap again with a layer of foil. To thaw, transfer the wrapped cakes to the refrigerator one day before decorating/serving.

Cheesecakes
Cool the cheesecake completely at room temperature before freezing. Remove the outer rim from the springform pan, leaving the cheesecake on the base. Cover it tightly with a layer of plastic wrap, followed by a layer of foil. Thaw in the refrigerator for at least 12 hours before serving. If you do not want to freeze the springform pan base, after the cheesecake has completely cooled, run a sharp knife underneath the crust to release it from the bottom of the pan. Carefully slide it onto a parchment paper–lined piece of cardboard or plate, then wrap and freeze as directed.

Cupcakes and Muffins
Freeze cupcakes without any frosting or icing. In groups of 2 or 4, wrap the cupcakes or muffins in plastic wrap and place the wrapped sets in a freezer-safe container or bag. Thaw in the refrigerator, then bring to room temperature before frosting and serving.

Pie and Pastry Dough
Wrap discs of pie dough or squares of folded puff pastry dough tightly in plastic wrap. Place the wrapped dough in a freezer-safe container or wrap again with a layer of foil. Thaw the wrapped dough in the refrigerator before rolling it out.

Pies, Quiches, Crisps, Crumbles, and Cobblers
Cover tightly with a layer of plastic wrap, followed by a layer of foil. Thaw covered pie in the refrigerator, then bring to room temperature before serving, if desired. Thaw covered quiches, crisps, crumbles, and cobblers in the refrigerator, then remove the plastic wrap and reheat, covered with foil, in a 350°F (177°C) oven for 20 to 30 minutes or until warmed through.

Cookies

Chewy Chocolate Chip Cookies

MAKES 22 TO 24 COOKIES

SKILL LEVEL: **Beginner**

PREP: **15 minutes**

BAKE: **13 to 14 minutes per batch**

TOTAL: **2 hours 45 minutes, including chilling**

Like a beloved book you read again and again, chocolate chip cookies are a comforting classic, as familiar as those dog-eared pages. I've been perfecting my recipe since 2013, and what you see here is a tried-and-true favorite, boasting a soft center, slightly crisp edges, and a buttery caramelized flavor throughout. Readers LOVE this recipe too, and I've heard about these cookies winning first prize at county fairs and selling out at bake sales. The dough is made from standard ingredients like flour, salt, sugar, butter, and eggs . . . it's the ratios and temperatures of those ingredients that make this recipe stand out from the rest. Using melted butter, an extra egg yolk, and more brown sugar than white sugar promises maximum chewiness, while a touch of cornstarch adds softness. Go ahead and dog-ear this page now!

2¼ cups all-purpose flour **(281g)**

1½ teaspoons cornstarch

1 teaspoon baking soda

½ teaspoon salt

12 tablespoons unsalted butter, melted and cooled for 5 minutes **(170g)**

¾ cup brown sugar **(150g)**

½ cup granulated sugar **(100g)**

1 large egg, at room temperature

1 large egg yolk, at room temperature

2 teaspoons vanilla extract

1¼ cups semi-sweet chocolate chips, plus more as needed **(225g)**

1. In a large bowl, whisk the flour, cornstarch, baking soda, and salt.

2. In a medium bowl, whisk the melted butter, brown sugar, and granulated sugar until no lumps remain. Whisk in the egg and egg yolk until combined, then whisk in the vanilla. The mixture should be thin. Pour the butter mixture into the flour mixture and mix with a large spoon or spatula. The dough should be soft, thick, and shiny. Fold in the chocolate chips. The chocolate chips may not stick to the dough because of the melted butter, but do your best to combine them.

3. Cover the dough tightly and refrigerate it for at least 2 hours or up to 3 days.

4. Preheat the oven to 325°F (163°C). Line baking sheets with parchment paper or silicone baking mats. If the dough has chilled for longer than 2 hours, let it sit at room temperature for about 15 minutes.

5. Scoop and roll the chilled cookie dough into balls, about 2 tablespoons (45g) each. Make sure the shape is taller than it is wide—almost like a cylinder (1). This helps the cookies bake up thicker. Arrange the cookies 3 inches apart on the prepared baking sheets (2).

6. Bake for 13 to 14 minutes or until the edges of the cookies are very lightly browned and set. The centers look very soft, but the cookies continue to set as they cool.

7. Cool the cookies on the baking sheet for 10 minutes before transferring to a cooling rack to cool completely. While the cookies are still warm, I like to press a few more chocolate chips into the tops—this is only for looks! Store covered tightly at room temperature for up to 1 week.

TIP: It may seem counterintuitive, but the lumpier and more misshapen the dough balls, the prettier the chocolate chip cookies! For beautiful, thick cookies, shape the cookie dough into tall, lumpy cylinders instead of perfectly rounded balls.

Tips for Success

COOKIE PERFECTION

- **Never skip the chilling step:** Chilling cookie dough in the refrigerator firms it, reducing cookie spread in the oven while also enhancing flavor.
- **Cool the baking sheets:** When baking in batches, let the baking sheets cool to room temperature between batches. Never place cookie dough on a hot baking sheet.
- **My secret to storing:** To keep cookies extra soft, store them in an airtight container with a slice of bread. The cookies absorb the bread's moisture, leaving the bread hard and the cookies extra soft.

TROUBLESHOOTING

- **If cookies are overspreading:** Remove the baking sheet from the oven and use a spoon to gently push the edges back toward the center of the cookie. Return to the oven, repeating the spoon trick if needed when the cookies are done.
- **If cookies aren't spreading at all:** When cookies aren't spreading, it's usually one of two things. There could be too much flour soaking up all the liquid. (Make sure you know how to properly measure; see Baking Basics: Principles, page 13). Or it could be because the dough is very cold. If you're in the middle of baking a batch and the cookies aren't spreading, remove the baking sheet from the oven and bang it on the counter two or three times to initiate spreading and return it to the oven. If you still have more dough to bake, microwave it at 50% power for 10 to 15 seconds to slightly warm it up before scooping/rolling/baking.

Crumb Cake Cookies

MAKES 24 COOKIES

When I started working on this cookbook, I had dreams of a soft and chewy cinnamon crumb–topped cookie (you dream about cookies too, right?). After at least six batches of test recipes going out to neighbors, friends, and mail carriers (yes!), I landed on a true winner. These have the exact flavor of crumb cake, with the soft, chewy center of a chocolate chip cookie. To get the perfect crumb-to-cookie ratio, use your fingers to pinch and press the dough ball until it resembles a shallow bowl, then use the dough "bowl" to scoop up the crumbly streusel. Vanilla icing is the *chef's kiss* on a cookie that could *almost* pass as a breakfast treat.

SKILL LEVEL: **Beginner**

PREP: **30 minutes**

BAKE: **12 to 14 minutes per batch**

TOTAL: **3 hours, including chilling**

Crumb Topping

½ cup all-purpose flour **(63g)**

⅓ cup brown sugar **(67g)**

1½ teaspoons ground cinnamon

4 tablespoons unsalted butter, at room temperature **(56g)**

Cookies

2¼ cups all-purpose flour **(281g)**

1 teaspoon cornstarch

1 teaspoon baking powder

½ teaspoon salt

¼ teaspoon baking soda

12 tablespoons unsalted butter, at room temperature **(170g)**

½ cup brown sugar **(100g)**

½ cup granulated sugar **(100g)**

1 large egg, at room temperature

1 large egg yolk, at room temperature

2 teaspoons vanilla extract

Icing

¾ cup powdered sugar, sifted **(90g)**

1 to 2 tablespoons milk

¼ teaspoon vanilla extract

1. Make the crumb topping: In a small bowl, whisk the flour, brown sugar, and cinnamon. Using a fork or a handheld mixer on low speed, mix in the butter until crumbly. Refrigerate the topping until the cookies are shaped.

2. Make the cookies: In a medium bowl, whisk the flour, cornstarch, baking powder, salt, and baking soda.

3. In a large bowl using a handheld or stand mixer fitted with the paddle, beat the butter, brown sugar, and granulated sugar on medium-high speed until the mixture is light and creamy, about 3 minutes. Add the egg, egg yolk, and vanilla and beat on high speed until combined, about 1 minute. Scrape down the sides of the bowl as needed. Add the flour mixture and beat on low speed until combined.

4. Cover the dough tightly and refrigerate it for at least 2 hours or up to 3 days.

5. Preheat the oven to 350°F (177°C). Line baking sheets with parchment paper or silicone baking mats. If the dough has chilled for longer than 2 hours, let it sit at room temperature for about 30 minutes.

6. Scoop and roll the chilled cookie dough into balls, about a scant 1½ tablespoons (30g) each. Using your fingers and thumbs, pinch and press a large indent in the center of the dough ball until it resembles a shallow bowl (1). Use the "bowl" of dough to scoop a generous amount of cold crumb topping to fill the cookie (2). Arrange them 3 inches apart on the prepared baking sheets (3).

7. Bake for 12 to 14 minutes or until the edges of the cookies are very lightly browned and set. Cool the cookies on the baking sheet for 10 minutes before transferring to a cooling rack to cool completely before icing.

8. Make the icing: In a small bowl, whisk the powdered sugar, 1 tablespoon milk, and vanilla. Add another tablespoon of milk to thin it out, if desired. Drizzle over the cooled cookies. The icing will set after about 2 hours. Store covered tightly at room temperature for up to 2 days or in the refrigerator for up to 1 week.

Strawberry Lemon Drops

MAKES 30 COOKIES

SKILL LEVEL: **Beginner**

PREP: **25 minutes**

BAKE: **15 minutes per batch**

TOTAL: **1 hour 10 minutes, including chilling**

These crumbly, melt-in-your-mouth cookies are similar to snowball cookies, which are also known as Russian tea cakes or Mexican wedding cookies. Freeze-dried strawberries are a must. Not only do they add pretty pink color to the coating, they also infuse concentrated flavor into the dough. Bonus: Only 30 minutes of dough chilling is required, so you'll be enjoying these little drops of sunshine in no time.

1 cup freeze-dried strawberries **(25g)**

16 tablespoons unsalted butter, at room temperature **(226g)**

1¼ cups powdered sugar, divided **(150g)**

1 teaspoon lemon zest

1½ tablespoons fresh lemon juice

1 teaspoon vanilla extract

2¼ cups all-purpose flour **(281g)**

¼ teaspoon salt

TIP: Freeze-dried strawberries, flash-frozen to remove all the moisture, are widely available in most grocery stores and online. Do not use "dried strawberries," which are chewy like raisins or dried apricots; they will not grind into a powder.

1. In a blender or food processor, process the freeze-dried strawberries into a fine powder. Measure ¼ cup (14g) of the powder for the dough and reserve the rest for the coating.

2. In a large bowl using a handheld or stand mixer fitted with the paddle, beat the butter for 1 minute on medium speed until smooth. Add ¾ cup (90g) of the powdered sugar and beat on low speed until incorporated, then increase the speed to medium-high and beat until the mixture is light and creamy, about 2 minutes. Scrape down the sides of the bowl as needed.

3. Add the lemon zest, lemon juice, and vanilla and beat on medium-high speed until combined. Add the flour, salt, and ¼ cup (14g) strawberry powder and mix on low speed until incorporated, then increase the speed to high and beat until fully combined.

4. Cover the dough tightly and refrigerate it for at least 30 minutes or up to 3 days.

5. Preheat the oven to 350°F (177°C). Line baking sheets with parchment paper or silicone baking mats. If the dough has chilled for longer than 2 hours, let it sit at room temperature for about 30 minutes before rolling.

6. Scoop and roll the cookie dough into balls, about 1 tablespoon (20g) each, and arrange them 2 inches apart on the prepared baking sheets.

7. Bake for 14 to 15 minutes or until the edges of the cookies are very lightly browned. Cool the cookies on the baking sheet for 5 minutes before coating.

8. In a shallow bowl, whisk the remaining ½ cup (60g) powdered sugar and the remaining strawberry powder. After the cookies have cooled for 5 minutes, very gently roll them in the strawberry sugar to coat. Place the cookies on cooling racks to cool completely. The coating will melt a bit and become sticky; that's okay.

9. Once the cookies have cooled, roll them in the strawberry sugar again. This is when the coating will really stick. If you have extra strawberry powder, you can sprinkle a little on top of the cookies after coating. Store covered tightly at room temperature for up to 1 week.

Soft Sugar Cookies

MAKES 24 (3- TO 4-INCH) COOKIES

This is my flagship recipe for cut-out sugar cookies. I've been baking them this exact way for over a decade, and many other bakers have been, too, as it's consistently the most popular cookie recipe on my website! With their characteristic flavors of vanilla and almond extracts, they feature thick, soft-baked centers *and* maintain their cookie cutter shapes in the oven. When baked, they have a flat, even surface so they're the perfect blank canvas for royal icing. Of course, if you don't want to dabble with royal icing, these cookies taste just as special with vanilla buttercream (see Soft & Moist White Vanilla Cake, page 84).

SKILL LEVEL: **Beginner**

PREP: **40 minutes**

BAKE: **11 to 12 minutes per batch**

TOTAL: **3 hours, including chilling**

2¼ cups all-purpose flour, plus more as needed **(281g)**

½ teaspoon baking powder

¼ teaspoon salt

12 tablespoons unsalted butter, at room temperature **(170g)**

¾ cup granulated sugar **(150g)**

1 large egg, at room temperature

2 teaspoons vanilla extract

¼ teaspoon almond extract (optional)

Tips for Success

SUGAR COOKIES

- The dough needs to be refrigerated so the cookies hold their shape in the oven, but it's imperative to roll it out *before* chilling it, because it's nearly impossible to roll out *after*.
- Rolling the dough on a silicone baking mat or parchment paper makes it easy to transfer the rolled-out dough to the refrigerator.

1. In a medium bowl, whisk the flour, baking powder, and salt.

2. In a large bowl using a handheld or stand mixer fitted with the paddle, beat the butter and sugar on high speed until the mixture is light and creamy, about 3 minutes. Add the egg, vanilla, and almond extract (if using) and beat on high speed until combined, about 1 minute. Scrape down the sides of the bowl as needed. Add the flour mixture and mix on low speed until combined. The dough should be soft. If it seems too soft and sticky for rolling, beat in 1 tablespoon more flour.

3. Divide the dough in half (1) and place each on a piece of lightly floured parchment paper or a lightly floured silicone baking mat. With a lightly floured rolling pin, roll the dough to about ¼-inch thickness (2). Use a bit more flour if the dough seems too sticky. The rolled-out dough can be any shape as long as it's ¼ inch thick.

4. Lightly flour one of the rolled-out dough portions. Place the second rolled-out dough portion, still on the parchment paper, on top of the first. (The stacking is more efficient for refrigerator storage.) Cover the dough tightly and refrigerate it for at least 2 hours or up to 2 days.

5. Preheat the oven to 350°F (177°C). Line baking sheets with parchment paper or silicone baking mats.

6. Remove the top piece of dough from the refrigerator. Using a cookie cutter, cut the dough into shapes (3). Gather the scraps, reroll, and continue cutting until all the dough is used. Repeat with the second piece of dough. Arrange the cookies 3 inches apart on the prepared baking sheets (4).

7. Bake for 11 to 12 minutes or until the edges of the cookies are very lightly browned and set. Let cool on the baking sheet for 5 minutes before transferring to a cooling rack to cool completely before decorating (5). Store iced or un-iced cookies covered tightly at room temperature for up to 5 days.

Royal Icing

MAKES 3 CUPS

SKILL LEVEL: **Intermediate**

PREP: **5 minutes**

TOTAL: **2 hours 5 minutes, including 2 hours for drying**

Royal icing is my top choice for decorating sugar cookies because it pipes easily and dries more quickly than other decorative icings. While many recipes call for raw egg whites, I prefer meringue powder. It contains pasteurized, dried egg whites that eliminate the need for raw eggs but still provide the same consistency and matte finish. Royal icing has a reputation for drying into a hard-as-cement texture, but my recipe dries enough to easily stack your decorated cookies but not so much that it will break your teeth! Use this recipe for both outlining the tops of the cookies and filling in the outline (a.k.a. flooding).

4 cups powdered sugar, sifted, plus more as needed (**480g**)

3 tablespoons meringue powder

9 tablespoons water, plus more as needed, at room temperature

1 teaspoon vanilla extract or 1/2 teaspoon of your favorite flavored extract, such as lemon, coconut, or peppermint (optional)

Gel food coloring (optional)

Sprinkles, for garnish (optional)

MAKE-AHEAD TIP: Royal icing can be made up to 3 days in advance. Transfer it to a smaller bowl or container, cover tightly, and refrigerate. When ready to use, let it come to room temperature, then give it a quick whisk to recombine. Whisk in a few drops of water if it has thickened.

1. In a large bowl using a handheld or stand mixer fitted with the whisk, mix the powdered sugar and meringue powder.

2. Add the water and a flavoring (if using) and whip on high speed for 1½ to 2 minutes. When lifting the whisk up off the icing, it should drizzle down and smooth out within 5 to 10 seconds. This is your target consistency (1). If it's too thick, whip in additional water, 1 tablespoon at a time. On particularly dry days, you may need up to 12 to 14 tablespoons total. Note that the longer you whip the royal icing, the thicker it becomes. If it is too thin, just keep whipping it to introduce more air, or you can add more sifted powdered sugar.

3. If you'd like to tint the icing, divide it into separate bowls for each color, or tint the entire batch one color. A little gel food coloring goes a long way, so use a toothpick to dot the gel into the icing. Stir it in and then add more to deepen the color if desired. Keep in mind that the more you stir, the thicker the icing becomes. If needed, stir in a few drops of water to maintain the target consistency.

Using Royal Icing

1. Fit a pastry bag with a small round piping tip (see Decorating Details, opposite, for recommended decorating tools). Fill the bag with icing, making sure to leave a few inches of space at the top of the bag. Twist to seal or use a rubber band or clip.

2. Holding the piping bag straight up and squeezing with medium pressure, pipe the icing in an outline around the edge of the cookie (2), then pipe icing in the center to cover the entire cookie (this step is called flooding, 3). Pop any air bubbles in the wet icing with a toothpick. If you're using sprinkles, add them while the icing is wet. When you're not actually working with the royal icing (for example, you are decorating cookies but you still have some icing left in the bowl that you intend to use next), place a damp paper towel directly on the surface to prevent it from hardening.

3. Let the decorated cookies sit at room temperature, uncovered, until the icing is dry. If the icing was applied in a thin layer, it will completely set in about 2 hours. If it is runny, or was thickly applied, it will take longer. If you decorate the cookies directly on a baking sheet, you can place it in the refrigerator to speed up the icing setting.

Decorating Details

Piping Tools: Use pastry bag(s) and tip(s) for decorating. You'll need a pastry bag for each color of icing, and small round piping tips such as Wilton piping tip #4. This is a versatile basic piping tip that can be used for outlining and flooding. For any fine decorative detail, use a thinner round tip such as Wilton piping tip #1. If you have multiple colors of icing and only 1 piping tip, use a piping tip coupler so you can easily transfer the tip between pastry bags.

Your Inner Artist: There are endless ways to decorate sugar cookies, and this is your chance to let your inner artist shine. A sprinkling of sanding sugar on top of the icing is always pretty, or have fun with colored icing and sprinkles. Instead of flooding the icing, you can pipe stripes, swirls, or dots. I love to layer icing, and while this method is easy, it takes extra time. Outline and then flood the icing onto your cookies, let that dry, and then pipe decorative designs on top of the dried icing (4).

Pistachio Crinkles

MAKES 28 TO 30 COOKIES

Sometimes, and I *really* mean sometimes, it's okay to ditch chocolate in favor of nuts. These soft, chewy "pistachio pillows" (as I fondly call them) are just like classic chocolate crinkle cookies but with a nutty and zesty twist. I like to use salted pistachios for a sweet and salty background, but unsalted nuts work, too. A drop of green food coloring brightens the color, but feel free to skip it.

SKILL LEVEL: **Beginner**

PREP: **25 minutes**

BAKE: **12 to 14 minutes per batch**

TOTAL: **1 hour 50 minutes, including chilling**

2⅓ cups all-purpose flour **(292g)**

1 cup salted pistachios, ground into fine crumbs **(130g)**

1 teaspoon baking soda

½ teaspoon salt

12 tablespoons unsalted butter, at room temperature **(170g)**

⅔ cup granulated sugar **(133g)**

½ cup brown sugar **(100g)**

1 large egg, at room temperature

1 large egg yolk, at room temperature

2 teaspoons orange zest

2 teaspoons fresh orange juice

1 teaspoon vanilla extract

1 teaspoon almond extract

1 drop green gel food coloring (optional)

½ cup powdered sugar, plus more as needed **(60g)**

TIP: As far as nut flavors go, pistachio is one of the more subtle. Almond extract often is added to enhance pistachio flavor, and I'm using that concept here.

1. In a medium bowl, whisk the flour, pistachios, baking soda, and salt.

2. In a large bowl using a handheld or stand mixer fitted with the paddle, beat the butter, granulated sugar, and brown sugar on medium-high speed until the mixture is light and creamy, about 3 minutes. Add the egg and egg yolk and beat on medium-high speed until combined. Add the orange zest, orange juice, vanilla, and almond extract, and beat on medium-high speed until combined. Scrape down the sides of the bowl as needed. Add the flour mixture and beat on low speed until combined. Add the green gel food coloring (if using) and beat until fully incorporated.

3. Cover the dough tightly and refrigerate it for at least 1 hour or up to 3 days.

4. Preheat the oven to 350°F (177°C). Line baking sheets with parchment paper or silicone baking mats. If the dough has chilled for longer than 3 hours, let it sit at room temperature for about 30 minutes before shaping and baking.

5. Put the powdered sugar in a small bowl. Scoop and roll the chilled cookie dough into balls, about 1½ tablespoons (35g) each, then roll in the powdered sugar to coat generously. Arrange the cookies 3 inches apart on the baking sheets.

6. Bake for 12 to 14 minutes or until the cookies are puffy and the edges are set.

7. Let cool on the baking sheet for 10 minutes before transferring to a cooling rack to cool completely. The powdered sugar coating melts into the warm cookies. If desired, use a fine-mesh sieve to dust a little more powdered sugar on the cooled cookies. Store covered tightly at room temperature for up to 1 week.

Chocolate Peppermint Sandwich Cookies

MAKES 28 SANDWICH COOKIES

Inspired by the iconic Oreo, these sandwich cookies combine cocoa powder, peppermint extract, and crushed candy canes for some festive winter flavor. This is a cut-out cookie, and you'll notice the rolling method is like that used for Soft Sugar Cookies (page 33). For the chocolate version, use cocoa powder instead of flour to dust your surface and rolling pin, so that the sticky dough stays dark and workable.

SKILL LEVEL: **Intermediate**

PREP: **1 hour 10 minutes**

BAKE: **11 to 12 minutes per batch**

TOTAL: **3 hours 30 minutes, including chilling**

Cookies

1½ cups all-purpose flour, plus more as needed **(188g)**

¾ cup unsweetened natural or Dutch-process cocoa powder, plus more as needed **(64g)**

1 teaspoon baking powder

⅛ teaspoon salt

12 tablespoons unsalted butter, at room temperature **(170g)**

1 cup granulated sugar **(200g)**

1 large egg, at room temperature

½ teaspoon vanilla extract

½ teaspoon peppermint extract

Peppermint Buttercream

10 tablespoons unsalted butter, at room temperature **(140g)**

2¾ cups powdered sugar **(330g)**

2 tablespoons milk, at room temperature

1 teaspoon vanilla extract

½ to ¾ teaspoon peppermint extract

⅛ teaspoon salt

Garnish

½ cup crushed peppermint candy canes **(60g)**

4 ounces semi-sweet or bittersweet chocolate, chopped **(113g)**

1. Make the cookies: In a medium bowl, whisk the flour, cocoa powder, baking powder, and salt.

2. In a large bowl using a handheld or stand mixer fitted with the paddle, beat the butter and sugar on high speed until the mixture is light and creamy, about 3 minutes. Add the egg, vanilla, and peppermint extract and beat on high speed until combined, about 1 minute. Scrape down the sides of the bowl as needed. Add the flour mixture and mix on low speed until combined. The dough should be soft. If it seems too soft and sticky for rolling, add 1 tablespoon more flour.

3. Divide the dough in half. Lightly dust a rolling pin and a piece of parchment paper or a silicone baking mat with cocoa powder. Roll out each half of the dough to about ¼-inch thickness; any shape is okay. Sprinkle lightly with cocoa powder if the dough seems too sticky.

4. Lightly dust one of the rolled-out dough portions with cocoa powder. Place the second rolled-out dough portion, still on the parchment paper, on top of the first. Cover the dough tightly and refrigerate it for at least 2 hours or up to 2 days.

5. Preheat the oven to 350°F (177°C). Line baking sheets with parchment paper or silicone baking mats.

6. Remove the top piece of dough from the refrigerator. Using a 2-inch round cookie cutter, cut the dough into rounds. Gather the scraps, reroll, and continue cutting until all the dough is used. Repeat with the second piece of dough. Arrange the cookies 2 inches apart on the prepared baking sheets.

7. Bake for 11 to 12 minutes or until the edges of the cookies are set. Cool the cookies on the baking sheet for 5 minutes before transferring to a cooling rack to cool completely.

8. Make the peppermint buttercream: In a large bowl using a handheld or stand mixer fitted with the paddle, beat the butter on medium speed until creamy, about 2 minutes. Add the powdered sugar, milk, vanilla, ½ teaspoon of the peppermint extract, and the salt. Beat on low speed for 30 seconds, then increase to medium-high speed and beat for 2 full minutes. Taste and beat in another ¼ teaspoon peppermint extract, if desired. Pipe or spread the peppermint buttercream over the bottom side of a cooled chocolate

recipe continues >

cookie, bringing it all the way to the edges. Place a second chocolate cookie on top, bottom side facing the filling, to make a sandwich. Repeat with the remaining cookies and buttercream.

9. Garnish the cookies: Put the crushed peppermint candy in a shallow dish. Roll the edges of the sandwich cookies in the crushed candy pieces, to coat the exposed buttercream.

10. Melt the chocolate (see Melting Chocolate, page 20). Drizzle the tops of the cookie sandwiches with melted chocolate. Refrigerate for 20 minutes or until the chocolate has set. Store covered tightly in the refrigerator for up to 5 days.

Chocolate Peanut Butter–Covered Shortbread Cookies

MAKES 42 TO 48 COOKIES

These slice-and-bake cookies start with a crispy, buttery shortbread. It's not too sweet, which makes for a great base under the peanut butter and chocolate topping. When you can't get your hands on a box of Girl Scout Tagalongs, these are the perfect solution. The recipe makes a lot, but I don't think you'll have trouble scouting out any taste testers!

SKILL LEVEL: **Beginner**

PREP: **50 minutes**

BAKE: **13 to 15 minutes per batch**

TOTAL: **3 hours 30 minutes, including chilling**

Cookies

12 tablespoons unsalted butter, at room temperature **(170g)**

¾ cup granulated sugar **(150g)**

1 large egg, at room temperature

2 teaspoons vanilla extract

2 cups + 2 tablespoons all-purpose flour, plus more as needed **(266g)**

½ teaspoon baking powder

¼ teaspoon salt

Topping

1¼ cups creamy peanut butter (the processed kind, not natural) **(313g)**

2 tablespoons unsalted butter, softened **(28g)**

1 cup powdered sugar **(120g)**

⅛ teaspoon salt

10 ounces milk chocolate or semi-sweet chocolate, coarsely chopped **(283g)**

Flaky sea salt, for garnish (optional)

1. Make the cookies: In a large bowl using a handheld or stand mixer fitted with the paddle, beat the butter and sugar on medium-high speed until the mixture is light and creamy, about 3 minutes. Add the egg and vanilla and beat on high speed until combined, about 1 minute. Add the flour, baking powder, and salt and beat on low speed until combined. You may think the dough won't come together, but keep the mixer running until the dough clumps up. The dough should be thick and slightly sticky. If you think it's too sticky to roll/shape, beat in 1 more tablespoon of flour.

2. Turn the dough out onto a floured surface and, with floured hands, divide it in half. Roll and shape each half into an 8-inch log, about 1½ inches in diameter. The measurements don't have to be exact. Tightly wrap the dough logs in plastic wrap and refrigerate for at least 3 hours or up to 3 days.

3. Preheat the oven to 350°F (177°C). Line baking sheets with parchment paper or silicone baking mats.

4. Slice the dough logs into rounds ¼ to ⅓ inch thick and arrange them 2 inches apart on the prepared baking sheets.

5. Bake for 13 to 15 minutes, or until the edges of the cookies are lightly browned and set. Cool the cookies on the baking sheets for 5 minutes before transferring to a cooling rack to cool completely.

6. Make the topping: In a large bowl using a handheld or stand mixer fitted with the paddle, beat the peanut butter and butter on medium-high speed until combined and smooth, about 1 minute. Add the powdered sugar and salt and start the mixer on low speed. Slowly increase the speed to medium-high as the powdered sugar is incorporated and beat until fully combined. Refrigerate the peanut butter mixture until ready to use.

7. Melt the chocolate (see Melting Chocolate, page 20). Set aside to cool slightly.

8. Line a baking sheet with parchment paper or a silicone baking mat. Using a table knife or small icing spatula, spread about 1½ teaspoons of the peanut butter mixture on top of each cooled cookie (1).

recipe continues >

9. Dip the peanut butter–topped cookies into the bowl of melted chocolate (or spoon chocolate on top), until the chocolate has fully coated the peanut butter layer (2). Place the cookies on the prepared baking sheet. Sprinkle the tops with a pinch of flaky sea salt (if using). Refrigerate for 20 minutes or until the chocolate has set. Store covered tightly at room temperature for up to 2 days or in the refrigerator for up to 1 week.

Maple Brown Sugar Cookies

MAKES 28 TO 30 COOKIES

A batch of these fall-favorite cookies is as necessary as a cozy blanket when the weather starts to cool down—though they can and should be enjoyed year-round! The cookies are mega-chewy and packed with nutty pecans and big maple flavor. Whenever I make them, family and friends gather around the cooling rack before I even finish icing them. Pure maple syrup alone isn't enough to guarantee that deep maple flavor, so make sure you use maple extract as well. Look for it in the baking aisle of your grocery store.

SKILL LEVEL: **Beginner**

PREP: **30 minutes**

BAKE: **12 to 13 minutes per batch**

TOTAL: **2 hours 50 minutes, including chilling**

Cookies

2⅓ cups all-purpose flour **(292g)**

1 teaspoon baking soda

⅛ teaspoon salt

8 tablespoons unsalted butter, at room temperature **(113g)**

1 cup dark brown sugar **(200g)**

1 large egg, at room temperature

⅓ cup pure maple syrup **(113g)**

1 teaspoon vanilla extract

1 teaspoon maple extract

1 cup chopped pecans **(120g)**

Maple Icing

2 tablespoons unsalted butter **(28g)**

⅓ cup pure maple syrup **(113g)**

1 cup sifted powdered sugar **(112g)**

Pinch of salt

TIP: If you have the time, toast the pecans before adding to the dough. See Toasting Nuts (page 21).

1. Make the cookies: In a medium bowl, whisk the flour, baking soda, and salt.

2. In a large bowl using a handheld or stand mixer fitted with the paddle, beat the butter and brown sugar on medium-high speed until the mixture is light and creamy, about 3 minutes. Add the egg and beat on high speed until combined, about 30 seconds. Scrape down the sides of the bowl as needed. Add the maple syrup, vanilla, and maple extract and beat until combined, about 1 minute. Add the flour mixture and beat on low speed until combined. Add the pecans and beat on low speed until just incorporated. The dough should be creamy and soft.

3. Cover the dough tightly and refrigerate it for at least 2 hours or up to 3 days.

4. Preheat the oven to 350°F (177°C). Line baking sheets with parchment paper or silicone baking mats. If the dough has chilled for longer than 3 hours, let it sit at room temperature for about 30 minutes before shaping.

5. Scoop and roll the chilled cookie dough into balls, about 1½ tablespoons (35g) each. Arrange the cookies 3 inches apart on the prepared baking sheets.

6. Bake for 12 to 13 minutes or until the edges of the cookies are lightly browned and set but the centers still look very soft. Cool the cookies on the baking sheet for 5 minutes before transferring to a cooling rack to cool completely.

7. Make the maple icing: In a small saucepan over low heat, melt the butter with the maple syrup, whisking occasionally. Remove from heat and whisk in the powdered sugar and salt. Drizzle over the cooled cookies. The icing will set after about 1 hour. Store covered tightly at room temperature for up to 2 days or in the refrigerator for up to 1 week.

Brown Butter Pumpkin Oatmeal Cookies

MAKES 24 COOKIES

SKILL LEVEL: **Beginner**

PREP: **45 minutes**

BAKE: **14 to 15 minutes per batch**

TOTAL: **1 hour 10 minutes**

These cookies have amassed a major fan base among my website followers. One reader calls them "the best fall cookie! Chewy, sweet, and just the perfect amount of spice." And many fans agree that "the brown butter takes these to the next level!" Because it takes some effort to achieve first place in the fall cookie contest, I want to call out two steps that will help the process. Pumpkin puree is very wet, which is excellent for Pumpkin Spice Latte Muffins (page 235) but can turn cookies into fluffy cakes. To keep the cookies chewy, blot excess moisture from the pumpkin. And to save a few minutes, brown the butter for the cookies and the glaze at the same time. Pumpkin pie spice is a frequent ingredient in my fall baking, and I have included a recipe for a homemade version here.

Cookies

1¼ cups canned pumpkin puree **(285g)**

16 tablespoons unsalted butter, cut into 16 pieces **(226g)**

2 cups rolled oats **(170g)**

1⅔ cups all-purpose flour **(208g)**

2 teaspoons pumpkin pie spice, homemade (recipe follows) or store-bought

1½ teaspoons ground cinnamon

1 teaspoon baking soda

½ teaspoon salt

1 cup granulated sugar **(200g)**

⅔ cup brown sugar **(133g)**

1 large egg yolk, at room temperature

2 teaspoons vanilla extract

Brown Butter Glaze

4 tablespoons unsalted butter, cut into 4 pieces **(56g)**

1½ cups powdered sugar **(180g)**

3 tablespoons milk

¼ teaspoon vanilla extract

Sprinkle of pumpkin pie spice (optional), for garnish

1. Line a medium bowl with a double layer of paper towels. Place the pumpkin puree in the bowl. Using another paper towel, press down to blot excess moisture from the pumpkin. You may need to repeat a couple of times with new paper towels. After blotting, you will have about 1 cup (225g) pumpkin puree. Set aside.

2. Brown the 16 tablespoons of butter for the cookies together with the 4 tablespoons for the glaze (see Browning Butter, page 20). Once browned, immediately remove from heat, and pour into a heat-safe glass bowl or liquid measuring cup, including all the browned solids at the bottom of the pan. Set aside 1 cup (226g/240ml) to use in the cookie dough, and reserve the rest for the glaze.

3. Make the cookies: Preheat the oven to 350°F (177°C). Line baking sheets with parchment paper or silicone baking mats.

4. In a large bowl, whisk the oats, flour, pumpkin pie spice, cinnamon, baking soda, and salt.

5. In another large bowl, whisk the reserved 1 cup (226g/240ml) brown butter, the granulated sugar, and brown sugar until combined. Whisk in the egg yolk and vanilla, and then the pumpkin puree. Slowly stir the oat mixture into the pumpkin mixture. The dough should be soft and very sticky.

6. Scoop the cookie dough, about 2 tablespoons (45g) of dough each, and arrange them 3 inches apart on the prepared baking sheets.

7. Bake for 14 to 15 minutes or until the edges of the cookies are lightly browned and set. Cool the cookies on the baking sheet for 10 minutes before transferring to a cooling rack to cool completely.

8. Make the brown butter glaze: Give the reserved brown butter a quick stir. If it's no longer thin and liquid, warm it gently on the stove or in the microwave. Whisk in the powdered sugar, milk, and vanilla until smooth. Lightly dip the top of each cookie into the glaze. Sprinkle a pinch of pumpkin pie spice (if using) on top of each glazed cookie. Return the cookies to the cooling rack and let sit until the glaze has set. Store covered tightly at room temperature for up to 2 days or in the refrigerator for up to 1 week.

Homemade Pumpkin Pie Spice

MAKES ABOUT 5 TABLESPOONS

This spice mixture lasts in a tightly sealed container until the individual spices' expiration dates, which is typically 1 to 2 years. Buy them all at once to ensure equal freshness and store in an airtight container at room temperature in a dry place.

3 tablespoons ground cinnamon

2 teaspoons ground ginger

1½ teaspoons ground nutmeg

1 teaspoon ground cloves

1 teaspoon ground allspice

Small pinch of freshly ground black pepper

Mix the cinnamon, ginger, nutmeg, cloves, allspice, and pepper until well combined.

Chocolate-Covered Cherry Thumbprints

MAKES 30 COOKIES

Sweet maraschino cherries strike just the right flavor balance in these deeply chocolatey cookies. I always love thumbprint cookies because they seem fancy and elevated, but you don't need any special decorating equipment or skills . . . just your thumb! One quick tip for these brownie-like treats: The dough gets a little sticky when shaping, so wipe your hands as needed as you work.

SKILL LEVEL: **Beginner**

PREP: **20 minutes**

BAKE: **12 to 14 minutes per batch**

TOTAL: **3 hours 45 minutes, including chilling**

30 maraschino cherries, without stems

1¼ cups all-purpose flour **(156g)**

⅔ cup unsweetened natural cocoa powder **(56g)**

1 teaspoon baking soda

⅛ teaspoon salt

8 tablespoons unsalted butter, at room temperature **(113g)**

½ cup granulated sugar **(100g)**

½ cup brown sugar **(100g)**

1 large egg, at room temperature

1 teaspoon vanilla extract

1 tablespoon juice from the maraschino cherry jar

¾ cup mini chocolate chips **(128g)**

4 ounces semi-sweet chocolate, finely chopped **(113g)**

1. Place the cherries on a paper towel–lined plate and gently blot any excess moisture. If your cherries are on the larger side, use only 15 and slice them in half. Set aside.

2. In a medium bowl, whisk the flour, cocoa powder, baking soda, and salt.

3. In a large bowl using a handheld or stand mixer fitted with the paddle, beat the butter, granulated sugar, and brown sugar on medium-high speed until the mixture is light and creamy, about 3 minutes. Add the egg and vanilla and beat on high speed until combined, about 1 minute. Scrape down the sides of the bowl as needed. Add the flour mixture and beat on low speed until combined. Beat in the maraschino cherry juice and mini chocolate chips. The dough should be thick and tacky.

4. Cover the dough tightly and refrigerate it for at least 3 hours or up to 3 days.

5. Preheat the oven to 350°F (177°C). Line baking sheets with parchment paper or silicone baking mats. If the dough has chilled for longer than 3 hours, let it sit at room temperature for about 20 minutes before rolling and baking.

6. Scoop and roll the chilled cookie dough into balls, about a heaping table-spoon (22g) each, and use your thumb to make an indent in the centers. Arrange them 2 to 3 inches apart on the prepared baking sheets. Place a cherry (or half a cherry) into the indent of each dough ball.

7. Bake for 12 to 14 minutes or until the edges of the cookies are set. Cool the cookies on the baking sheet for 5 minutes before transferring to a cooling rack to cool completely.

8. Melt the chocolate (see Melting Chocolate, page 20). Drizzle the tops of the cookies with melted chocolate. Refrigerate for 20 minutes or until the chocolate has set. Store covered tightly at room temperature for up to 2 days or in the refrigerator for up to 1 week.

Cracked Pepper Parmesan Cookies

MAKES 28 TO 32 COOKIES

SKILL LEVEL: **Beginner**

PREP: **10 minutes**

BAKE: **14 to 16 minutes per batch**

TOTAL: **1 hour 35 minutes, including chilling**

A savory cookie! These slice-and-bake cookies skip the sugar in favor of salty Parmesan cheese, fragrant thyme, and sharp black pepper. They're mega flavorful, taste incredible with fig jam spread on top, and fit right in on cheese-and-charcuterie boards. I love the hearty pops of flavor from freshly cracked black peppercorns, but if you aren't a spice fan, feel free to reduce the amount. If you don't have a pepper grinder/mill and need to use finely ground black pepper, reduce the amount to ¼ teaspoon.

1¼ cups all-purpose flour, plus more as needed **(156g)**

1 cup (4 ounces) freshly grated Parmesan cheese **(113g)**

8 tablespoons unsalted butter, cubed and at room temperature **(113g)**

1½ teaspoons dried thyme

¾ teaspoon freshly ground black pepper

½ teaspoon salt

1 tablespoon water, plus more as needed

1. In a food processor, combine the flour, Parmesan, butter, thyme, pepper, and salt and pulse until a dough begins to form in small clumps. Add the water and pulse a few more times, just until the dough comes together. It should still be crumbly.

2. Turn the dough out onto a floured surface (1) and use your hands to roughly shape it into a large clump. Knead the dough for about 30 seconds to help it come together. If it remains crumbly, flick a few drops of water on the dough to moisten it so it holds together. Roll and shape the dough into an 8-inch-long log (2). Tightly wrap in plastic wrap and refrigerate it for at least 1 hour or up to 3 days.

3. Preheat the oven to 350°F (177°C). Line baking sheets with parchment paper or silicone baking mats.

4. Slice the dough log into rounds ¼ to ⅓ inch thick (3) and arrange them 2 inches apart on the prepared baking sheets. Bake for 14 to 16 minutes or until the edges of the cookies are lightly browned.

5. Cool the cookies on the baking sheet for 10 minutes before transferring to a cooling rack to cool completely. Store covered tightly at room temperature for up to 1 week.

Freezing Cookie Dough

Drop Cookie Dough: After shaping the dough as the recipe directs, arrange on a parchment-lined baking sheet or plate, set close but not touching, and freeze for 1 hour. The frozen dough balls can then be transferred to a freezer-safe container. Bake from frozen, adding 1 to 2 minutes to the bake time.

Coated Cookie Dough: Before rolling in a coating such as powdered sugar, freeze the unbaked cookie dough balls (see above). When ready to bake, let the cookie dough sit at room temperature for 30 minutes, and then roll in the topping. Add 1 to 2 minutes to the bake time.

Slice-and-Bake Cookie Dough: Wrap logs of cookie dough tightly in plastic wrap. Place the wrapped dough in a freezer-safe container or wrap again with aluminum foil. Thaw the wrapped dough in the refrigerator overnight, then slice and bake.

Roll-Out Cookie Dough: Prepare the dough, divide in half, flatten both portions into discs, wrap each in plastic wrap, and freeze. Thaw the wrapped discs in the refrigerator, then bring to room temperature, about 1 hour. Roll out the dough as directed in the recipe, then chill the rolled-out dough in the refrigerator for 45 minutes to 1 hour before cutting into shapes and baking.

Banana Walnut Cookies

MAKES 30 COOKIES

SKILL LEVEL: **Beginner**

PREP: **30 minutes**

BAKE: **13 to 15 minutes per batch**

TOTAL: **50 minutes**

Until this recipe, I had never successfully made a batch of deliciously chewy, naturally flavored banana cookies. Previous attempts were always cakey, or they tasted bland. The secret? I borrowed my trick for making Strawberry Cake (page 89), cooking the fruit on the stove to concentrate the flavor. Because of extra moisture from the bananas, the dough uses only an egg yolk instead of a whole egg. The cookie dough requires no refrigeration, and just wait until you taste the flavor on day two!

1 cup mashed bananas (about 2 large ripe bananas) **(230g)**

2 cups all-purpose flour **(250g)**

1½ cups rolled oats **(128g)**

1½ teaspoons ground cinnamon

1 teaspoon baking soda

½ teaspoon salt

¼ teaspoon ground nutmeg

16 tablespoons unsalted butter, melted and slightly cooled **(226g)**

¾ cup brown sugar **(150g)**

½ cup granulated sugar **(100g)**

1 large egg yolk, at room temperature

2 teaspoons vanilla extract

1¼ cups chopped walnuts, plus more for garnish (optional) **(150g)**

TIP: Enjoy the cookies plain or top with the maple icing from the Maple Brown Sugar Cookies (page 45) or the brown butter glaze from the Brown Butter Pumpkin Oatmeal Cookies (page 46).

1. In a small saucepan over medium heat, bring the mashed banana to a simmer. Reduce the heat to medium-low and cook, stirring occasionally, until the banana is reduced by a quarter, to around ¾ cup (173g), about 10 minutes. Set aside to cool.

2. Preheat the oven to 350°F (177°C). Line baking sheets with parchment paper or silicone baking mats.

3. In a large bowl, whisk the flour, oats, cinnamon, baking soda, salt, and nutmeg.

4. In a medium bowl, whisk the melted butter, brown sugar, and granulated sugar until no lumps remain. Whisk in the egg yolk and then the reduced banana and the vanilla. Pour the banana mixture into the flour mixture and mix until combined. Fold in the walnuts.

5. Scoop the cookie dough, about 1½ tablespoons (35g) each, and arrange them 3 inches apart on the prepared baking sheets.

6. Bake for 13 to 15 minutes or until the edges of the cookies are lightly browned and set. The centers will look very soft.

7. Cool the cookies on the baking sheet for 10 minutes before transferring to a cooling rack to cool completely. While the cookies are still warm, I like to press a few more walnut pieces into the tops—this is only for looks! Store covered tightly at room temperature for up to 1 week.

Brownies

& Bars

Thick & Fudgy Brownies

MAKES 16 BROWNIES

I include this recipe first because it's the foundation for two others in this chapter. When I was writing this cookbook, I dedicated myself to experimenting with numerous new brownie recipes, introducing slight modifications to achieve a perfectly thick and fudgy brownie with exceptional flavor. You can bake them as is, or as Birthday Brookies (page 58) or Crème de Menthe Brownies (page 61). If you love nuts in your brownies, replace half of the chocolate chips with chopped walnuts.

SKILL LEVEL: **Beginner**
PREP: **15 minutes**
BAKE: **35 minutes**
TOTAL: **50 minutes, plus cooling**

Let me explain a few details about this recipe:

- Whisking sugar into warm butter begins to dissolve it. Then, during baking, the dissolved sugar rises, forming a shiny, crackly top.
- Eggs provide structure, and the extra yolk in the batter adds fat for a chewier, fudgier texture.
- Using Dutch-process cocoa powder instead of natural cocoa results in a smoother, less acidic chocolate flavor.

12 tablespoons unsalted butter, melted and hot **(170g)**

3 tablespoons vegetable oil

1½ cups granulated sugar **(300g)**

2 large eggs, at room temperature

1 egg yolk, at room temperature

1½ teaspoons vanilla extract

1 cup unsweetened Dutch-process cocoa powder **(84g)**

¾ cup all-purpose flour **(94g)**

1 tablespoon hot water

½ teaspoon salt

1½ cups semi-sweet chocolate chips **(270g)**

1. Preheat the oven to 350°F (177°C). Line a 9-inch square metal baking pan with parchment paper, leaving a few inches of overhang on two opposite sides.

2. In a large heat-safe bowl, whisk the hot melted butter, oil, and sugar. Let sit for 3 to 5 minutes to slightly cool. Whisk in the eggs, egg yolk, and vanilla. Mix well, then whisk in the cocoa powder, flour, hot water, and salt. The batter should be thick. Fold in the chocolate chips, then spread the batter evenly in the prepared pan.

3. Bake for 35 minutes or until a toothpick inserted in the center comes out with only a few moist crumbs. Err on the side of underbaking, as the brownies continue to set as they cool. Cool the brownies completely in the pan set on a cooling rack.

4. Lift the brownies out of the pan by gripping the parchment paper overhang; transfer to a cutting board and cut into squares. Store covered tightly at room temperature for up to 1 week.

Birthday Brookies

MAKES 18 TO 24 BARS

SKILL LEVEL: **Beginner**

PREP: **25 minutes**

BAKE: **32 minutes**

TOTAL: **1 hour, plus cooling**

This half-brownie, half-bar cookie hybrid gets the birthday party treatment with colorful rainbow sprinkles. White chocolate chips add a creamy sweetness that balances the richness of the brownies. A touch of almond extract adds a little extra sugar cookie flavor, but feel free to skip it.

Cookie Dough

8 tablespoons unsalted butter, at room temperature **(113g)**

⅓ cup brown sugar **(67g)**

⅓ cup granulated sugar **(67g)**

1 large egg, at room temperature

1 teaspoon vanilla extract

¼ teaspoon almond extract (optional)

1¼ cups all-purpose flour **(156g)**

½ teaspoon baking powder

⅛ teaspoon salt

½ cup white chocolate chips **(90g)**

⅓ cup rainbow sprinkles, plus more for sprinkling on top **(57g)**

Brownie Batter

Thick & Fudgy Brownies (page 57)

1. Preheat the oven to 350°F (177°C). Line a 9 × 13-inch metal baking pan with parchment paper, leaving a few inches of overhang on two opposite sides.

2. Make the cookie dough: In a large bowl using a handheld or stand mixer fitted with the paddle, beat the butter, brown sugar, and granulated sugar on medium-high speed until the mixture is light and creamy, about 3 minutes. Add the egg, vanilla, and almond extract (if using), and beat on high speed until combined, about 1 minute. Scrape down the sides of the bowl as needed. Add the flour, baking powder, and salt and beat on low speed until combined. Beat in the white chocolate chips and sprinkles. The dough should be thick and sticky.

3. Make the brownie batter: Make the batter as directed, but spread it in the prepared baking pan.

4. Press about ¼ cup (70g) of the cookie dough into a flat disc and place it on top of the brownie batter. Repeat with the remaining cookie dough, covering the surface of the brownie layer but leaving some chocolate parts exposed. Lightly press down on the cookie dough to make an even layer as best you can. Top with extra sprinkles, if desired.

5. Bake for 32 to 36 minutes or until the top is lightly browned. If the top browns too quickly, loosely tent aluminum foil over the pan. Err on the side of underbaking, as the brookies continue to set as they cool. Cool the brookies completely in the pan set on a cooling rack.

6. Lift the brookies out of the pan by gripping the parchment paper overhang; transfer to a cutting board and cut into squares. Store covered tightly at room temperature for up to 1 week.

Crème de Menthe Brownies

MAKES 18 TO 24 BARS

In a parade of holiday cookies, these minty brownies took center stage when I was growing up. Mom made them every December, and I distinctly remember fighting with my sisters over who got the last one. It was a sweet sibling rivalry that always ended with a triumphant grin . . . usually not from me, since I was the youngest. I still love making mint brownies like Mom did (and am much more apt to share them now!), because they're downright delicious.

SKILL LEVEL: **Beginner**
PREP: **35 minutes**
BAKE: **20 minutes**
TOTAL: **1 hour, plus cooling**

Brownie Batter

Thick & Fudgy Brownies (page 57)

Mint Buttercream

8 tablespoons unsalted butter, at room temperature **(113g)**

2 cups powdered sugar **(240g)**

2 tablespoons green crème de menthe syrup (see Tip)

Chocolate Topping

6 ounces semi-sweet chocolate, chopped **(170g)**

4 tablespoons unsalted butter **(56g)**

½ cup chopped Andes chocolate mints **(70g)**

TIP: Crème de menthe syrup is a green nonalcoholic syrup often sold in the ice cream toppings section of the grocery store. If you can't find it, use a mixture of 2 tablespoons milk, 1¼ teaspoons peppermint extract, and 1 drop of green gel food coloring instead.

1. Preheat the oven to 350°F (177°C). Line a 9 × 13-inch metal baking pan with parchment paper, leaving a few inches of overhang on two opposite sides.

2. Make the brownies: Make the brownie batter as directed, but spread it in the prepared baking pan. Bake for 20 to 23 minutes or until a toothpick inserted in the center comes out with only a few moist crumbs. Err on the side of underbaking, as the brownies continue to set as they cool. Cool the brownies completely in the pan set on a cooling rack.

3. Make the mint buttercream: In a large bowl using a handheld or stand mixer fitted with the paddle, beat the butter on medium speed until creamy, about 2 minutes. Scrape down the sides of the bowl as needed. Add the powdered sugar and crème de menthe syrup and beat on low speed for 30 seconds, then increase to medium-high speed and beat for 2 minutes until creamy.

4. Using a small offset icing spatula, spread the mint buttercream in an even layer over the cooled brownies. Place the pan in the refrigerator.

5. Make the chocolate topping: Melt the chocolate with the butter, stirring until smooth and fully combined (see Melting Chocolate, page 20). Pour the warm chocolate topping over the mint buttercream and spread it into an even layer (1). Gently tap the pan on the counter a few times to help smooth out the surface. Sprinkle the chopped Andes mints over the chocolate (2). Refrigerate, uncovered, for at least 1 hour to set the chocolate.

6. Lift the brownies out of the pan by gripping the parchment paper overhang; transfer to a cutting board and cut into squares. Store covered tightly at room temperature for up to 2 days or in the refrigerator for up to 1 week.

Chai Spice Blondies

MAKES 16 BARS

SKILL LEVEL: **Beginner**

PREP: **20 minutes**

BAKE: **30 minutes**

TOTAL: **55 minutes, plus cooling**

Blondies are "blond brownies." Instead of chocolate, they use brown sugar and a hefty dose of vanilla for a butterscotch-like flavor. An extra egg yolk plays a crucial role in the texture, adding a boost of chewiness, richness, and moisture. Inspired by the delicious comfort of coffeehouse chai lattes, these generously spiced blondies are a cozy upgrade from a plain blondie.

Blondies

2 cups all-purpose flour **(250g)**

½ teaspoon baking powder

½ teaspoon ground cinnamon

½ teaspoon salt

¼ teaspoon ground cardamom

¼ teaspoon ground ginger

⅛ teaspoon ground allspice

⅛ teaspoon ground nutmeg

Pinch of freshly ground black pepper

1 cup brown sugar **(200g)**

14 tablespoons unsalted butter, melted **(196g)**

½ cup granulated sugar **(100g)**

1 large egg, at room temperature

1 large egg yolk, at room temperature

1 tablespoon vanilla extract

4 ounces white chocolate, chopped, or ⅔ cup white chocolate chips **(113g)**

Topping

1 tablespoon granulated sugar

Pinch of ground cardamom

Pinch of ground cinnamon

2 ounces white chocolate, chopped **(57g)**

1. Make the blondies: Preheat the oven to 350°F (177°C). Line a 9-inch square metal baking pan with parchment paper, leaving a few inches of overhang on two opposite sides.

2. In a large bowl, whisk the flour, baking powder, cinnamon, salt, cardamom, ginger, allspice, nutmeg, and pepper.

3. In a medium bowl, whisk the brown sugar, melted butter, and granulated sugar. Whisk in the egg, egg yolk, and vanilla and mix until combined. Pour the butter mixture into the flour mixture and whisk to combine. The batter should be thick. Using a spatula, fold in the 4 ounces (113g) chopped white chocolate and spread the batter evenly in the prepared pan.

4. Make the topping: In a small bowl, stir together the sugar, cardamom, and cinnamon. Sprinkle the topping evenly over the blondies.

5. Bake for 30 to 32 minutes or until a toothpick inserted in the center comes out with only a few moist crumbs. Cool the blondies completely in the pan set on a cooling rack.

6. Melt the 2 ounces (57g) chopped white chocolate (see Melting Chocolate, page 20). Drizzle over the cooled blondies, then place the pan in the refrigerator for about 20 minutes to set the white chocolate.

7. Lift the blondies out of the pan by gripping the parchment paper overhang; transfer to a cutting board and cut into squares. Store covered tightly at room temperature for up to 1 week.

Jammin' Strawberry Crumb Bars

MAKES 16 BARS

This recipe went through more rounds of testing than expected! The perfect crumb-topped strawberry bar had to meet my high standards of epic strawberry flavor, incredible texture, and holding their shape when cut. The winning recipe is below, and it incorporates jam to enhance the sweet strawberry flavor and ensure that the bars hold together. I appreciate, as I'm sure you will too, that both the crust and topping come from the same dough mixture.

SKILL LEVEL: **Beginner**

PREP: **20 minutes**

BAKE: **45 minutes**

TOTAL: **1 hour 5 minutes, plus cooling**

2 cups all-purpose flour **(250g)**

1½ cups rolled oats **(128g)**

¾ cup brown sugar **(150g)**

1 teaspoon baking powder

1 teaspoon lemon zest

½ teaspoon ground cinnamon

½ teaspoon salt

1 teaspoon vanilla extract

14 tablespoons unsalted butter, cut into 14 pieces, at room temperature **(198g)**

1 cup strawberry jam or preserves **(300g)**

1 cup thinly sliced fresh strawberries **(about 150g)**

1. Preheat the oven to 350°F (177°C). Line a 9-inch square metal baking pan with parchment paper, leaving a few inches of overhang on two opposite sides.

2. In a large bowl using a handheld or stand mixer fitted with the paddle, beat the flour, oats, brown sugar, baking powder, lemon zest, cinnamon, and salt on medium speed until combined. Beat in the vanilla. With the mixer running on low speed, add the butter, one piece at a time. Let the mixer run until the butter has broken down into smaller, flour-coated pieces about the size of a pea. The mixture should be crumbly.

3. Press about two-thirds of the crumb mixture into the prepared pan. Using the flat bottom of a metal measuring cup, pack down tightly to form a crust. Bake for 10 minutes.

4. Spread the jam in an even layer over the warm crust. Arrange the sliced strawberries in a single layer over the jam. Sprinkle the remaining crumb mixture evenly over the top, and use a spatula to lightly press it down.

5. Bake for 45 to 50 minutes or until the crust is golden brown and the jam filling is bubbling up around the sides of the pan. Cool the bars completely in the pan set on a cooling rack.

6. Lift the bars out of the pan by gripping the parchment paper overhang; transfer to a cutting board and cut into squares. Store covered tightly at room temperature for up to 3 days or in the refrigerator for up to 1 week.

Gingerbread Cookie Bars

MAKES 18 TO 24 BARS

SKILL LEVEL: **Beginner**

PREP: **20 minutes**

BAKE: **23 minutes**

TOTAL: **2 hours 15 minutes, including cooling and chilling**

These soft gingerbread cookie bars are really easy to make—no dough chilling, no rolling pin, no cookie cutters, no stress! They're chewy like brownies, with a deep and distinctive gingerbread flavor. This holiday treat offers big reward for minimal effort, which is why the recipe has become a beloved staple on my website.

Cookie Bars

2¼ cups all-purpose flour **(281g)**

2 teaspoons ground ginger

1½ teaspoons baking soda

1 teaspoon ground cinnamon

¼ teaspoon ground allspice

¼ teaspoon ground cloves

¼ teaspoon ground nutmeg

¼ teaspoon salt

Small pinch of freshly ground black pepper

12 tablespoons unsalted butter, melted **(170g)**

½ cup dark brown sugar **(100g)**

½ cup granulated sugar **(100g)**

⅓ cup unsulfured molasses **(113g)**

1 large egg, at room temperature

1 teaspoon vanilla extract

Spiced Cream Cheese Frosting

6 ounces full-fat brick cream cheese, at room temperature **(170g)**

2 tablespoons unsalted butter, at room temperature **(28g)**

1½ cups powdered sugar **(180g)**

1 teaspoon vanilla extract

Small pinch of ground allspice

Small pinch of ground cinnamon

Small pinch of ground ginger

Pinch of salt, as needed

Sprinkles, for garnish (optional)

1. Preheat the oven to 350°F (177°C). Line a 9 × 13-inch metal baking pan with parchment paper, leaving a few inches of overhang on two opposite sides.

2. **Make the cookie bars:** In a large bowl, whisk the flour, ginger, baking soda, cinnamon, allspice, cloves, nutmeg, salt, and pepper.

3. In a medium bowl, whisk the melted butter, brown sugar, granulated sugar, and molasses until no lumps remain. Whisk in the egg and vanilla. Pour the butter mixture into the flour mixture and mix with a large spoon or spatula until no traces of flour remain. The dough should be thick and shiny. Transfer the dough to the prepared baking pan and press it into a smooth, even layer.

4. Bake for 23 to 26 minutes or until the top is set but still looks quite soft and a toothpick inserted in the center comes out with only a few moist crumbs. Err on the side of underbaking. Bars puff up in the oven and then settle and firm up as they cool. Cool the bars in the pan set on a cooling rack for at least 1 hour.

5. **Make the spiced cream cheese frosting:** In a large bowl using a handheld or stand mixer fitted with the paddle, beat the cream cheese and butter on medium-high speed until smooth, about 2 minutes. Scrape down the sides of the bowl as needed. Add the powdered sugar, vanilla, allspice, cinnamon, and ginger. Beat on low speed for 30 seconds, then increase to high speed and beat for 2 minutes until completely combined and creamy. Taste and beat in a pinch of salt if the frosting is too sweet. Spread the frosting on the cooled bars. Top with sprinkles (if using). To help set the frosting, refrigerate for 30 minutes.

6. Lift the bars out of the pan by gripping the parchment paper overhang; transfer to a cutting board and cut into squares. Store covered tightly in the refrigerator for up to 5 days.

Chewy Tahini Granola Bars

MAKES 18 BARS

Tahini is sesame seed paste and has a mild earthy flavor that fits perfectly in baked goods. Here it's combined with chewy oats, tart dried cherries, sweet honey, and chocolate, in seeded bars that pack a ton of flavor, for an exceptionally satisfying treat. After I perfected this recipe, the wholesome bars quickly became a repeat favorite, and I dubbed them the Official Snack of Sally's Cookbook.

SKILL LEVEL: **Beginner**
PREP: **25 minutes**
BAKE: **20 minutes**
TOTAL: **45 minutes, plus cooling**

Granola Bars

2 cups rolled oats **(170g)**

½ cup unsweetened shredded coconut **(50g)**

½ cup roughly chopped dried cherries **(85g)**

⅓ cup raw pepitas (green pumpkin seeds) **(50g)**

¼ cup mini chocolate chips **(43g)**

2 tablespoons chia seeds

½ teaspoon ground cinnamon

¼ teaspoon salt

½ cup honey **(170g)**

⅓ cup tahini **(85g)**

¼ cup coconut oil, melted **(56g)**

1 teaspoon vanilla extract

Topping

⅓ cup mini chocolate chips or regular chocolate chips, or 2 ounces chopped chocolate **(57g)**

½ teaspoon coconut oil

Sesame seeds, for sprinkling (optional)

1. Make the granola bars: Preheat the oven to 350°F (177°C). Line a 9-inch square metal baking pan with parchment paper, leaving a few inches of overhang on two opposite sides.

2. In a blender or food processor, combine the oats and coconut and pulse about 10 times until the mixture is coarsely and uniformly chopped. Transfer to a large bowl and stir in the dried cherries, pepitas, mini chocolate chips, chia seeds, cinnamon, and salt.

3. In a medium bowl, whisk the honey, tahini, coconut oil, and vanilla. Pour this mixture over the oat mixture and stir until completely combined. Press the mixture into the prepared pan and use the bottom of a metal measuring cup to pack it down as firmly as possible.

4. Bake for 20 to 25 minutes or until the edges are lightly browned. Cool the bars completely in the pan set on a cooling rack.

5. Make the topping: Melt the chocolate chips with the coconut oil, stirring until smooth and fully combined (see Melting Chocolate, page 20). Drizzle over the cooled granola bars and sprinkle with sesame seeds (if using). Refrigerate uncovered for at least 20 minutes to set the chocolate.

6. Lift the bars out of the pan by gripping the parchment paper overhang; transfer to a cutting board and cut into bars. Store covered tightly at room temperature for up to 5 days or in the refrigerator for up to 1 week.

Key Lime Cheesecake Bars

MAKES 18 TO 24 BARS

SKILL LEVEL: **Beginner**

PREP: **35 minutes**

BAKE: **50 minutes**

TOTAL: **7 hours 30 minutes, including cooling and chilling**

Here we have three dreamy layers that combine the refreshing flavor of key lime pie with the creamy decadence of cheesecake. I add extra flavor to the crust by browning the butter, a less-than-10-minute step that packs an impressive amount of flavor. Though you don't have to bake the bars in a water bath, letting them cool in the oven with the door ajar helps prevent the surface from cracking. This vibrant dessert is perfect for summer potlucks, BBQs, and any warm-weather gathering where a cold treat just hits the spot!

Crust

2 cups graham cracker crumbs (about 16 full-sheet graham crackers) **(240g)**

⅓ cup granulated sugar **(67g)**

8 tablespoons unsalted butter, cut into 8 pieces **(113g)**

Filling

24 ounces full-fat brick cream cheese, at room temperature **(678g)**

1¼ cups granulated sugar **(250g)**

1 cup full-fat sour cream, at room temperature **(240g)**

½ cup lime or key lime juice, at room temperature **(120g/ml)**

2 tablespoons lime or key lime zest

2 teaspoons vanilla extract

4 large eggs, at room temperature

Topping

1½ cups heavy cream, cold **(360g/ml)**

3 tablespoons powdered sugar

1 teaspoon vanilla extract

½ teaspoon lime or key lime zest, plus more for garnish

1. Preheat the oven to 350°F (177°C). Line a 9 × 13-inch metal baking pan with parchment paper, leaving a few inches of overhang on two opposite sides.

2. Make the crust: In a large bowl, stir the graham cracker crumbs and sugar. Set aside.

3. Brown the butter (see Browning Butter, page 20). Once browned, immediately remove from heat and pour the butter over the graham cracker mixture, scraping up all the browned solids at the bottom of the pan and adding them as well. Stir until the crumbs are uniformly moistened, breaking up any clumps. The mixture should be thick, coarse, and sandy.

4. Pour the mixture into the prepared baking pan. Pat and press the crumbs down to make an even, compact crust. Bake the crust for 10 minutes. Place on a cooling rack while you make the filling. **Reduce the oven temperature to 325°F (163°C).**

5. Make the filling: In a large bowl using a handheld or stand mixer fitted with the paddle, beat the cream cheese and sugar on medium-high speed until smooth and creamy, about 2 minutes. Beat in the sour cream, lime juice, lime zest, and vanilla. Scrape down the sides of the bowl as needed. With the mixer running on medium speed, add the eggs one at a time, beating after each addition just until combined. Pour the cheesecake batter over the warm crust and use a spatula to smooth it into an even layer.

6. Bake for 40 to 45 minutes or until the center is almost set. When done, the center of the cheesecake bars will wobble slightly if you gently tap the pan.

7. Turn off the oven and leave the cheesecake bars in the oven for 1 hour with the door ajar. After 1 hour, transfer the pan to a cooling rack and allow the bars to cool for 1 hour.

8. Make the topping: In a large bowl using a handheld or stand mixer fitted with the whisk, beat the cream, powdered sugar, vanilla, and lime zest on medium-high speed until medium-stiff peaks form, 3 to 4 minutes. Spread the whipped cream evenly over the cheesecake bars and sprinkle with extra lime zest. Refrigerate, uncovered, for at least 4 hours or up to 1 day. If refrigerating for longer than 4 hours, cover the bars.

9. Lift the bars out of the pan by gripping the parchment paper overhang; transfer to a cutting board and cut into squares. Store covered tightly in the refrigerator for up to 5 days.

Vanilla Bean Shortbread Bars

MAKES 16 BARS

Smooth, melt-in-your-mouth, mildly sweet shortbread is a simple delight, and this is the best way I know how to make it. Without other added flavorings, butter and vanilla take the spotlight. Along with the flour, cornstarch provides the shortbread with structure, but its main job is keeping the bars extra soft, tender, and light. Thanks to the confinement of the baking pan, there's no risk of this dough overspreading, a common issue with shortbread cookies. And as a nice bonus, there's no need to chill the dough!

SKILL LEVEL: **Beginner**

PREP: **10 minutes**

BAKE: **28 minutes**

TOTAL: **1 hour 15 minutes, including cooling**

16 tablespoons unsalted butter, at room temperature **(226g)**

⅔ cup granulated sugar **(133g)**

2 cups all-purpose flour **(250g)**

¼ cup cornstarch **(28g)**

1½ teaspoons vanilla extract

Seeds scraped from ½ of a vanilla bean

½ teaspoon salt

Coarse sparkling sugar, for topping

1. Preheat the oven to 350°F (177°C). Line a 9-inch square metal baking pan with parchment paper, leaving a few inches of overhang on two opposite sides.

2. In a large bowl using a handheld or stand mixer fitted with the paddle, beat the butter and granulated sugar on medium-high speed until the mixture is light and creamy, about 3 minutes. Add the flour, cornstarch, vanilla, vanilla bean seeds, and salt, and beat on low speed until combined. The dough should be thick and stiff.

3. Press the dough evenly into the prepared pan, smoothing out the surface as much as possible. Sprinkle lightly with coarse sugar and prick the surface a few times with a fork.

4. Bake for 28 to 32 minutes or until the edges are golden brown. Cool in the pan set on a cooling rack for 30 minutes.

5. Lift the shortbread out of the pan by gripping the parchment paper overhang; transfer to a cutting board and cut into squares while still slightly warm. Store covered tightly at room temperature for up to 1 week.

Millionaire's Shortbread Bars

MAKES 16 BARS

SKILL LEVEL: **Intermediate**

PREP: **35 minutes**

BAKE: **20 minutes**

TOTAL: **3 hours 10 minutes, including 2 hours chilling**

Playfully called millionaire's shortbread because of how lavish they taste, these triple-layer bars feature a wealth of decadence. I tested plenty of variations to perfect each element. The result is an extra soft yet sturdy shortbread base, a buttery caramel layer that cuts neatly, and a smooth chocolate topping that sets just right. Sweetened condensed milk is the secret to achieving a soft, perfectly sliceable caramel layer, while corn syrup helps prevent crystallization and gives the caramel a chewier consistency. I can't promise the big bucks, but after one bite you'll feel like you've won the dessert lottery!

Crust

12 tablespoons unsalted butter, at room temperature **(170g)**

½ cup granulated sugar **(100g)**

1⅓ cups all-purpose flour **(167g)**

2 tablespoons cornstarch

1 teaspoon vanilla extract

¼ teaspoon salt

Caramel

1 (14-ounce) can sweetened condensed milk **(396g)**

⅔ cup brown sugar **(133g)**

8 tablespoons unsalted butter, cut into 8 pieces **(113g)**

¼ cup light corn syrup or Lyle's Golden Syrup **(85g)**

½ teaspoon vanilla extract

¼ teaspoon salt

Chocolate Topping

6 ounces semi-sweet chocolate, chopped **(170g)**

4 tablespoons unsalted butter **(56g)**

Flaky sea salt, for topping (optional)

1. Preheat the oven to 350°F (177°C). Line a 9-inch square metal baking pan with parchment paper, leaving a few inches of overhang on two opposite sides.

2. Make the crust: In a large bowl using a handheld or stand mixer fitted with the paddle, beat the butter and sugar on medium-high speed until the mixture is light and creamy, about 3 minutes. Add the flour, cornstarch, vanilla, and salt, and beat on low speed until combined. The mixture will look sandy at first but will eventually come together as the mixer runs. Press the dough evenly into the prepared pan (1), smoothing out the surface as much as possible.

3. Bake for 20 to 23 minutes or until the crust just begins to brown around the edges. Place the pan on a cooling rack while you make the caramel.

4. Make the caramel: In a medium saucepan, combine the condensed milk, brown sugar, butter, and corn syrup. Whisk over medium heat until the butter is melted and the mixture comes to a boil. Boil, whisking occasionally, until the caramel pulls away from the sides of the pan and the mixture reaches a temperature of 225°F (107°C), 5 to 7 minutes. Remove from heat and whisk in the vanilla and salt.

5. Pour the caramel over the shortbread in a smooth, even layer (2). Refrigerate, uncovered, for 1 hour or until the top has set.

6. Make the chocolate topping: Melt the chocolate with the butter, stirring until smooth and fully combined (see Melting Chocolate, page 20). Pour and spread the topping over the caramel layer (3) and gently tap the pan on the counter a few times to smooth out the surface. Sprinkle lightly with flaky sea salt (if using). Refrigerate, uncovered, for at least 1 hour.

7. Lift the bars out of the pan by gripping the parchment paper overhang; transfer to a cutting board and cut into squares. For neat squares, use a sharp knife and wipe it clean between each cut. Store covered tightly at room temperature for up to 2 days or in the refrigerator for up to 1 week.

Salted Brown Butter Pecan Pie Bars

MAKES 18 TO 24 BARS

For many, Thanksgiving just isn't the same without pecan pie. These bars deliver all the nostalgic flavor (and then some) but with half the effort and in a fraction of the time. For the crust, I use a simple press-in shortbread dough. Browning the butter for the crust gives it a toasty, nutty flavor that complements the maple and pecan filling.

SKILL LEVEL: **Beginner**

PREP: **30 minutes**

BAKE: **40 minutes**

TOTAL: **1 hour 15 minutes, including cooling**

Crust

16 tablespoons unsalted butter, cut into 16 pieces **(226g)**

½ cup granulated sugar **(100g)**

2 tablespoons water

1 teaspoon vanilla extract

½ teaspoon salt

2 cups all-purpose flour **(250g)**

1 tablespoon cornstarch

Topping

½ cup pure maple syrup **(170g)**

½ cup dark brown sugar **(100g)**

6 tablespoons unsalted butter **(85g)**

¼ cup heavy cream **(60g/ml)**

2 large eggs, beaten, at room temperature

3 cups chopped pecans **(360g)**

Flaky sea salt, for sprinkling

1. Preheat the oven to 350°F (177°C). Line a 9 × 13-inch metal baking pan with parchment paper, leaving a few inches of overhang on two opposite sides.

2. **Make the crust:** Brown the butter (see Browning Butter, page 20). Once browned, immediately remove from heat and pour it into a large heat-safe glass bowl. Scrape up all the browned solids at the bottom of the skillet and add them as well. Allow to cool for about 10 minutes. Do not rinse out the skillet.

3. Add the sugar, water, vanilla, and salt to the slightly cooled brown butter and stir until combined. Add the flour and cornstarch and mix until the flour disappears. The mixture should be slick. Press the crust evenly into the prepared baking pan.

4. Bake for 15 minutes or until lightly browned on the edges. Place the pan on a cooling rack while you make the topping. Leave the oven on.

5. **Make the topping:** Return the skillet to medium heat and add the maple syrup, brown sugar, butter, and cream. Melt the butter, whisking constantly to combine the ingredients. When the butter has melted, remove the pan from heat and pour the mixture into a large heat-safe bowl. Cool for 5 minutes. Whisk in the beaten eggs, then fold in the pecans. Pour the topping over the warm crust and spread it into an even layer. Lightly sprinkle with flaky sea salt.

6. Bake for 25 to 28 minutes or until a toothpick inserted in the center comes out mostly clean. If the top is browning too quickly, loosely tent aluminum foil over the pan. Cool the bars completely in the pan set on a cooling rack.

7. Lift the bars out of the pan by gripping the parchment paper overhang; transfer to a cutting board and cut into squares. Store covered tightly at room temperature for up to 1 week.

Cakes of

All Sorts

Chocolate Ganache Cake: 2 Ways

SERVES 12

The ultimate chocolate cake has made its grand entrance. This supremely moist cake with rich, bold chocolate flavor can be layered with either creamy peanut butter frosting or fluffy chocolate mousse. Whichever filling you choose, you'll enrobe the layered cake with silky chocolate ganache that keeps the sweetness pleasantly balanced. Both the peanut butter and chocolate mousse versions have received glowing reviews on my website and are truly the crown jewels of my cake-baking career.

> **SKILL LEVEL: Intermediate**
>
> **PREP: 40 minutes to 3 hours, depending on filling**
>
> **BAKE: 24 minutes**
>
> **TOTAL: 5 to 7 hours, including cooling and chilling**

Cake

Nonstick spray or butter, for the pan

1¾ cups all-purpose flour **(219g)**

1¾ cups granulated sugar **(350g)**

¾ cup unsweetened natural cocoa powder **(64g)**

2 teaspoons instant espresso powder (optional)

2 teaspoons baking soda

1 teaspoon baking powder

1 teaspoon salt

¾ cup full-fat sour cream, at room temperature **(180g)**

½ cup vegetable oil **(113g/120ml)**

2 large eggs, at room temperature

½ cup buttermilk, at room temperature **(120g/ml)**

2 teaspoons vanilla extract

½ cup hot water or hot black coffee **(120g/ml)**

1 cup mini chocolate chips tossed in 1 tablespoon flour **(170g)**

Chocolate Mousse Filling

½ cup hot water **(120g/ml)**

¼ cup unsweetened natural or Dutch-process cocoa powder **(21g)**

8 ounces semi-sweet chocolate, finely chopped **(226g)**

2 cups heavy cream, cold **(480g/ml)**

2 tablespoons powdered sugar

½ teaspoon vanilla extract

Chocolate Ganache

8 ounces semi-sweet chocolate, finely chopped **(226g)**

1 cup heavy cream **(240g/ml)**

Fresh berries or chopped peanut butter cups, for garnish (optional)

TIP: When time is an issue, note that the peanut butter frosting takes just 5 minutes while the chocolate mousse requires more than 2 hours of chilling time. To get ahead, you can make both the cake layers and mousse filling up to 2 days in advance.

1. Preheat the oven to 350°F (177°C). Grease three 9-inch round cake pans with nonstick spray, line with parchment paper rounds, and grease the parchment (see Lining a Round Cake Pan . . . , page 82).

2. Make the cake: In a large bowl, whisk the flour, sugar, cocoa powder, espresso powder (if using), baking soda, baking powder, and salt.

3. In another large bowl using a handheld or stand mixer fitted with the whisk, mix the sour cream, oil, and eggs on medium-high speed. Add the buttermilk and vanilla and mix until combined. Pour the flour mixture into the buttermilk mixture and add the hot water. Whisk on low speed until combined. Fold in the floured chocolate chips. The batter should be thin and you may see some air bubbles on the surface—that's normal. Divide the batter evenly among the prepared pans and smooth the tops.

4. Bake for 24 to 26 minutes or until a toothpick inserted in the center comes out clean. Cool the cakes in the pans set on a cooling rack for 1 hour. Run a knife around the edges to help loosen the sides, remove the cakes from the pans, peel off the parchment, and place on the cooling rack to finish cooling.

5. Make the chocolate mousse filling: In a small bowl, whisk the hot water and cocoa powder until smooth. Melt the chocolate (see Melting Chocolate, page 20). Pour the cocoa mixture into the melted chocolate and stir until thick and smooth; set aside. In a large bowl using a handheld or stand mixer fitted with the whisk, whip the cream, powdered sugar, and vanilla on medium-high speed until medium peaks form, about 3 minutes. Pour in the chocolate mixture and gently fold together with a spatula until combined. Do not overmix, as this could deflate it. Cover the mousse and refrigerate for at least 2 hours or up to 2 days before using.

recipe continues >

6. Assemble the cake: (For a detailed description of the steps, see Assembling Layer Cakes, page 88.) Level the layers. Place one on a serving plate and spread with 1½ cups (200g) of the chocolate mousse filling (1) (or 1 cup [240g] of the peanut butter frosting). Top with the second cake layer, upside down, and spread the same amount of filling as on the first layer. Top with the third cake layer, right side up, and spread the remaining filling on top and around the sides. Run a bench scraper around the cake to help smooth out the sides (2). Refrigerate the cake for at least 1 hour or up to 4 hours to set.

7. Make the chocolate ganache: Place the chocolate in a medium heat-safe bowl. In a small saucepan, heat the cream over medium heat just until it begins to simmer. Do not let it come to a full boil—that's too hot! Pour the cream over the chocolate and let it sit for 2 to 3 minutes. With a metal spoon or small spatula, slowly stir until the chocolate has melted and the mixture is smooth. Refrigerate the ganache for at least 30 minutes or up to 1 hour to thicken.

8. Spoon or pour the thickened ganache on the chilled cake (3) and use a large icing spatula to spread it evenly over the top and sides. Garnish with berries or peanut butter cups (if using). Serve immediately or cover and refrigerate for up to 1 day before serving. The cake can be served at room temperature or chilled. Store covered in the refrigerator for up to 5 days.

ALTERNATE FILLING
Peanut Butter Frosting
12 tablespoons unsalted butter, at room temperature **(170g)**

1¾ cups creamy peanut butter (the processed kind, not natural) **(440g)**

1¾ cups powdered sugar **(210g)**

1 teaspoon vanilla extract

Pinch of salt

3 tablespoons heavy cream, at room temperature

In a large bowl using a handheld or stand mixer fitted with the paddle, beat the butter on medium speed until creamy, about 2 minutes. Add the peanut butter and beat until combined, about 1 minute. Scrape down the sides of the bowl as needed. Add the powdered sugar, vanilla, and salt. With the mixer running on low speed, pour in the cream. Increase to medium-high speed and beat for 2 minutes. Use as instructed in step 6.

Lining a Round Cake Pan with Parchment Paper Rounds

1. Set one of the cake pans on a sheet of parchment and trace around it with a pencil. Trace as many rounds as needed for the number of pans you're using.

2. Cut out the rounds, just inside the pencil line.

3. Very lightly grease the cake pan(s) with butter or nonstick spray.

4. Place a parchment round inside a pan, pressing it to adhere to the bottom.

5. Lightly grease the parchment. Greasing both the pan and parchment round creates an ultra-nonstick environment so the cake won't stick to the pan, and the parchment round won't stick to the cake.

Soft & Moist White Vanilla Cake

SERVES 10 TO 12

SKILL LEVEL: **Beginner**

PREP: **30 minutes**

BAKE: **24 minutes**

TOTAL: **4 hours, including cooling**

To say I treasure this cake recipe is an understatement. It yields a pristine white vanilla cake with a light, fluffy crumb thanks to the careful combination of cake flour, egg whites, and sour cream. Since developing the recipe in 2017, I have used the batter as the base for many other variations, including Strawberry Cake (page 89). I always decorate this with vanilla buttercream, but you can swap it for chocolate buttercream from the Marble Cake recipe (page 87) or whipped cream cheese frosting used with the Red Velvet Cupcakes (page 118).

Cake

Nonstick spray or butter, for the pan

2½ cups cake flour **(295g)**

2 teaspoons baking powder

1 teaspoon salt

½ teaspoon baking soda

12 tablespoons unsalted butter, at room temperature **(170g)**

1¾ cups granulated sugar **(350g)**

5 large egg whites, at room temperature

½ cup full-fat sour cream, at room temperature **(120g)**

1 tablespoon vanilla extract

1 cup whole milk, at room temperature **(240g/ml)**

Vanilla Buttercream

20 tablespoons unsalted butter, at room temperature **(282g)**

5 cups powdered sugar **(600g)**

⅓ cup heavy cream, half-and-half, or whole milk, at room temperature **(80g/ml)**

2 teaspoons vanilla extract

⅛ teaspoon salt, as needed

1. Preheat the oven to 350°F (177°C). Grease two 9-inch round cake pans with nonstick spray, line with parchment paper rounds, and grease the parchment.

2. **Make the cake:** In a medium bowl, whisk the flour, baking powder, salt, and baking soda.

3. In a large bowl using a handheld or stand mixer fitted with the paddle, beat the butter and sugar on high speed until the mixture is light and creamy, about 3 minutes. Add the egg whites and beat on high speed until combined, about 2 minutes. Scrape down the sides of the bowl as needed. Add the sour cream and vanilla and beat on medium-high speed until combined, about 1 minute. Add the flour mixture and then, with the mixer on low speed, slowly pour in the milk and beat just until combined. Whisk the batter by hand a few times to ensure there are no lumps at the bottom of the bowl. Do not overmix. The batter should be slightly thick. Pour the batter evenly into the prepared pans and smooth the tops.

4. Bake for 24 to 25 minutes or until a toothpick inserted in the center comes out clean. Cool the cakes in the pans set on a cooling rack for 1 hour. Run a knife around the edges to help loosen the sides, remove the cakes from the pans, peel off the parchment, and place on the cooling rack to finish cooling.

5. **Make the vanilla buttercream:** (See American-Style Buttercream, opposite, for tips.) In a large bowl using a handheld or stand mixer fitted with the paddle, beat the butter on medium speed until creamy, about 2 minutes. Sift in the powdered sugar and then add the cream and vanilla. Beat on low speed for 30 seconds, then increase to medium-high speed and beat for 2 full minutes. Taste; beat in the salt if the frosting is too sweet.

6. **Assemble the cake:** (For a detailed description of the steps, see Assembling Layer Cakes, page 88.) Level the layers. Place one on a serving plate and spread ¾ to 1 cup (180 to 240g) of the vanilla buttercream in an even layer. Top with the second cake layer, upside down, and spread the top and sides with 1 cup (240g) buttercream in a very thin layer to make the crumb coat. If desired, run a bench scraper around the cake to help smooth out the buttercream on the sides. Refrigerate the cake until the crumb coat has set, about 20 minutes. Finish by spreading the top and sides with the remaining buttercream.

7. Slice and serve immediately or keep at room temperature for a few hours before serving. Store covered in the refrigerator for up to 5 days.

Tips for Success

AMERICAN-STYLE BUTTERCREAM

The vanilla buttercream (page 84), chocolate buttercream (page 87), and mocha buttercream (page 111) are American-style buttercreams. They do not require cooking and they use powdered sugar to both sweeten and thicken. Review the following tips before you begin:

- **Use These Tools:** An electric mixer creams the butter into a smooth, sturdy base. A fine-mesh sieve aerates the powdered sugar (and cocoa powder for chocolate and mocha buttercreams) and rids any large lumps.
- **Pop the Bubbles:** During the beating process, air is introduced into the buttercream. For perfectly smooth buttercream, use the paddle instead of the whisk attachment of a stand mixer and don't overmix. To ensure that the buttercream has a smooth, creamy texture on the cake, you can pop the air bubbles. Grab a wooden spoon or spatula and mash the frosting up against the side of the bowl. Do this until most of the air bubbles deflate. This trick requires a lot of arm muscle!

- **Switch It Up:** You can use these buttercreams on a variety of cake and cupcake recipes. Each yields 3 to 4 cups (720 to 960g) of frosting, which is enough to generously frost 12 to 16 cupcakes or a 9- or 8-inch round 2-layer cake.
- **Tint Your Vanilla Buttercream:** You can tint vanilla buttercream with food coloring. I recommend gel food coloring over liquid because you don't need much, and it won't throw off the consistency. Add it with the cream.
- **Darken Your Chocolate Buttercream:** The longer you whip buttercream, the lighter in color it becomes. For darker chocolate buttercream with a glossy finish, briefly heat a portion of the frosting, which helps the cocoa powder absorb more liquid. Place about 1 cup of the prepared buttercream in a heat-safe bowl and microwave it at 50% power for 10 seconds, then stir it back into the rest of the buttercream.

Strawberry Cake

SERVES 10 TO 12

This is the lush strawberry cake recipe I developed when I no longer wished to settle for artificial flavoring. Expectations were low as my final test cake cooled; it's difficult to pack enough natural flavor into cakes without compromising the texture. But when I took that first bite, I just about cried tears of joy. (Or were those actual tears because I had just dirtied every dish with all this recipe testing?) Moist yet light, the cake is supreme strawberry perfection with its flavor coming from reduced strawberry puree in the cake and freeze-dried strawberry powder in the frosting. My efforts have been majorly rewarded since that first bite (and all those dishes), because I've made this cake dozens of times, posted it on my website, and witnessed enthusiastic oohs and ahhs from family, friends, and bakers around the world. What a triumph! See page 90 for visuals.

SKILL LEVEL: Intermediate

PREP: 1 hour 30 minutes

BAKE: 24 minutes

TOTAL: 6 hours, including cooling

Cake

1 pound fresh strawberries, rinsed and hulled **(454g)**

Nonstick spray or butter, for the pans

2½ cups cake flour **(295g)**

2 teaspoons baking powder

1 teaspoon salt

½ teaspoon baking soda

12 tablespoons unsalted butter, at room temperature **(170g)**

1¾ cups granulated sugar **(350g)**

5 large egg whites, at room temperature

⅓ cup full-fat sour cream or plain 2% Greek yogurt, at room temperature **(80g)**

2 teaspoons vanilla extract

½ cup whole milk, at room temperature **(120g/ml)**

1 to 2 drops red or pink gel food coloring (optional)

Strawberry Cream Cheese Frosting

1 cup freeze-dried strawberries **(25g)**

8 ounces full-fat brick cream cheese, at room temperature **(226g)**

8 tablespoons unsalted butter, at room temperature **(113g)**

3 cups powdered sugar **(360g)**

1 tablespoon whole milk, at room temperature

1 teaspoon vanilla extract

Pinch of salt, as needed

Fresh strawberries, for garnish (optional)

1. In a blender or food processor, puree the fresh strawberries (1). You should have a little more than 1 cup (about 270g). Transfer the puree to a small saucepan over medium-low heat. Simmer, stirring occasionally, until it's reduced to ½ cup (about 135g). This usually takes 25 to 35 minutes but could take longer depending on your pan or the ripeness of the strawberries. Remove from heat, pour into a heat-safe bowl, and cool completely before using (2).

2. Preheat the oven to 350°F (177°C). Grease two 9-inch round cake pans with nonstick spray, line with parchment paper rounds, and grease the parchment.

3. Make the cake: In a medium bowl, whisk the flour, baking powder, salt, and baking soda.

4. In a large bowl using a handheld or stand mixer fitted with the paddle, beat the butter and sugar on high speed until the mixture is light and creamy, about 3 minutes. Add the egg whites and beat on high speed until combined, about 2 minutes. Scrape down the sides of the bowl as needed. Add the sour cream and vanilla and beat on medium-high speed until combined, about 1 minute. Add the flour mixture and then, with the mixer on low speed, slowly pour in the milk and beat just until combined. Do not overmix. Whisk in the cooled strawberry puree (3) and food coloring (if using), making sure there are no lumps at the bottom of the bowl. The batter should be slightly thick. Pour the batter evenly into the prepared pans and smooth the tops (4).

recipe continues >

5. Bake for 24 to 25 minutes or until a toothpick inserted in the center comes out clean. Cool the cakes in the pans set on a cooling rack for 1 hour. Run a knife around the edges to loosen the sides, remove the cakes from the pans, peel off the parchment, and place on the cooling rack to finish cooling.

6. **Make the strawberry cream cheese frosting:** In a blender or food processor, process the freeze-dried strawberries to a fine powder. If any larger bits remain, sift the powder through a fine-mesh sieve.

7. In a large bowl using a handheld or stand mixer fitted with the paddle, beat the cream cheese and butter on medium-high speed until smooth, about 2 minutes. Scrape down the sides of the bowl as needed. Add the powdered sugar, strawberry powder, milk, and vanilla. Beat on low speed for 30 seconds, then increase to high speed and beat for 3 minutes until completely combined and creamy. Taste. Beat in the salt if the frosting is too sweet. Cover and refrigerate it for at least 1 hour or up to 8 hours before using.

8. **Assemble the cake:** (For a detailed description of the steps, see Assembling Layer Cakes, page 88.) Level the layers. Place one on a serving plate and spread ¾ to 1 cup (180 to 240g) of the frosting in an even layer on top. Top with the second cake layer, upside down, and spread the top and sides with 1 cup (240g) of the frosting in a very thin layer to make the crumb coat. If desired, run a bench scraper around the cake to help smooth out the frosting on the sides. Refrigerate the cake until the crumb coat has set, about 20 minutes. Cover the top and sides with the remaining frosting. Garnish with fresh strawberries (if using).

9. Before slicing and serving, refrigerate the cake, uncovered, for at least 20 minutes to set the frosting. Or you can cover and store it in the refrigerator for up to 2 days before serving. If you refrigerated the cake for longer than 4 hours, take it out of the refrigerator 2 hours before serving so it can mostly come to room temperature. Store covered in the refrigerator for up to 5 days.

The Only Carrot Cake Recipe You Need

SERVES 12

Calling this cake a fan favorite isn't giving it enough credit. Even a quick glance at the rave reviews on my website proves this is a *fan obsession.* In fact, I've both experienced it myself and have been told that one taste transforms carrot cake skeptics into enthusiasts. I developed the recipe in 2015, and it has been my birthday cake every year since. I love it just as much as my readers do because it's fluffy, dense, spiced, and sweet with an off-the-charts moist crumb. The cream cheese frosting is lusciously smooth and tangy, and because it's refrigerated before using, it holds the cake together nicely. The recipe here is perfect, but if you want to make one change, you can swap the applesauce for canned crushed pineapple.

> SKILL LEVEL: **Beginner**
>
> PREP: **30 minutes**
>
> BAKE: **20 minutes**
>
> TOTAL: **3 hours 30 minutes, including cooling**

Cake

Nonstick spray or butter, for the pans

1½ cups brown sugar **(300g)**

1 cup vegetable oil **(226g/240ml)**

4 large eggs, at room temperature

¾ cup smooth unsweetened applesauce **(180g)**

½ cup granulated sugar **(100g)**

1 teaspoon vanilla extract

2½ cups all-purpose flour **(313g)**

2 teaspoons baking powder

1½ teaspoons ground cinnamon

1 teaspoon baking soda

1 teaspoon ground ginger

½ teaspoon salt

¼ teaspoon ground cloves

¼ teaspoon ground nutmeg

2 cups freshly grated peeled carrots (about 4 large carrots) **(260g)**

2 cups chopped walnuts or pecans, toasted (see Toasting Nuts, page 21), divided **(240g)**

Cream Cheese Frosting

16 ounces full-fat brick cream cheese, at room temperature **(452g)**

8 tablespoons unsalted butter, at room temperature **(113g)**

4 cups powdered sugar **(480g)**

1½ teaspoons vanilla extract

Pinch of salt

1. Preheat the oven to 350°F (177°C). Grease three 9-inch round cake pans with nonstick spray, line with parchment paper rounds, and grease the parchment.

2. Make the cake: In a large bowl, whisk the brown sugar, oil, eggs, applesauce, granulated sugar, and vanilla until no lumps remain.

3. In another large bowl, whisk the flour, baking powder, cinnamon, baking soda, ginger, salt, cloves, and nutmeg. Add the applesauce mixture to the flour mixture and, using a spatula, mix and fold the ingredients until combined, making sure there are no pockets of dry ingredients at the bottom of the bowl. Fold in the carrots and 1 cup (about 120g) of the toasted nuts. The batter should be slightly thick and a few lumps are okay. Pour the batter evenly into the prepared pans and smooth the tops.

4. Bake for 20 to 25 minutes or until a toothpick inserted in the center comes out clean. Cool the cakes in the pans set on a cooling rack for 1 hour. Run a knife around the edges to help loosen the sides, remove the cakes from the pans, peel off the parchment, and place on the cooling rack to finish cooling.

5. Make the cream cheese frosting: In a large bowl using a handheld or stand mixer fitted with the paddle, beat the cream cheese and butter on medium-high speed until smooth, about 2 minutes. Scrape down the sides of the bowl as needed. Add the powdered sugar, vanilla, and salt. Beat on low speed for 30 seconds, then increase to high speed and beat for 3 minutes until completely combined and creamy. Cover and refrigerate it for at least 1 hour or up to 8 hours.

6. Assemble the cake: (For a detailed description of the steps, see Assembling Layer Cakes, page 88.) Level the layers. Place one on a serving plate and spread ¾ to 1 cup (180 to 240g) of the frosting in an even layer on top. Top with the second cake layer, upside down, and spread the same amount of frosting as on the first layer. Top with the third cake layer, right side up, and spread the top and sides with 1 cup (240g) frosting in a very thin layer to make the crumb coat. If desired, run a bench scraper around the cake to help smooth out the frosting on the sides. Refrigerate the cake until the crumb coat has set, about 20 minutes. Cover the top and sides with the remaining frosting. Garnish with the remaining nuts.

7. Before slicing and serving, refrigerate the cake, uncovered, for at least 20 minutes to set the frosting. If you refrigerated the cake for longer than 4 hours, take it out of the refrigerator 2 hours before serving so it can mostly come to room temperature. Store covered in the refrigerator for up to 5 days.

Berries & Cream Pavlova Cake

SERVES 8 TO 10

SKILL LEVEL: **Intermediate**

PREP: **30 minutes**

BAKE: **1 hour 20 minutes**

TOTAL: **7 hours, including cooling**

Pavlova is a meringue-based dessert that's crisp on the edges, chewy on top, and marshmallow-soft in the center. That's three different textures in one single bite and, yes, it's extraordinary! It also makes a lovely layer cake and happens to be naturally gluten-free. Bake the meringue layers low and slow, and after they cool in the oven, layer them with fluffy lemon-hinted whipped cream and juicy berries. I like to doll up the Pavlova with white chocolate curls and fresh mint sprigs.

Meringues

Nonstick spray, for the pans

1⅓ cups granulated sugar **(267g)**

6 large egg whites, at room temperature

1 teaspoon vanilla extract

1½ teaspoons cornstarch

½ teaspoon cream of tartar

Berry Topping

3 cups mixed fresh berries (if using strawberries, slice thin) **(about 450g)**

1 tablespoon granulated sugar

1 teaspoon lemon zest

Whipped Cream Topping

2 cups heavy cream, cold **(480g/ml)**

3 tablespoons granulated sugar

2 tablespoons fresh lemon juice

1 teaspoon vanilla extract

Optional Garnishes

White chocolate curls

Fresh mint sprigs

MAKE-AHEAD TIP: Once the meringue layers are cool, you can store them, covered, at room temperature for up to 2 days, but be aware that humid or rainy weather may cause them to soften. For best taste and texture, I do not recommend freezing this cake.

1. Preheat the oven to 350°F (177°C). Using a pencil, trace around an 8-inch round cake pan on two sheets of parchment paper. Flip the sheets over and place them pencil side down on two baking sheets. Grease each lightly with nonstick spray.

2. Make the meringues: In a food processor or blender, process the sugar until it is very fine, about 1 minute.

3. In a large bowl using a handheld or stand mixer fitted with the whisk, beat the egg whites on medium-high speed until soft peaks form, about 3 minutes. Add half of the sugar and beat for 30 seconds. Add the remaining sugar and the vanilla and beat on high speed until stiff, glossy peaks form, 2 to 3 minutes (1). The peaks should be stiff enough that you can hold the bowl upside down and they won't move. Using a spatula, gently fold in the cornstarch and cream of tartar until combined.

4. Divide the egg white mixture evenly between the two circles. Using an offset spatula, gently spread it in an even layer to the edges of the circles (2).

5. Place both baking sheets in the oven. As soon as you close the oven door, **reduce the oven temperature to 200°F (93°C).** Bake until the meringues are firm and dry, about 1 hour 20 minutes. Halfway through baking, swap the pans between racks and rotate them 180 degrees.

6. Turn off the oven and open the oven door slightly. With the door ajar, let the meringues cool completely in the oven, about 4 hours.

7. Make the berry topping: In a large bowl, gently toss the berries, sugar, and lemon zest.

8. Make the whipped cream topping: In a large bowl using a handheld or stand mixer fitted with the whisk, whip the cream, sugar, lemon juice, and vanilla on medium-high speed until medium peaks form, about 3 minutes. You want the peaks to be somewhat soft so the whipped cream spreads nicely.

9. Using a thin metal spatula, carefully lift a cooled meringue off the parchment and place on a cake stand or serving plate. Using an offset spatula, spread about half of the whipped cream over top, then add half of the berries (3). Repeat with the second meringue (4) and remaining whipped cream and berries. Garnish with white chocolate curls and mint (if using).

10. Slice and serve immediately or refrigerate, uncovered, for up to 4 hours before serving. Store covered in the refrigerator for up to 2 days. The meringues may start to weep droplets of liquid after a few hours, but this does not affect the taste.

TIP: You will need to bake the two layers on separate baking sheets. Bake them on the center and lower oven racks. If your oven isn't large enough, bake and cool them one at a time.

Caramel Sheet Cake

SERVES 12

Brown sugar–hinted with a tender, moist crumb, this buttermilk cake stole my heart when I developed the recipe. As the icing sets, it thickens to the consistency of caramel fudge candy, a perfect counterpoint to the soft cake. To enhance the flavor in both the cake and icing, my top recommendation is to use dark brown sugar instead of light brown. The cake is sweet but not cloyingly so, thanks to the salt and tangy buttermilk.

SKILL LEVEL: **Intermediate**
PREP: **30 minutes**
BAKE: **30 minutes**
TOTAL: **3 hours 30 minutes, including cooling**

Cake

Nonstick spray or butter, for the pans

2⅓ cups cake flour **(275g)**

2 teaspoons baking powder

¾ teaspoon salt

¼ teaspoon baking soda

12 tablespoons unsalted butter, at room temperature **(170g)**

1 cup granulated sugar **(200g)**

½ cup dark brown sugar **(100g)**

2 large eggs, at room temperature

2 teaspoons vanilla extract

1½ cups buttermilk, at room temperature **(360g/ml)**

Caramel Icing

1½ cups powdered sugar **(180g)**

¾ cup dark brown sugar **(150g)**

5 tablespoons unsalted butter, cut into 5 pieces **(71g)**

¼ cup buttermilk, at room temperature **(60g/ml)**

1 teaspoon vanilla extract

Pinch of salt

Flaky sea salt, for garnish (optional)

1. Preheat the oven to 350°F (177°C). Grease a 9 × 13-inch glass or metal baking pan with nonstick spray, line with parchment paper, and grease the parchment.

2. Make the cake: In a medium bowl, whisk the flour, baking powder, salt, and baking soda.

3. In a large bowl using a handheld or stand mixer fitted with the paddle, beat the butter, granulated sugar, and brown sugar on high speed until the mixture is light and creamy, about 3 minutes. Add the eggs and vanilla and beat on high speed until combined, about 2 minutes. Scrape down the sides of the bowl as needed. Add about half of the flour mixture and then, with the mixer on low speed, slowly pour in half the buttermilk and beat just until combined. Add the remaining flour mixture and then, with the mixer on low speed, slowly pour in the remaining buttermilk and beat just until combined. Whisk the batter by hand a few times to ensure that there are no lumps at the bottom of the bowl. The batter should be slightly thick. Pour the batter into the prepared pan and smooth the top.

4. Bake for 30 to 34 minutes, tenting with aluminum foil after about 20 minutes to prevent the top from becoming too brown. The cake is done when the edges are lightly browned and a toothpick inserted in the center comes out clean. Cool the cake in the pan set on a cooling rack while you make the icing. The cake can still be slightly warm when the icing is added.

5. Make the caramel icing: Sift the powdered sugar into a large heat-safe bowl. Set aside.

6. In a medium saucepan, stir the brown sugar and butter over medium heat until the mixture comes to a boil. If the butter separates from the sugar, remove the pan from heat, whisk vigorously to combine, and return to medium heat. Slowly add the buttermilk and stand back a bit; the mixture will rapidly bubble up. Whisking constantly, boil for 1 minute. Remove from heat and stir in the vanilla and salt.

7. Pour the mixture over the powdered sugar and whisk until smooth. Allow to cool and thicken for 15 to 20 minutes. Pour the warm icing over the cake and use an icing spatula to spread it to the edges. Sprinkle lightly with flaky sea salt (if using).

8. Cool completely before slicing and serving. The icing will thicken as it cools. Store covered tightly in the refrigerator for up to 5 days.

Blueberry Bundt Cake

SERVES 12

SKILL LEVEL: **Beginner**

PREP: **25 minutes**

BAKE: **55 minutes**

TOTAL: **3 hours, including cooling**

Bursting with blueberries and brightened with lemon, this super-moist cake is a flavor-packed dream! Sour cream is imperative to achieving its fluffy, tender crumb. Bundt cakes tend to stick to the pan, so to help ensure the cake seamlessly releases, grease *and* flour the pan before adding the batter.

Cake

Nonstick spray or butter and flour, for the pan

2 cups fresh blueberries, washed and patted dry **(280g)**

2¾ cups + 1 tablespoon all-purpose flour, divided **(344g)**

1½ teaspoons baking powder

¾ teaspoon salt

½ teaspoon baking soda

16 tablespoons unsalted butter, at room temperature **(226g)**

1¾ cups granulated sugar **(350g)**

3 large eggs, at room temperature

1 cup full-fat sour cream, at room temperature **(240g)**

⅓ cup fresh lemon juice, at room temperature **(80g/ml)**

2 tablespoons lemon zest

1 teaspoon vanilla extract

Creamy Lemon Icing

1 cup powdered sugar, sifted **(120g)**

1½ tablespoons fresh lemon juice

1 tablespoon heavy cream

Lemon zest, for garnish (optional)

1. Preheat the oven to 350°F (177°C). Grease a 10- to 12-cup Bundt pan with nonstick spray and lightly coat with flour.

2. Make the cake: In a medium bowl, gently toss the blueberries with 1 tablespoon of the flour. In a second medium bowl, whisk the remaining flour, baking powder, salt, and baking soda.

3. In a large bowl using a handheld or stand mixer fitted with the paddle, beat the butter and sugar on medium-high speed until the mixture is light and creamy, about 3 minutes. Scrape down the sides of the bowl as needed. Add the eggs and beat until combined. Add the sour cream, lemon juice, lemon zest, and vanilla, and beat on medium-high speed until combined, about 1 minute. The mixture will look a bit curdled. Add the flour mixture and beat on low speed until combined. The batter should be thick and creamy. Gently fold in the floured blueberries. Pour the batter into the prepared pan and smooth the top.

4. Bake for 55 to 60 minutes or until the edges of the cake are golden brown and a toothpick inserted in the center comes out clean. Cool the cake in the pan set on a cooling rack for 1 hour.

5. Run a knife around the edges to help loosen the cake from the pan, and then invert the cake onto a large plate, cake stand, or platter. Cool for at least 30 minutes more before icing.

6. Make the creamy lemon icing: In a medium bowl, whisk the powdered sugar, lemon juice, and cream until smooth. Drizzle the icing on the cake and garnish with lemon zest (if using). Store covered at room temperature for up to 2 days or in the refrigerator for up to 5 days.

Almond Poppy Seed Loaf Cake

MAKES 1 LOAF

During the time I was testing recipes for this book, my younger daughter was three years old. As one can imagine, she was overjoyed by the Baked Chocolate Cake Donuts (page 205), but this is the recipe she loved the most. "It's my faaaavorite!!" she repeatedly exclaimed in a sing-songy voice. Buttery moist and sweet, this almond extract–kissed loaf cake has added texture from poppy seeds in the crumb and toasty almonds on top. Almond simple syrup was a last-minute addition, and now I can't imagine the loaf without that glorious finishing touch. Pour it over the warm cake before slicing, take that first bite, and you might find a new "faaaavorite" too!

> SKILL LEVEL: **Beginner**
> PREP: **20 minutes**
> BAKE: **50 minutes**
> TOTAL: **1 hour 45 minutes, including cooling**

Cake

Nonstick spray or butter, for the pan

2 cups all-purpose flour **(250g)**

1½ tablespoons poppy seeds

1 teaspoon baking powder

½ teaspoon baking soda

½ teaspoon salt

8 tablespoons unsalted butter, at room temperature **(113g)**

1 cup granulated sugar **(200g)**

2 large eggs, at room temperature

⅓ cup full-fat sour cream, at room temperature **(80g)**

⅓ cup milk, at room temperature **(80g/ml)**

¼ cup vegetable oil **(56g/60ml)**

1 teaspoon almond extract

⅓ cup sliced almonds, for topping **(42g)**

Almond Simple Syrup

¼ cup water **(60g/ml)**

¼ cup granulated sugar **(50g)**

¼ teaspoon almond extract

1. Preheat the oven to 350°F (177°C). Grease a 9 × 5-inch loaf pan with non-stick spray.

2. **Make the cake:** In a medium bowl, whisk the flour, poppy seeds, baking powder, baking soda, and salt.

3. In a large bowl using a handheld or stand mixer fitted with the paddle, beat the butter and sugar on medium-high speed until the mixture is light and creamy, about 3 minutes. Add the eggs, sour cream, milk, oil, and almond extract and beat until combined. Scrape down the sides of the bowl as needed. Add the flour mixture and beat on low speed just until the flour disappears. Pour the batter into the prepared pan, smooth the top, and sprinkle with the almonds.

4. Bake for 50 to 55 minutes, tenting with aluminum foil after about 30 minutes to prevent the top from becoming too brown. The cake is done when a toothpick inserted in the center comes out clean. Cool the cake in the pan set on a cooling rack set over parchment paper or a baking sheet for 20 minutes. Remove the cake from the pan and return it to the rack.

5. **Make the almond simple syrup:** In a small saucepan, whisk the water, sugar, and almond extract. Bring to a boil over medium heat, stirring constantly, until the sugar is dissolved. Remove from heat and pour the syrup into a heat-safe glass liquid measuring cup. Cool for 5 minutes and then pour over the warm cake. Let it soak in for at least 10 minutes before slicing and serving. Store covered tightly at room temperature for up to 5 days or in the refrigerator for up to 1 week.

Lemon Lavender Olive Oil Cake

SERVES 8

SKILL LEVEL: **Beginner**
PREP: **30 minutes**
BAKE: **30 minutes**
TOTAL: **2 hours 10 minutes, including cooling**

Introducing a one-layer cake that's suitable any time of day . . . perfect for brunch, charming alongside afternoon tea, and an elegant addition to any dessert spread. Lemon-forward with an aromatic floral note, this olive oil–based cake is a breeze to make with no complicated assembly required. To ensure the delicate lavender flavor shines through, take a moment to pulse the dried lavender and lemon zest with the sugar. And for an extra burst of flavor, brush the warm cake with refreshing lemon lavender simple syrup. As a bonus, the syrup keeps the cake moist for days!

Lemon Lavender Simple Syrup

⅓ cup fresh lemon juice **(80g/ml)**

⅓ cup granulated sugar **(67g)**

1 teaspoon dried culinary lavender buds

Cake

Nonstick spray or butter, for the pan

1 cup granulated sugar **(200g)**

1 tablespoon lemon zest

1 teaspoon dried culinary lavender buds

2 large eggs, at room temperature

⅔ cup extra-virgin olive oil **(150g/160ml)**

½ cup plain 2% Greek yogurt or full-fat sour cream, at room temperature **(120g)**

¼ cup fresh lemon juice **(60g/ml)**

¼ cup milk, at room temperature **(60g/ml)**

1 teaspoon vanilla extract

1¾ cups cake flour **(207g)**

1 teaspoon baking powder

½ teaspoon salt

¼ teaspoon baking soda

Lemon slices and culinary lavender buds, for garnish (optional)

TIP: Purchase food-grade dried lavender buds—sometimes sold as "culinary lavender"—in specialty kitchen shops or online.

1. Make the lemon lavender simple syrup: In a small saucepan, whisk the lemon juice and sugar. Bring to a boil over medium heat, stirring constantly. Once boiling, reduce the heat to low, add the lavender, and simmer for 10 minutes. Remove from heat and strain the syrup through a fine-mesh sieve over a heat-safe glass liquid measuring cup. Discard the lavender and set the syrup aside.

2. Preheat the oven to 350°F (177°C). Grease a 9-inch springform pan with nonstick spray.

3. Make the cake: In a food processor, combine the sugar, lemon zest, and lavender and pulse several times to combine. The sugar is aromatic and moist like brown sugar. Pour it into a large bowl and add the eggs. Whisk until well combined, then whisk in the olive oil, yogurt, lemon juice, milk, and vanilla.

4. In a medium bowl, whisk the flour, baking powder, salt, and baking soda. Add to the egg mixture and whisk lightly just until combined. The batter should be slightly thick. Pour the batter into the prepared pan and smooth the top.

5. Bake for 30 to 35 minutes or until a toothpick inserted in the center comes out clean. Cool the cake in the pan set on a cooling rack for 10 minutes.

6. Pour the simple syrup over the warm cake, then set aside to cool for at least 1 hour. Remove the outer ring of the pan and garnish the cake with lemon slices and a scattering of lavender buds (if using). Slice and serve. Store covered tightly at room temperature for up to 5 days or in the refrigerator for up to 1 week.

Tiramisu Cake Roll

SERVES 10

Soaked with espresso, filled with mascarpone cream, spiked with alcohol, and finished with cocoa powder, traditional tiramisu is pure indulgence! Here I'm using the same flavors and serving it as a rolled sponge cake. Though it requires a few mixing bowls and specialty tools such as a pastry brush and sieve or sifter, this is a stunning cake with showstopper appeal. It is best made in advance so the cake can set. See the visuals on page 106 for help with the assembly.

SKILL LEVEL: **Advanced**

PREP: **45 minutes**

BAKE: **13 minutes**

TOTAL: **7 hours, including cooling and chilling**

Cake

Nonstick spray or butter, for the pan

1 cup cake flour **(118g)**

1 teaspoon baking powder

½ teaspoon salt

4 large eggs, separated, at room temperature

¾ cup granulated sugar, divided **(150g)**

¼ cup vegetable oil **(56g/60ml)**

1½ teaspoons vanilla extract

1 teaspoon instant espresso powder

¼ cup powdered sugar, for rolling the cake **(30g)**

Mascarpone Cream

1 cup heavy cream, cold **(240g/ml)**

⅓ cup powdered sugar, divided **(40g)**

1½ teaspoons vanilla extract

8 ounces mascarpone cheese, cold **(226g)**

Assembly

3 tablespoons hot black coffee or espresso

1 tablespoon amaretto liqueur, dark rum, sweet Marsala wine, or coffee

2 tablespoons unsweetened natural or Dutch-process cocoa powder

1. Preheat the oven to 350°F (177°C). Grease a 10 × 15-inch baking pan with nonstick spray, line with parchment paper, and grease the parchment.

2. Make the cake: Sift the flour, baking powder, and salt into a medium bowl.

3. In a large bowl using a handheld or stand mixer fitted with the whisk, beat the egg whites and ¼ cup (50g) of the sugar on high speed for 4 to 5 minutes or until stiff peaks form. Gently transfer to another bowl.

4. To the mixing bowl used for the egg whites, add the egg yolks, remaining ½ cup (100g) sugar, the oil, vanilla, and espresso powder. Beat on high speed for 3 to 4 minutes or until creamy and thickened. Add half of the whipped egg whites to the egg yolk mixture. Beat on low speed for 10 seconds. Add the remaining egg whites and beat on low speed for 10 seconds. Sift in the flour mixture, then fold the batter together with a spatula just enough to combine. Do not overmix.

5. Pour the batter into the prepared pan and smooth the top (1). Give the pan a shake to make sure the batter is level and fills the corners. Lightly tap the pan on the counter once or twice to pop any air bubbles.

6. Bake for 13 to 15 minutes or until the cake springs back when lightly pressed with a finger. Do not overbake.

7. Meanwhile, prepare for rolling the cake: Lay an 18-inch-long piece of parchment on the counter and sift the powdered sugar evenly on top.

8. As soon as the cake is removed from the oven, invert it onto the sugar-dusted parchment. Remove the pan and peel off and discard the baking parchment. Starting with a short end, slowly and gently roll up the warm cake with the sugared parchment (2). Allow the cake to cool completely rolled up in the parchment, about 4 hours.

9. Make the mascarpone cream: In a large bowl using a handheld or stand mixer fitted with the whisk, whip the cream, 3 tablespoons of the powdered sugar, and the vanilla on medium-high speed until medium-stiff peaks form, about 3 minutes. In a small bowl, use a fork to gently mix the mascarpone and remaining powdered sugar just until combined. Take care not to over-mix, as the mascarpone could break or curdle and become grainy. Gently fold the mascarpone mixture into the whipped cream just until combined. Refrigerate the mascarpone cream until you are ready to assemble the cake.

recipe continues >

10. To assemble: Slowly and gently unroll the cooled cake. In a small bowl, stir together the coffee and amaretto. Use a small pastry brush to brush the mixture over the cake. Leaving a ½-inch border around the cake, spread about two-thirds of the chilled mascarpone cream (just eyeball it) evenly over the cake (3). Gently roll the cake back up, peeling the parchment off as you roll (4). Use a bench scraper to help pick up the cake and place it on a cutting board or serving platter. Spread the remaining mascarpone cream over the top and sides of the cake roll and dust with cocoa powder.

11. Refrigerate, uncovered, for at least 2 hours or up to 2 days, before slicing and serving. If refrigerating for longer than 2 hours, cover tightly. For best taste and texture, I do not recommend freezing this cake.

Coconut Hi-Hat Cupcakes

MAKES 16 CUPCAKES

These are chocolate-dipped, Swiss meringue buttercream–frosted coconut cupcakes. And yes, they are quite the decadent treat! Coconut extract, canned coconut milk, and shredded coconut add deep layers of flavor. Use canned coconut milk, not the beverage mixer, and give it a whisk before measuring because it can separate in the can. Swiss meringue buttercream is my top choice for these because it holds its shape even when dunked in chocolate. It requires attention to detail, but the payoff is a smooth-as-silk frosting that's less sweet than American-style buttercream. See page 110 for success tips and visuals.

SKILL LEVEL: **Advanced**
PREP: **1 hour 15 minutes**
BAKE: **20 minutes**
TOTAL: **4 hours 10 minutes, including cooling**

Cupcakes

1¾ cups cake flour **(207g)**

¾ teaspoon baking powder

¼ teaspoon baking soda

¼ teaspoon salt

8 tablespoons unsalted butter, at room temperature **(113g)**

1 cup granulated sugar **(200g)**

2 large eggs, at room temperature

½ cup full-fat sour cream, at room temperature **(120g)**

1 teaspoon vanilla extract

1 teaspoon coconut extract

½ cup canned full-fat coconut milk, at room temperature **(120g/ml)**

¾ cup sweetened shredded coconut **(60g)**

Swiss Meringue Buttercream

4 large egg whites, at room temperature

1⅓ cups granulated sugar **(267g)**

16 tablespoons unsalted butter, slightly softened but still cool (about 60°F/16°C) and cut into 16 pieces **(226g)**

1½ teaspoons vanilla extract, or 1 teaspoon vanilla + ½ teaspoon coconut extract

⅛ teaspoon salt

Topping

¼ cup sweetened shredded coconut **(20g)**

12 ounces semi-sweet chocolate, coarsely chopped **(340g)**

1½ tablespoons vegetable oil

1. Preheat the oven to 350°F (177°C). Line a 12-cup muffin pan with cupcake liners. Line a second pan with 4 liners (or bake in batches).

2. **Make the cupcakes:** In a medium bowl, whisk the flour, baking powder, baking soda, and salt.

3. In a large bowl using a handheld or stand mixer fitted with the paddle, beat the butter and sugar on high speed until the mixture is light and creamy, about 3 minutes. Add the eggs and beat on high speed until combined, about 2 minutes. Scrape down the sides of the bowl as needed. Add the sour cream, vanilla, and coconut extract and beat on medium-high speed until combined, about 1 minute. Add the flour mixture and then, with the mixer on low speed, slowly pour in the coconut milk and beat just until combined. Fold in the shredded coconut. Do not overmix. The batter should be slightly thick. Spoon the batter into the cupcake liners, filling about two-thirds full (about 3 tablespoons of batter).

4. Bake for 20 to 23 minutes or until a toothpick inserted in the center comes out clean. Cool the cupcakes in the pan set on a cooling rack for 20 minutes, then remove from the pan and return to the rack to cool completely before frosting.

5. **Make the Swiss meringue buttercream:** Set up a double boiler (see page 20). To the upper pot or bowl, add the egg whites and sugar. Position the pot or bowl over, but not touching, the simmering water below. Whisking constantly, cook the egg white mixture until the sugar has dissolved and the temperature reaches 160°F (71°C) on an instant-read thermometer.

6. Transfer to a large heat-safe bowl (if using a hand mixer) or the bowl of a stand mixer fitted with the whisk. Cool for 5 minutes, then beat on high speed until stiff, glossy peaks form, 10 to 12 minutes (1). Switch the stand mixer to the paddle attachment (if using a hand mixer, keep using the beaters). On medium-high speed add the butter, 1 piece at a time, waiting for each piece to fully incorporate before adding more. After all the butter has been added, reduce the speed to medium and beat in the vanilla, coconut extract (if using), and salt until incorporated, about 30 seconds.

7. Fit a pastry bag with a large round piping tip (I use Ateco #808), fill with buttercream, and pipe it on the cooled cupcakes (2). Place the frosted cupcakes in the freezer for 15 minutes before dipping them so the frosting adheres to the cupcakes.

recipe continues >

8. Make the topping: Preheat the oven to 300°F (149°C). Line a baking sheet with parchment paper or a silicone baking mat.

9. Spread the coconut on the prepared baking sheet and bake for 5 to 7 minutes or until lightly toasted. Give the pan a shake halfway through so the coconut browns evenly. Set aside.

10. Melt the chocolate with the oil (see Melting Chocolate, page 20). Let the mixture cool for 5 minutes before dipping.

11. Place a cooling rack on a baking sheet. Holding a cupcake by its bottom, carefully and quickly dip the top into the chocolate to coat the frosting (3). Place the dipped cupcakes on the rack over the baking sheet and sprinkle the tops with toasted coconut (4). Refrigerate the cupcakes for 30 minutes to set the chocolate. Store covered in the refrigerator for up to 3 days.

Tips for Success

SWISS MERINGUE BUTTERCREAM (SMBC)

To begin this frosting, egg whites and sugar are cooked into a syrup; this makes it safe to eat and also stabilizes the Swiss meringue. It's worth noting that cream of tartar is included in some meringue recipes for stability, including in the Berries & Cream Pavlova Cake (page 94), but it's unnecessary here, as we're taking it a step further to make buttercream. Off heat, the mixture is then whipped to stiff, glossy peaks before beating in butter to make a thick, smooth frosting.

Review these success tips before getting started:

- **Aim for Stiff Peaks:** After several minutes of mixing, the meringue should form stiff, glossy peaks. This means the meringue holds sharp points in the bowl or on the lifted whisk attachment. Stiff peaks do not droop down.

- **If Your Meringue Won't Reach Stiff Peaks:** The meringue will never reach stiff peaks if there was a drop of egg yolk (fat) or grease in the egg whites, in the mixing bowl, or on any tools you are using. Wipe down all your tools with lemon juice or white vinegar before using. Use an egg separator, and separate and add the egg whites one at a time. It's also helpful to avoid making this on particularly humid days when there's extra moisture in the air.

- **Patience and Trust:** These are your best friends here. About halfway through adding the butter, the mixture will look soupy, but don't give up! Let the mixer run until the buttercream is creamy and thick.

- **If Your SMBC Separates or Is Too Thick:** If your meringue has separated or is too thick after you mix in all the butter, just keep beating because it will eventually come together. If it's only getting thicker and chunkier, there's a quick fix. Place the mixture in the top of a double boiler (see page 20) and place it over simmering water. Without stirring, let the edges of the mixture warm up and become liquid (the center will still be solid), 1 to 2 minutes. Remove from heat and return the mixture to the mixer. Beat on low speed for 30 seconds, then increase to medium-high speed and beat until smooth, about 2 minutes.

- **How to Fix Thin SMBC:** After all of the butter has been added, it should only take a minute or two of mixing to be creamy and thick. If it's not thickening, place the bowl in the refrigerator for 20 minutes to cool down, then return it to the mixer and beat on medium-high speed until thickened. Don't refrigerate for longer than 20 minutes or the butter will solidify.

PERFECT CONSISTENCY

TOO THIN

TOO THICK

Espresso Chocolate Truffle Cupcakes

MAKES 14 CUPCAKES

Who needs a coffee shop when you can get your java fix in cupcake form? I use my vanilla cupcakes as a starting point, add espresso powder, and top with silky mocha buttercream. As if that combination weren't sensational enough, there's also a surprise filling! You'll make a simple chocolate ganache, and as it cools, the ganache thickens to a rich chocolate truffle consistency. See page 121 for visuals of filling cupcakes.

SKILL LEVEL: **Beginner**

PREP: **50 minutes**

BAKE: **19 minutes**

TOTAL: **3 hours 10 minutes, including cooling**

Cupcakes

1¾ cups cake flour **(207g)**

1 tablespoon instant espresso powder

¾ teaspoon baking powder

¼ teaspoon baking soda

¼ teaspoon salt

8 tablespoons unsalted butter, at room temperature **(113g)**

1 cup granulated sugar **(200g)**

3 large egg whites, at room temperature

½ cup full-fat sour cream, at room temperature **(120g)**

2 teaspoons vanilla extract

½ cup whole milk, at room temperature **(120g/ml)**

Chocolate Truffle Filling

4 ounces semi-sweet chocolate, finely chopped **(113g)**

⅔ cup heavy cream **(160g/ml)**

Mocha Buttercream

¼ cup lukewarm whole milk (about 90°F/32°C) **(60g/ml)**

2 teaspoons instant espresso powder

16 tablespoons unsalted butter, at room temperature **(226g)**

3⅔ cups powdered sugar **(440g)**

⅓ cup unsweetened natural or Dutch-process cocoa powder **(28g)**

1 teaspoon vanilla extract

Pinch of salt, as needed

Chocolate-covered espresso beans, for garnish (optional)

1. Preheat the oven to 350°F (177°C). Line a 12-cup muffin pan with cupcake liners. Line a second pan with 2 liners (or bake in batches).

2. **Make the cupcakes:** In a medium bowl, whisk the flour, espresso powder, baking powder, baking soda, and salt.

3. In a large bowl using a handheld or stand mixer fitted with the paddle, beat the butter and sugar on high speed until the mixture is light and creamy, about 3 minutes. Add the egg whites and beat on high speed until smooth and fully combined, about 2 minutes. Scrape down the sides of the bowl as needed. Add the sour cream and vanilla and beat on medium-high speed until combined, about 1 minute. Add the flour mixture and then, with the mixer on low speed, slowly pour in the milk and beat just until combined. Whisk the batter by hand a few times to make sure there are no lumps at the bottom of the bowl. Do not overmix. The batter should be slightly thick. Spoon the batter into the cupcake liners, filling only about two-thirds full (about 3 tablespoons of batter).

4. Bake for 19 to 22 minutes or until a toothpick inserted in the center comes out clean. Cool the cupcakes in the pan set on a cooling rack for 20 minutes, then remove them from the pan and return to the rack to cool completely before filling and frosting.

5. **Make the chocolate truffle filling:** Place the chocolate in a medium heat-safe bowl. In a small saucepan, heat the cream over medium heat until it just begins to simmer. Do not let it come to a full boil—that's too hot! Pour over the chocolate and let it sit for 2 to 3 minutes. With a metal spoon or small spatula, slowly stir until the mixture is smooth. The ganache is thin. Refrigerate it for at least 30 minutes to thicken before filling the cupcakes.

6. Using a sharp knife, cut a circle into the center of the cooled cupcakes to create a little cone-shaped pocket about 1 inch deep. Spoon some of the filling inside each carved-out cupcake; 1 to 2 teaspoons will fit inside. Slice off the pointy end of the cone-shaped piece of cake you removed, and gently press the round piece back on top of the filling to close the hole.

recipe continues >

7. Make the mocha buttercream: (See American-Style Buttercream, page 85, for tips.) In a small bowl, combine the lukewarm milk and espresso powder, stirring to dissolve.

8. In a large bowl using a handheld or stand mixer fitted with the paddle, beat the butter on medium speed until creamy, about 2 minutes. Sift in the powdered sugar and cocoa powder, then add the espresso-milk mixture and vanilla. Beat on low speed for 30 seconds, then increase to medium-high speed and beat for 2 full minutes. Taste; beat in the salt if the frosting is too sweet.

9. Fit a pastry bag with a piping tip (I use Ateco #849), fill with buttercream, and pipe it on the cooled cupcakes. An icing spatula or knife also can be used to frost the cupcakes. Garnish with chocolate-covered espresso beans (if using). Store covered in the refrigerator for up to 3 days.

Red Velvet Cupcakes
page 118

Simply Perfect Vanilla
Cupcakes
page 117

Espresso Chocolate
Truffle Cupcakes
page 111

Simply Perfect Vanilla
Cupcakes
page 117

**Cream-Filled Chocolate
Cupcakes**
page 121

**Simply Perfect Vanilla
Cupcakes**
page 117

Coconut Hi-Hat Cupcakes
page 107

Simply Perfect Vanilla Cupcakes

MAKES 14 CUPCAKES

If you learn anything from this cookbook, let it be this: Deviating from the ingredients in a baking recipe will change the desired results. This is proven with my vanilla cupcakes, a fan-favorite recipe on my website that readers have described as "spectacular," "unequaled," and "hands-down the best." The batter uses the same key ingredients as my Soft & Moist White Vanilla Cake (page 84) for cupcakes that are light, airy, flavorful, and perfect for any occasion! They're an outstanding base for a variety of frosting flavors; I have them pictured here with vanilla buttercream that's been tinted with gel food coloring.

SKILL LEVEL: **Beginner**

PREP: **45 minutes**

BAKE: **19 minutes**

TOTAL: **3 hours, including cooling**

Cupcakes

1¾ cups cake flour **(207g)**

¾ teaspoon baking powder

¼ teaspoon baking soda

¼ teaspoon salt

8 tablespoons unsalted butter, at room temperature **(113g)**

1 cup granulated sugar **(200g)**

3 large egg whites, at room temperature

½ cup full-fat sour cream, at room temperature **(120g)**

2 teaspoons vanilla extract

Seeds scraped from ½ of a vanilla bean (optional)

½ cup whole milk, at room temperature **(120g/ml)**

Frosting

Vanilla Buttercream (page 84)

Sprinkles, for garnish (optional)

TIP: Do not fill the cupcake liners all the way to the top. If you do, the cupcakes will spill over the sides and you'll be left with sad mushroom-shaped cupcakes. For cupcakes that expand evenly, fill the liners about two-thirds full, which is about 3 tablespoons of batter each.

1. Preheat the oven to 350°F (177°C). Line a 12-cup muffin pan with cupcake liners. Line a second pan with 2 liners (or bake in batches).

2. Make the cupcakes: In a medium bowl, whisk the flour, baking powder, baking soda, and salt.

3. In a large bowl using a handheld or stand mixer fitted with the paddle, beat the butter and sugar on high speed until the mixture is light and creamy, about 3 minutes. Add the egg whites and beat on high speed until smooth and well combined, about 2 minutes. Scrape down the sides of the bowl as needed. Add the sour cream, vanilla, and vanilla bean seeds (if using) and beat on medium-high speed until combined, about 1 minute. Add the flour mixture and then, with the mixer on low speed, slowly pour in the milk and beat just until combined. Whisk the batter by hand a few times to ensure no lumps remain at the bottom of the bowl. Do not overmix. The batter should be slightly thick. Spoon the batter into the cupcake liners (1), filling about two-thirds full (about 3 tablespoons of batter).

4. Bake for 19 to 22 minutes or until a toothpick inserted in the center comes out clean. Cool the cupcakes in the pan set on a cooling rack for 20 minutes, then remove them from the pan and return to the rack to cool completely before frosting.

5. Frost the cupcakes: Fit a pastry bag with a piping tip (I use Wilton #1M), fill with vanilla buttercream, and pipe it on the cooled cupcakes. An icing spatula or knife also can be used to frost the cupcakes. Garnish with sprinkles (if using). Store covered in the refrigerator for up to 3 days.

Red Velvet Cupcakes

MAKES 14 CUPCAKES

SKILL LEVEL: **Beginner**
PREP: **40 minutes**
BAKE: **20 minutes**
TOTAL: **2 hours 50 minutes, including cooling**

Is red velvet a mystery flavor to you? It used to be for me, too, until I enjoyed a magnificent slice of red velvet cake at a friend's wedding several years ago. It's truly unique, carefully balancing the flavors of mild cocoa, tangy buttermilk, and sweet vanilla. These cupcakes pack all those fabulous flavors in a super-moist and velvety crumb. It's best to use gel food coloring instead of liquid, and to help the color stand out, use a touch of white vinegar (rest assured, you can't taste it!). Red velvet is often paired with cream cheese frosting; I've opted to lighten it into a whipped cream cheese frosting that really lets the flavors shine!

Cupcakes

1½ cups cake flour **(177g)**

2 tablespoons unsweetened natural cocoa powder

1 teaspoon baking powder

¼ teaspoon baking soda

¼ teaspoon salt

5 tablespoons unsalted butter, melted and slightly cooled **(71g)**

1 cup granulated sugar **(200g)**

¼ cup vegetable oil **(56g/60ml)**

1 large egg, at room temperature

2 teaspoons vanilla extract

½ teaspoon distilled white vinegar

½ cup buttermilk, at room temperature **(120g/ml)**

¾ teaspoon red gel food coloring

Whipped Cream Cheese Frosting

1 cup heavy cream, cold **(240g/ml)**

12 ounces full-fat brick cream cheese, at room temperature **(340g)**

1⅓ cups powdered sugar **(160g)**

1 teaspoon vanilla extract

1. Preheat the oven to 350°F (177°C). Line a 12-cup muffin pan with cupcake liners. Line a second pan with 2 liners (or bake in batches).

2. Make the cupcakes: In a large bowl, whisk the flour, cocoa powder, baking powder, baking soda, and salt.

3. In a medium bowl, whisk the melted butter, sugar, oil, egg, vanilla, and vinegar until well combined. Pour this mixture into the flour mixture, whisk lightly, then pour in the buttermilk. Add the red gel food coloring and stir with a spatula until combined. The batter should be thick. Spoon the batter into the cupcake liners, filling about halfway (a little less than 3 tablespoons).

4. Bake for 20 to 23 minutes or until a toothpick inserted in the center comes out clean. Cool the cupcakes in the pan set on a cooling rack for 20 minutes, then remove them from the pan and return to the rack to cool completely before frosting.

5. Make the whipped cream cheese frosting: In a large bowl using a handheld or stand mixer fitted with the whisk, whip the cream on medium-high speed until stiff peaks form, 3 to 4 minutes. Transfer the whipped cream to a medium bowl.

6. In the same bowl used for the whipped cream (no need to wash it), beat the cream cheese on medium-high speed until smooth and creamy. Scrape down the sides of the bowl as needed. Add the powdered sugar and vanilla and beat until smooth, about 2 minutes. Add the whipped cream to the cream cheese mixture and gently fold together with a spatula just until combined. Do not overmix.

7. Fit a pastry bag with a piping tip (I use Ateco #849), fill with frosting, and pipe it on the cooled cupcakes. An icing spatula or knife also can be used to frost the cupcakes. Store covered in the refrigerator for up to 3 days.

Cream-Filled Chocolate Cupcakes

MAKES 15 CUPCAKES

SKILL LEVEL: **Beginner**

PREP: **50 minutes**

BAKE: **20 minutes**

TOTAL: **3 hours 10 minutes, including cooling**

A few years ago, I set out to make a homemade version of the iconic Hostess CupCakes, and after one bite of my final test batch, I discovered a dessert so good my eyes automatically closed in pure bliss. Hot liquid in the batter helps "bloom" the cocoa powder, drawing out its flavor, something you also do in Chocolate Ganache Cake: 2 Ways (page 81). I use hot coffee for the cupcakes, but you can substitute hot water. After the cupcakes cool, fill them with fluffy whipped buttercream and then top them with a two-ingredient satiny ganache. I dare you to try to keep your eyes open when you take that first bite!

Cupcakes

1 cup all-purpose flour **(125g)**

½ cup unsweetened natural cocoa powder **(43g)**

1 teaspoon baking soda

½ teaspoon baking powder

½ teaspoon salt

1 cup granulated sugar **(200g)**

½ cup buttermilk, at room temperature **(120g/ml)**

⅓ cup vegetable oil **(75g/80ml)**

1 large egg, at room temperature

1 teaspoon vanilla extract

½ cup hot black coffee (decaf or regular) or hot water **(120g/ml)**

Chocolate Ganache

6 ounces semi-sweet chocolate, finely chopped **(170g)**

⅔ cup heavy cream **(160g/ml)**

Whipped Vanilla Buttercream Filling

8 tablespoons unsalted butter, at room temperature **(113g)**

2 cups powdered sugar **(240g)**

3 tablespoons heavy cream

2 teaspoons vanilla extract

Pinch of salt, as needed

1. Preheat the oven to 350°F (177°C). Line a 12-cup muffin pan with cupcake liners. Line a second pan with 3 liners (or bake in batches).

2. Make the cupcakes: In a large bowl, whisk the flour, cocoa powder, baking soda, baking powder, and salt.

3. In a medium bowl, whisk the sugar, buttermilk, oil, egg, and vanilla until well combined, then pour into the flour mixture along with the hot coffee and whisk until the batter is smooth. The batter should be thin. Pour or spoon the batter into the cupcake liners, filling about two-thirds full (about 3 tablespoons of batter).

4. Bake for 20 to 22 minutes or until a toothpick inserted in the center comes out clean. Cool the cupcakes in the pan set on a cooling rack for 20 minutes, then remove them from the pan and return to the rack to cool completely before frosting. If the tops of the cooled cupcakes are sticky after cooling, refrigerate them for 20 to 30 minutes before filling.

5. Make the chocolate ganache: Put the chocolate in a medium heat-safe bowl. In a small saucepan, heat the cream over medium heat until it just begins to simmer. Do not let it come to a full boil—that's too hot! Pour it over the chocolate and let it sit for 2 to 3 minutes. With a metal spoon or small spatula, slowly stir until the mixture is smooth. Place the ganache in the refrigerator for 30 to 60 minutes to chill and thicken before using.

6. Make the whipped vanilla buttercream filling: In a large bowl using a handheld or stand mixer fitted with the paddle, beat the butter on medium speed until creamy, about 2 minutes. Add the powdered sugar, cream, and vanilla. Beat on low speed for 30 seconds, then increase to medium-high speed and beat for 3 full minutes. Taste; beat in the salt if the frosting is too sweet.

7. Using a sharp knife, cut a circle into the center of the cooled cupcakes to create a little cone-shaped pocket about 1 inch deep (1). Spoon or pipe the buttercream inside each carved-out cupcake, using enough frosting to fill it without overflowing (2). Slice off the pointy end of the cone-shaped piece of cake you removed and gently press the round piece over the filling to close the hole (3).

8. With a knife or small icing spatula, spread a thick layer of ganache on top of each cupcake (4). If you have filling left over, fit a pastry bag with a small round piping tip (I use Wilton #6), fill with the remaining buttercream, and pipe it on the ganache topping. Store covered in the refrigerator for up to 3 days.

Classic Cheesecake with Cherry Sauce Topping

SERVES 12

This is my beloved velvety-smooth, delightfully dense, tangy-rich cheesecake, and the recipe I turn to when I need a slice of this timeless dessert. Paired with a buttery-sweet graham cracker crust, it's the ultimate in simple decadence. It's so popular around here that I stopped asking which dessert I should make for holiday feasts. Because the answer is always THIS, especially after I began serving it with an easy homemade cherry topping.

SKILL LEVEL: **Intermediate**

PREP: **1 hour**

BAKE: **1 hour 5 minutes**

TOTAL: **8 hours, including cooling and chilling**

Graham Cracker Crust

1½ cups graham cracker crumbs (about 12 full-sheet graham crackers) **(180g)**

¼ cup granulated sugar **(50g)**

5 tablespoons unsalted butter, melted **(71g)**

Cheesecake

32 ounces full-fat brick cream cheese, at room temperature **(904g)**

1 cup granulated sugar **(200g)**

1 cup full-fat sour cream, at room temperature **(240g)**

2 teaspoons fresh lemon juice

1 teaspoon vanilla extract

3 large eggs, at room temperature

Optional Cherry Sauce Topping

1½ tablespoons cornstarch

1½ tablespoons water, at room temperature

1 teaspoon fresh lemon juice

2½ cups fresh or unthawed frozen pitted sour cherries **(375g)**

½ cup granulated sugar **(100g)**

⅛ teaspoon salt

1 teaspoon vanilla extract

TIP: If you opt for the cherry topping, sour cherries are key; it tastes a bit flat with sweet cherries.

1. Adjust the oven rack to the lower-middle position and preheat the oven to 350°F (177°C). Wrap one or two large pieces of heavy-duty aluminum foil around an ungreased 9- or 10-inch springform pan. Have ready a shallow roasting pan large enough to hold the springform pan.

2. Make the graham cracker crust: In a medium bowl, combine the graham cracker crumbs and sugar. Stir in the melted butter and break up any large clumps. The mixture should be sandy. Pour into the prepared springform pan. Using your hand, pat the crumbs into the bottom and partly up the sides to make a compact crust. Bake the crust for 10 minutes. Remove the pan from the oven and set aside while you prepare the filling. Leave the oven on.

3. Make the cheesecake: In a large bowl using a handheld or stand mixer fitted with the paddle, beat the cream cheese and sugar on medium-high speed until smooth and creamy, about 2 minutes. Beat in the sour cream, lemon juice, and vanilla and mix until fully combined. Scrape down the sides of the bowl as needed. With the mixer on medium speed, add the eggs one at a time, beating after each addition just until combined. Stop the mixer as soon as the final egg is fully mixed into the batter; overmixing will deflate the cheesecake. The batter should be thick.

4. Boil a kettle of water. Place the wrapped springform pan, with the warm prebaked crust, in the roasting pan. Pour the cheesecake batter into the crust and use a spatula to smooth it into an even layer. Carefully pour 1 inch of boiling water into the roasting pan and place it in the oven. If it's easier, you can pull out the oven rack, place the roasting pan with the cheesecake in the oven, then add the hot water. See page 126 for visuals.

5. Bake for 55 to 70 minutes or until the center is almost set. When the cheesecake is done, the center should still slightly wobble if you gently tap the pan. If the top of the cheesecake is browning too quickly, tent it with foil halfway through baking.

6. Turn off the oven and open the oven door slightly, leaving the cheesecake and water bath in place. With the door ajar, let the cheesecake cool in the oven for 1 hour. Remove the cheesecake from the water bath, discard the foil, and place the springform pan on a cooling rack to cool completely. When it has cooled, cover and refrigerate the cheesecake for at least 4 hours or up to 2 days.

recipe continues >

Tips for Success

CHEESECAKE

I've made many cheesecakes over the years, and I'm happy to share three insider tips:

- **Do Not Overmix:** For best results, don't overmix once you begin adding the eggs, otherwise you'll beat too much air into the batter and the cheesecake will sink as the air escapes.

- **Use a Water Bath:** Don't skip the water bath (see page 126 for more info).

- **Be Patient:** Let the cheesecake cool in the oven for 1 hour with the oven door slightly open. The recipe certainly takes a while, but most of the time is spent waiting for it to bake, cool, and chill. If you can muster up the patience, you'll be generously rewarded with a cheesecake that looks as good as it tastes.

7. Make the cherry sauce topping (if using): In a small bowl, mix the cornstarch, water, and lemon juice, stirring to dissolve the cornstarch.

8. In a medium saucepan, combine the cherries, sugar, and salt. Cook over medium heat, stirring occasionally, until the cherries begin to release their juices, 4 to 6 minutes. Stir in the cornstarch mixture, then bring to a boil, stirring often. Once it has reached the boil, cook for 1 minute. Remove from heat and stir in the vanilla. Pour the sauce into a heat-safe bowl and let stand at room temperature until completely cool; the mixture will thicken as it cools. The topping can be made up to 3 days in advance and refrigerated.

9. Run a knife around the edges of the springform pan to help loosen the cheesecake, then remove the outer ring. To serve, cut into slices with a sharp knife. For neat slices, wipe the knife clean and dip it into warm water between each slice. Spoon cooled cherry sauce topping over each slice. Store covered tightly in the refrigerator for up to 4 days.

Pumpkin Cheesecake

SERVES 12

If you're looking for a grandiose dessert for the holiday table, let this creamy pumpkin cheesecake be your hero. During the recipe testing phase, I discovered that blotting the pumpkin puree is beneficial (a step also taken for Brown Butter Pumpkin Oatmeal Cookies, page 46). Significant moisture in pumpkin puree can keep the cheesecake from setting up properly, so be sure not to skip the blotting step. To complement the brilliant flavor, I use Biscoff cookies for the crust and Homemade Pumpkin Pie Spice (page 47) in the batter. The spice mix works wonders in the whipped cream, too!

SKILL LEVEL: **Intermediate**
PREP: **45 minutes**
BAKE: **1 hour 20 minutes**
TOTAL: **8 hours, including cooling and chilling**

Crust

32 Biscoff cookies (8.8 ounces) **(250g)**

5 tablespoons unsalted butter, melted **(71g)**

Cheesecake

1 (15-ounce) can pumpkin puree **(425g)**

32 ounces full-fat brick cream cheese, at room temperature **(904g)**

1 cup brown sugar **(200g)**

½ cup granulated sugar **(100g)**

⅓ cup full-fat sour cream, at room temperature **(80g)**

1½ tablespoons cornstarch

1½ teaspoons ground cinnamon

1½ teaspoons pumpkin pie spice, homemade (page 47) or store-bought

1 teaspoon vanilla extract

4 large eggs, at room temperature

Spiced Whipped Cream

1 cup heavy cream, cold **(240g/ml)**

2 tablespoons brown sugar

½ teaspoon vanilla extract

¼ teaspoon pumpkin pie spice

1. Adjust the oven rack to the lower-middle position and preheat the oven to 350°F (177°C). Wrap one or two large pieces of heavy-duty aluminum foil around an ungreased 9- or 10-inch springform pan (1). Have ready a shallow roasting pan large enough to hold the springform pan.

2. **Make the crust:** In a food processor or blender, grind the cookies into fine crumbs. Put the crumbs in a medium bowl and stir in the melted butter. The mixture should be sandy. Pour into the prepared springform pan. Using your hand, pat the crumbs into the bottom and partly up the sides to make a compact crust (2). Bake the crust for 10 minutes. Remove the pan from the oven and set aside to slightly cool as you prepare the filling. Leave the oven on.

3. **Make the cheesecake:** Line a medium bowl with two layers of paper towels. Place the pumpkin puree in the bowl. Using another paper towel, press down to blot excess moisture from the pumpkin. Repeat a few times until the pumpkin looks drier. After blotting, you will have a heaping cup (about 300g) of pumpkin. Set aside.

4. In a large bowl using a handheld or stand mixer fitted with the paddle, beat the cream cheese, brown sugar, and granulated sugar on medium-high speed until smooth and creamy, about 2 minutes. Beat in the pumpkin, sour cream, cornstarch, cinnamon, pumpkin pie spice, and vanilla until fully combined. Scrape down the sides of the bowl as needed. With the mixer on medium speed, add the eggs one at a time, beating after each addition just until combined. Stop as soon as the final egg is mixed into the batter; over-mixing will deflate the cheesecake.

5. Boil a kettle of water. Place the wrapped springform pan, with the warm prebaked crust, in the roasting pan. Pour the cheesecake batter into the crust and use a spatula or spoon to smooth it into an even layer (3). Carefully pour 1 inch of boiling water into the roasting pan and place it in the oven (4). If it's easier, you can pull out the oven rack, place the roasting pan with the cheesecake in the oven, then pour in the hot water.

6. Bake for 70 to 80 minutes or until the center is almost set. When the cheesecake is done, the center will still slightly wobble if you gently tap the pan.

recipe continues >

7. Turn the oven off and open the oven door slightly, leaving the cheesecake and water bath in place. With the door ajar, let the cheesecake cool in the oven for 1 hour. Remove the cheesecake from the water bath, discard the foil, and place the springform pan on a cooling rack to cool completely. Once it has cooled, cover and refrigerate the cheesecake for at least 5 hours or up to 2 days.

8. Make the spiced whipped cream: In a bowl using a hand mixer or stand mixer fitted with the whisk, whip the cream, brown sugar, vanilla, and pumpkin pie spice on medium-high speed until medium peaks form, about 3 minutes. Spread or pipe the topping onto the cheesecake.

9. Run a knife around the edges of the springform pan to help loosen the cheesecake, then remove the outer ring. To serve, cut into slices with a sharp knife. For neat slices, wipe the knife clean and dip it into warm water between each slice. Store covered tightly in the refrigerator for up to 4 days.

Cheesecake Water Bath

To prevent a cheesecake from cracking, sinking, or baking unevenly, bake it in a water bath. Don't worry—you don't have to buy any special equipment or a fancy bathtub-size baking appliance! It simply means placing the filled springform pan, well-wrapped in aluminum foil so that no water can seep in, inside a larger pan with hot water in it. This is how the recipe here is written. However, if you want to skip baking the cheesecake in water, you can just create a humid environment a different way (see far right). It's not as reliable, as I've still had a few cheesecakes crack on the surface. But it works about 90 percent of the time!

Water bath alternative: Place the cheesecake (no need to wrap in foil) on the middle oven rack. Place a large ovenproof pan (not glass) on the bottom oven rack. Pour about 1 inch of hot water into the empty pan on the bottom rack. Quickly shut the oven door and bake the cheesecake. This alternate method adds steam to the oven without having the cheesecake pan sit inside the water itself. The cooling and chilling instructions are the same.

Pies

& Beyond

Rolling Out Pie Dough

The pie recipes in this book provide specific instructions, but here's some guidance that can help you, especially if you're a pie crust beginner.

Tips for Success

- If you're making a double-crust pie, work with one crust at a time and keep the other in the refrigerator until you're ready to roll it out.

- Lightly flour the surface, rolling pin, your hands, and the dough. Use gentle-to-medium pressure with your rolling pin. Start from the center and work your way out in all directions, turning the dough with your hands as you go. Between passes of the rolling pin, rotate the dough and flip it over to make sure it's not sticking to your surface. Sprinkle more flour if it begins to stick.

- If the dough becomes misshapen as you roll it, use your hands to help mold it back into an even circle. Roll the dough into a 12-inch circle about ⅛ inch thick, which is the perfect size to fit a 9-inch pie dish.

- When you're rolling, don't be concerned about visible specks of butter in the dough. They are perfectly normal and expected.

- To move the rolled dough to the pie dish, carefully roll one end of the dough gently onto your rolling pin, rolling it back toward you, and slowly peeling it off the surface as you go. Pick it up and carefully roll it back out over the top of the pie dish.

Troubleshooting

- **Pie dough is cracking around the edges:** If you overwork the butter into the dry ingredients, the dough will feel too wet before you can add enough water. So do not overwork the butter—you want those crumbles. If the edges crack as you roll out the dough, dip your fingers in ice-cold water and gently press the edges back together. Wait a minute and then try rolling it out again.

- **Pie dough is crumbling all over:** There may be too much butter and not enough flour and water. Again, this is usually a result of butter being worked in too much, which can easily happen if the ingredients aren't cold enough. If the pie dough is crumbling as you roll it out, try adding more water AND more flour. Sprinkle a bit of ice-cold water and flour onto the crumbled pieces and gently work it in with your fingers. Wait a minute and then try rolling it out again.

How to Make a Pie Crust Shield

A pie crust shield is a covering that prevents the edges from burning. You can buy a metal one or easily make one from aluminum foil. Fold a 12-inch square of foil in half and cut a half-circle in the center of the folded edge. When unfolded, you'll have a foil square with a circle cut out of the center. If the edges of the crust start to brown much faster than the center, carefully place the shield over the pie to protect the edges (1) while keeping the center of the pie uncovered (2).

How to Make a Lattice Pie Crust

See visuals, opposite, for help with assembly.

1. On a lightly floured surface with a floured rolling pin, roll out the chilled pie dough to a roughly 12-inch circle about ⅛ inch thick. Using a pastry wheel, sharp knife, or pizza cutter, cut twelve 1-inch-wide strips of dough (1).

2. Evenly space six strips over the top of your filled pie (2). Use the longer strips in the center and the shorter strips on the ends. Fold every other strip (three in total) back over themselves so they're almost falling off the pie. Lay one of the remaining six strips on top, perpendicular to the others (3). Unfold the three vertical strips back so they lie over the perpendicular strip (4). Fold the other three vertical strips back. Lay one of the remaining five strips perpendicular on top (5). Unfold the three vertical strips back so they lie over the perpendicular strip (6). You're now beginning to see the beautiful woven pattern.

3. Repeat with the last four strips, weaving the strips over and under one another (7). Use a paring knife or kitchen shears to trim excess dough, leaving about 1½ inches of overhang (8). Fold the overhang back toward the center of the pie and pinch the edges to adhere the top and bottom crusts together (9).

How to Crimp & Flute Pie Crust

Crimping and fluting are techniques to add a decorative edge to a pie. They also help prevent the edges of the crust from sinking down into the pie dish and help to seal in a juicy pie filling.

1. Fit the pie dough into the pie dish, then use a paring knife or kitchen shears to trim excess dough, leaving 1 to 1½ inches of overhang. For a double-crust pie, wait until after you add the top pie crust to trim the edges.

2. Fold the overhang back over and pinch it to make a thick, compact edge. For a double-crust pie, roll and pinch the top and bottom crust edges together.

> **To Crimp (1):** Using a fork, press the tines down into the edges of the crust, continuing all the way around the pie.

> **To Flute (2):** Using the knuckle of your index finger on your dominant hand, and your index finger and thumb of your other hand, pinch the edges of the dough around the knuckle of your dominant hand. Turn the pie dish as you go. Lightly flour your fingers if the dough becomes sticky.

How to Parbake Pie Crust

When a recipe calls for parbaking, it means you should partially bake the crust before filling.

1. After you've chilled your shaped pie crust, crumple up a 12-inch square of parchment paper and line the chilled pie crust with it (1). Crumpling it up first will help it lie flat and fit the dish.

2. Fill it with 1 pound (454g) of ceramic pie weights or dried beans (2). Bake the crust for 10 minutes at the oven temperature specified in the recipe.

3. Carefully lift the parchment paper with the pie weights from the crust (3).

4. Prick the bottom of the crust all over with a fork to create steam vents (4) and return the crust, without weights, to the oven to bake for 7 to 8 more minutes or until the bottom is just beginning to brown.

You can parbake the crust up to 3 days ahead of time. Cool completely, then cover and refrigerate until ready to use. No need to bring to room temperature before filling and baking.

Double Pie Crust

MAKES 1½ POUNDS (680G) DOUGH, ENOUGH FOR 2 PIE CRUSTS

SKILL LEVEL: **Intermediate**

PREP: **15 minutes**

TOTAL: **2 hours 15 minutes**

Pie dough, the foundation for so many delicious bakes, has a reputation for being fussy and finicky. Once you have a solid recipe (I've been fine-tuning this one for years!) and build confidence, the door opens to an entire baking category. The ingredient list for mine is short and simple. It's an all-butter dough, so it's extra flaky and, you guessed it, very buttery. A little sugar is added to help break down the butter, but the crust isn't sweet; it works just as well with savory fillings. The instructions are thorough and you'll find lots of helpful information in Pie Crust Basics (page 131), but my biggest piece of advice is to keep everything cold every step of the way. I usually combine the dry ingredients and place the mixture in the freezer while I cube the cold butter. Use ice-cold water and refrigerate the dough for at least 2 hours before rolling it out. See visuals, opposite.

2½ cups all-purpose flour, plus more as needed **(313g)**

2 teaspoons granulated sugar

1 teaspoon salt

16 tablespoons unsalted butter, very cold and cubed **(226g)**

½ cup ice-cold water, plus more as needed **(120g/ml)**

TIP: I recommend using a glass pie dish. It conducts heat evenly, which allows the bottom to bake thoroughly. As a bonus, you can see when the sides and bottom of the crust have browned.

1. In a large bowl, whisk the flour, sugar, and salt. Using a pastry blender or two forks, cut the butter into the mixture (1, 2) until it resembles coarse meal; pea-sized bits with a few larger bits of butter is okay (3). You can use a food processor to pulse the mixture, but take care not to overwork the ingredients.

2. Drizzle the water over the entire surface of the flour mixture, 1 tablespoon at a time (4), and stir with a spatula after every tablespoon has been added until the dough begins to come together in large clumps (5). Do not add any more water than needed to achieve this.

3. Transfer the dough to a floured surface. Using floured hands, gently bring the dough mixture together into a ball (6). Avoid overworking the dough. If it feels too dry or is too crumbly to form a ball, dip your fingers in cold water and then continue bringing the dough together. If it feels too sticky, sprinkle on a little more flour and continue bringing it together. Using a sharp knife or bench scraper, cut the dough in half (7, 8). Gently flatten each half into a 1-inch-thick disc (9). Wrap each tightly in plastic wrap. Refrigerate for at least 2 hours and up to 5 days. After refrigerating, the dough is ready to roll out and use in a pie recipe.

Classic Apple Pie

SERVES 8 TO 10

You're looking at my favorite dessert on the planet. As someone who bakes as a hobby and profession, I understand the pressure that puts on a pie! After years of refining this recipe, I have some helpful apple pie tips for you. First, cut the apples into ¼-inch slices; you do not want them paper thin. Second, precook the filling for a few minutes on the stove so the apples are fork-tender. And finally, use a mix of tart and sweet apples such as Granny Smith, Honeycrisp, and Fuji, and do not skip the lemon—it makes the flavors sing! See visuals on page 140 for help with assembly.

> SKILL LEVEL: **Intermediate**
>
> PREP: **3 hours, including pie crust**
>
> BAKE: **1 hour**
>
> TOTAL: **7 hours, including chilling and cooling**

Crust

Double Pie Crust (page 136)

Filling

10 cups ¼-inch-thick apple slices (about 8 large apples, peeled and cored) **(1.25kg)**

½ cup granulated sugar **(100g)**

¼ cup all-purpose flour **(31g)**

1 tablespoon fresh lemon juice

1½ teaspoons ground cinnamon

¼ teaspoon ground allspice

¼ teaspoon ground nutmeg

Assembly

Egg wash: 1 large egg beaten with 1 tablespoon milk

Coarse sugar, for sprinkling (optional)

For Serving (Optional)

Vanilla ice cream

Salted Caramel Sauce (recipe follows)

TIP: Instead of the top pie crust, you can use the crumb topping from Sour Cherry Crumb Pie (page 145), adding ½ teaspoon ground cinnamon to the flour. The bake time remains the same.

1. Make and chill the pie crust dough as directed.

2. If you're new to working with pie dough, review Rolling Out Pie Dough (page 131). On a floured surface, roll out one of the discs of chilled dough to a 12-inch circle, giving the dough a quarter-turn after every few rolls to keep it even. Carefully place the dough into a 9-inch pie dish (1). Tuck and pat it in place with your fingers, making sure it is smooth. Place the pie shell in the refrigerator as you work on the filling.

3. Make the filling: In a large bowl, toss the apple slices with the sugar, flour, lemon juice, cinnamon, allspice, and nutmeg. Pour the apple filling into a very large skillet or Dutch oven. Cook over medium heat, stirring gently, until the apples begin to soften, about 5 minutes. Set aside to slightly cool.

4. Preheat the oven to 400°F (204°C). Place a baking sheet on the bottom oven rack to catch any juices that may bubble over.

5. Roll the second disc of dough to a 12-inch circle. Spoon or pour the warm filling into the bottom crust (2), making sure there are no large gaps between the slices. It's a lot of filling! Make a lattice top (see How to Make a Lattice Pie Crust, page 132). Crimp or flute the edges to seal (see page 134).

6. Finish the crust: Lightly brush the top and edges of the pie crust with egg wash (3). Sprinkle the top with coarse sugar (if using, 4).

7. Bake for 25 minutes. Add a pie crust shield (see page 132) to prevent the edges from browning too quickly, and **reduce the oven temperature to 375°F (191°C)**. Bake for an additional 35 to 45 minutes or until the crust is golden brown and juices are bubbling through the lattice. If needed toward the end of bake time, remove the pie crust shield and tent a large piece of aluminum foil over the top if it is getting too brown.

8. Cool the pie on a cooling rack for at least 3 hours before slicing.

9. Serve plain or with a scoop of vanilla ice cream and a drizzle of Salted Caramel Sauce (if using). Store covered tightly at room temperature for up to 1 day or in the refrigerator for up to 5 days.

recipe continues >

Salted Caramel Sauce

MAKES 1 CUP

1 cup granulated sugar **(200g)**

6 tablespoons unsalted butter,
  at room temperature and cut into
  6 pieces **(85g)**

½ cup heavy cream, at room
  temperature **(120g/ml)**

1 teaspoon salt

1. In a medium heavy-duty stainless-steel saucepan (do not use nonstick) over medium heat, cook the sugar, stirring constantly with a heat-resistant silicone spatula or wooden spoon. The sugar will form clumps and eventually melt into an amber-colored liquid. On my stove, this takes about 6 minutes. Stir constantly, especially around the bottom edges, and be careful not to let it burn.

2. Once the sugar is fully melted, reduce the heat to low and stir in the butter; it will quickly bubble up. Cook and stir constantly until the butter is melted and well combined. If the butter separates or the sugar clumps up, remove the pan from heat and vigorously whisk until it's combined, then return it to the heat.

3. Very slowly and carefully pour in the cream, stirring constantly the entire time. It will bubble up again and let off a puff of steam. When all the cream has been added, stop stirring, increase the heat to medium, and let it boil for 1 minute. If you'd like to be precise and use a candy thermometer, the temperature should reach 220°F (104°C).

4. Remove from heat and stir in the salt. The caramel will be a thin liquid at this point. Allow to slightly cool and thicken before using. Cover tightly and refrigerate for up to 1 month. The sauce will solidify. Reheat in the microwave or on the stove to a smooth, flowing consistency.

How to Assemble the Pie

It's the Great Pumpkin Pie

SERVES 8 TO 10

SKILL LEVEL: **Beginner**

PREP: **2 hours 45 minutes, including pie crust**

BAKE: **1 hour 12 minutes**

TOTAL: **6 hours 50 minutes, including chilling and cooling**

Long before all the trendy pumpkin spice–flavored foods came along, the humble yet mighty pumpkin pie reigned. Bursting with generously spiced pumpkin flavor and a velvet-smooth texture, my version has secured a permanent spot on our Thanksgiving menu. The secret touch? A pinch of black pepper to embolden the spice flavor, a trick I learned from the brilliant cooks at King Arthur Baking. If you make Homemade Pumpkin Pie Spice (page 47), you can use that here instead of the ginger, nutmeg, cloves, and pepper; you will still add the cinnamon. Classic, timeless, and always imitated . . . this is the Great Pumpkin Pie.

Crust

Double Pie Crust (page 136)

Egg wash: 1 large egg beaten with 1 tablespoon milk

Filling

1 (15-ounce) can pumpkin puree (425g)

1 cup brown sugar (200g)

2 large eggs

⅔ cup heavy cream (160g/ml)

⅓ cup milk (80g/ml)

1 tablespoon cornstarch

1½ teaspoons ground cinnamon

½ teaspoon ground ginger

½ teaspoon salt

¼ teaspoon ground nutmeg

⅛ teaspoon freshly ground black pepper

⅛ teaspoon ground cloves

Optional Garnishes

Sugared Cranberries (page 209)

Classic Whipped Cream (page 154)

MAKE-AHEAD TIP: You can prepare the filling 1 day in advance, cover tightly, and refrigerate until ready to use. No need to bring it to room temperature before baking.

1. Make and chill the pie crust dough as directed. You will only need 1 disc for this pie (save the second disc for another use).

2. If you're new to working with pie dough, review Rolling Out Pie Dough (page 131). On a floured surface, roll out the dough to a 12-inch circle, giving the dough a quarter-turn after every few rolls to keep it even. Carefully place the dough into a 9-inch pie dish. Tuck and pat it in place with your fingers, making sure it is smooth. Crimp or flute the edges (see page 134). Lightly brush the edges of the crust with egg wash. Chill the crust in the refrigerator for 20 minutes.

3. Preheat the oven to 375°F (191°C).

4. Parbake the crust (see page 135).

5. **Make the filling:** In a large bowl, whisk the pumpkin, brown sugar, and eggs. Add the cream, milk, cornstarch, cinnamon, ginger, salt, nutmeg, pepper, and cloves. Whisk vigorously until everything is smooth and combined. The filling should be a creamy, pourable consistency. Pour the filling into the warm crust.

6. Bake for 25 minutes. Add a pie crust shield (see page 132) and continue baking the pie for another 30 to 35 minutes or until the center is just about set. A small part of the center will still be wobbly when it's done—that's okay. Cool the pie on a cooling rack for at least 3 hours.

7. Decorate with Sugared Cranberries and Classic Whipped Cream (if using). Slice and serve. Store covered tightly in the refrigerator for up to 3 days.

Sour Cherry Crumb Pie

SERVES 8 TO 10

My grandmother was a hardworking soul with a big, infectious laugh . . . and she made the BEST cherry pie. It was a little different every time she made it, because she kept the recipe half scribbled on paper and half in her head! This pie is my tribute to her. I love pairing the juicy, sweet-tart filling with a crunchy, buttery brown-sugar crumble on top. Precooking the sour cherry filling on the stove ensures that the filling will set and be perfectly sliceable. Allowing the pie to cool completely before slicing is a non-negotiable . . . and so is a scoop of vanilla ice cream, because Grandma wouldn't have it any other way!

SKILL LEVEL: **Beginner**

PREP: **3 hours, including pie crust**

BAKE: **55 minutes**

TOTAL: **8 hours, including chilling and cooling**

Crust
Double Pie Crust (page 136)

Crumb Topping
1 cup all-purpose flour **(125g)**

½ cup brown sugar **(100g)**

⅛ teaspoon salt

4 tablespoons unsalted butter, melted **(56g)**

Filling
3 tablespoons cornstarch

6 cups fresh or unthawed frozen pitted sour cherries **(900g)**

¾ cup granulated sugar **(150g)**

1 teaspoon fresh lemon juice

1 tablespoon all-purpose flour

½ teaspoon vanilla extract

½ teaspoon almond extract

Assembly
Egg wash: 1 large egg beaten with 1 tablespoon milk

For Serving (Optional)
Vanilla ice cream

1. Make and chill the pie crust dough as directed. You will only need 1 disc for this pie (save the second disc for another use).

2. **Make the crumb topping:** In a small bowl, combine the flour, brown sugar, and salt. Stir in the melted butter until it comes together. The mixture should be sandy and crumbly. Cover and refrigerate until needed.

3. **Make the filling:** Place the cornstarch in a small bowl and set within reach of the stove. In a medium saucepan, combine the cherries, sugar, and lemon juice. Cook over medium-low heat, stirring occasionally, until the cherries begin to release their juices, about 5 minutes. As the cherries cook, remove ¼ cup (60g/ml) of the juice from the pan and add it to the cornstarch. Using a fork, mix the cornstarch and cherry juice until the cornstarch is dissolved. Pour the mixture into the saucepan with the cherries, stir in the flour, and bring to a boil. Boil for 5 minutes, stirring occasionally. Remove from heat and stir in the vanilla and almond extracts. Set aside to slightly cool and thicken.

4. **Finish the crust:** If you're new to working with pie dough, review Rolling Out Pie Dough (page 131). On a floured surface, roll out the dough to a 12-inch circle, giving the dough a quarter-turn after every few rolls to keep it even. Carefully place the dough into a 9-inch pie dish. Tuck and pat it in place with your fingers, making sure it is smooth. Crimp or flute the edges (see page 134). Lightly brush the edges of the crust with egg wash. Refrigerate the crust as the oven preheats.

5. Preheat the oven to 400°F (204°C). Place a baking sheet on the bottom rack to catch any juices that may bubble over.

6. Spoon the cherry filling into the crust, smoothing it into an even layer. Sprinkle the cold crumb topping evenly over the top.

7. Bake for 20 minutes. Add a pie crust shield (see page 132) and **reduce the oven temperature to 375°F (191°C)**. Bake for an additional 35 to 40 minutes or until the crumb topping is golden brown and the filling juices are bubbling around the edges. If needed toward the end of bake time, remove the pie crust shield and tent a large piece of foil over the top if it is getting too brown.

8. Cool the pie on a cooling rack for at least 4 hours before slicing. Serve with a scoop of vanilla ice cream (if using). Store covered tightly at room temperature for up to 1 day or in the refrigerator for up to 5 days.

Butternut Squash & Sage Chicken Pot Pie

SERVES 8

SKILL LEVEL: **Intermediate**

PREP: **2 hours 50 minutes,** including pie crust

BAKE: **32 minutes**

TOTAL: **3 hours 35 minutes,** including chilling and cooling

Chicken pot pie has long been one of the most comforting meals when the outside temperature drops. The combination of golden flaky crust, creamy rich sauce, and oodles of herbed vegetables and chicken feels like a giant hug from the kitchen. Here I've packed even more flavor into this comfort food classic by adding butternut squash, kale, and fresh sage. For a vegetarian version, substitute vegetable broth for the chicken broth, omit the chicken meat, and add 1 cup (120g) roughly chopped mushrooms when you add the onions.

Crust

Double Pie Crust (page 136)

Filling

3 tablespoons unsalted butter **(43g)**

1½ cups small-cubed butternut squash **(210g)**

¾ cup chopped carrots **(90g)**

¾ cup chopped celery **(90g)**

½ cup diced yellow onions **(65g)**

3 garlic cloves, minced

¼ cup all-purpose flour **(31g)**

2 tablespoons chopped fresh sage

2 teaspoons fresh thyme leaves

1 teaspoon salt

½ teaspoon freshly ground black pepper

2 cups chicken broth **(480g/ml)**

½ cup whole milk **(120g/ml)**

2 cups chopped cooked chicken, light or dark meat, or a mix **(250g)**

1 cup chopped kale leaves **(35g)**

Assembly

Egg wash: 1 large egg beaten with 1 tablespoon milk

1. Make and chill the pie crust dough as directed.

2. **Make the filling:** In a large skillet, melt the butter over medium heat. Add the squash, carrots, celery, onions, and garlic and cook, stirring occasionally, until the vegetables begin to soften, about 5 minutes.

3. Add the flour, sage, thyme, salt, and pepper and stir until the flour has absorbed all the liquid. Pour in the chicken broth and milk and simmer for 8 minutes or until the mixture has thickened into a creamy gravy-like consistency. Stir in the chicken and kale and remove from heat. Cool for 15 minutes.

4. Preheat the oven to 425°F (218°C).

5. **Finish the crust:** If you're new to working with pie dough, review Rolling Out Pie Dough (page 131). On a floured surface, roll out one of the discs of chilled dough (keep the other one in the refrigerator until it is needed) to a 12-inch circle, giving the dough a quarter-turn after every few rolls to keep it even. Carefully place the dough into a 9-inch pie dish. Tuck and pat it in place with your fingers, making sure it is smooth. Spoon the filling into the pie crust.

6. Roll out the second disc of chilled pie dough to a 12-inch circle. Cover the pie with the second crust. Crimp or flute the edges to seal (see page 134). Cut a few small vents in the top crust to allow steam to escape, and lightly brush the top and edges of the pie with egg wash.

7. Bake for 20 minutes. Add a pie crust shield (see page 132) to prevent the edges from browning too quickly. Bake for an additional 12 to 18 minutes or until the crust is golden brown. Cool for at least 15 minutes before slicing and serving. Store covered tightly in the refrigerator for up to 3 days.

Caramelized Onion, Fig & Goat Cheese Galette

SERVES 8

A galette is a free-form pie; it's an excuse to break the rules because there's no careful shaping involved. This thyme-flecked dough needs to chill in the refrigerator, which gives ample time to cook the onions to caramelized perfection. A splash of balsamic vinegar captures any flavorful bits the onions left behind and, together with goat cheese, introduces a touch of tanginess to the filling. You can serve this as a substantial appetizer or a meat-free main dish. (And I won't fight you if you want a slice for dessert!) I don't use this word often when describing baked goods, but this galette's flavor is truly *triumphant*!

SKILL LEVEL: **Beginner**

PREP: **1 hour 50 minutes**

BAKE: **38 minutes**

TOTAL: **2 hours 40 minutes, including some cooling**

Crust

1 cup all-purpose flour, plus more as needed **(125g)**

½ cup whole-wheat flour **(65g)**

1 teaspoon dried thyme

1 teaspoon granulated sugar

¼ teaspoon salt

8 tablespoons unsalted butter, cold and cubed **(113g)**

¼ cup ice-cold water, plus more as needed **(60g/ml)**

Filling

1 tablespoon butter

1 teaspoon extra-virgin olive oil

1 pound sweet onions, peeled and sliced (about 2 medium onions) **(454g)**

½ teaspoon granulated sugar

¼ teaspoon salt

1 tablespoon balsamic vinegar

¼ teaspoon dried thyme

4 ounces crumbled soft goat cheese **(113g)**

8 ounces fresh figs, stems removed and sliced into ¼-inch rounds (about 1½ cups slices) **(226g)**

Assembly

Egg wash: 1 large egg beaten with 1 tablespoon milk

Flaky sea salt

Optional Garnishes

Drizzle of honey

Fresh thyme

1. Make the crust: In a medium bowl, whisk both flours, the thyme, sugar, and salt. Add the butter. Using a pastry blender or two forks, cut in the butter until coarse crumbs form. Add the cold water and stir until the flour is moistened and a dough forms. Be careful not to overmix. If the dough seems dry, add more water, 1 tablespoon at a time, until it begins to mass together. Turn the dough out onto a lightly floured surface and, using lightly floured hands, gently form the dough into a ball and then flatten it into a thick disc. Wrap the dough in plastic wrap and refrigerate it for at least 1 hour or up to 3 days.

2. Make the filling: In a large skillet over medium-low heat, melt the butter with the olive oil, swirling to coat the bottom of the pan. Add the onions and cook, stirring frequently, until they begin to turn translucent, about 10 minutes. Reduce the heat to low, stir in the sugar and salt, and cook, stirring frequently, until the onions are very soft and golden brown, 15 to 20 minutes. Add a splash of water if the onions are sticking—don't let them burn or get too dark. Stir in the vinegar and thyme, then remove the pan from heat. Let the onions cool for at least 5 minutes.

3. Preheat the oven to 400°F (204°C). Line a large baking sheet with parchment paper or a silicone baking mat.

4. On a lightly floured surface, roll the dough to a 12-inch circle. Carefully transfer the rolled dough to the prepared baking sheet.

5. Assemble the galette: Leaving a 2-inch border around the edge, spread the onions over the crust. Sprinkle the goat cheese over the onions, then arrange the figs on top. Fold the edges of the dough over the filling, pleating as needed. Brush the top of the crust with egg wash and sprinkle lightly with flaky sea salt.

6. Bake until the filling is bubbling and the crust is golden brown, 38 to 42 minutes. Cool on the baking sheet for 10 minutes. Before slicing and serving, drizzle with honey and sprinkle with fresh thyme (if using). Store covered tightly in the refrigerator for up to 3 days.

TIP: If you can't find fresh figs, use ¾ cup (about 115g) chopped dried Turkish figs (often labeled Smyrna) with the stems removed.

Fresh Peach Mascarpone Pie

SERVES 8 TO 10

SKILL LEVEL: **Beginner**

PREP: **40 minutes**

BAKE: **10 minutes**

TOTAL: **8 hours 50 minutes, including chilling**

My family and I go peach picking at a local farm every summer, a tradition we started in 2020 when looking for fun outdoor activities. Though biting into a juicy farm-fresh peach is one of summer's finest delights, we also love sinking our teeth into this creamy peach pie. When mixed with vanilla, mascarpone's delicately sweet flavor complements the peach layers, all of which sits atop a crunchy graham cracker crumb crust.

Crust

1½ cups graham cracker crumbs (about 12 full-sheet graham crackers) **(180g)**

¼ cup granulated sugar **(50g)**

6 tablespoons unsalted butter, melted **(85g)**

Cream Filling

1¼ cups heavy cream, cold **(300g/ml)**

¼ cup granulated sugar, divided **(50g)**

1 teaspoon vanilla extract

Seeds scraped from ½ of a vanilla bean

8 ounces mascarpone cheese, at room temperature **(226g)**

Peach Layers

5 cups ¼-inch-thick peach slices (about 8 peaches, peeled and pitted) **(750g)**

¼ cup granulated sugar **(50g)**

1 tablespoon fresh lemon juice

Peach glaze: 2 tablespoons peach or apricot preserves mixed with 1 tablespoon water

TIP: You want slightly firm peaches with no soft spots. Your best bet is to place about 10 firm peaches in a paper bag for a couple days to ripen. Some may develop soft spots, which is why I suggest buying more than you need. Eat any overly soft peaches and use the rest in this peachy pie! I do not recommend thawed frozen peaches because the pie will not set up.

1. Preheat the oven to 350°F (177°C).

2. Make the crust: In a medium bowl, mix the graham cracker crumbs and sugar, then stir in the melted butter. The mixture should be thick, coarse, and sandy. Break up any large chunks. Pour the mixture into a 9-inch pie dish and press in evenly to form a crust. Bake the crust for 10 minutes. Place on a cooling rack to cool completely.

3. Make the cream filling: In a large bowl using a handheld or stand mixer fitted with the whisk, whip the cream, 3 tablespoons of the sugar, the vanilla, and vanilla bean seeds on medium-high speed until stiff peaks form, 3 to 4 minutes. In a small bowl, gently mix the mascarpone with the remaining sugar just until the mixture is smooth. Be careful not to overmix, as this could curdle the mascarpone. Gently fold the mascarpone mixture into the whipped cream until combined. Refrigerate the cream mixture while you prepare the peaches.

4. Make the peach layers: In a large bowl, gently toss the peach slices with the sugar and lemon juice until coated.

5. Spoon about half of the cream filling into the cooled crust and spread it into an even layer. Arrange about half of the peaches in concentric circles over the top. Repeat with the remaining cream filling and peaches. Cover loosely with plastic wrap and refrigerate for at least 8 hours or up to 1 day.

6. Immediately before slicing and serving, lightly brush the top peach layer with the peach glaze. Store covered tightly in the refrigerator for up to 3 days.

Tips for Success

CRUMB CRUSTS

- Using your hand, press the crumbs into the bottom and up the sides of the pie dish to make a compact crust.

- Do not pack down with heavy pressure or the crust will be too hard.

- Run a spoon around the bottom "corner" where the side and bottom of the pie dish meet to make a rounded crust (1)—this helps prevent the crust from falling apart when you cut the pie.

1

Sky-High Chocolate Mousse Pie

SERVES 8 TO 10

This towering pie features a chocolaty cookie-crumb crust, smooth chocolate mousse layered with a ribbon of Oreo cookie crumbs, and billowy fresh whipped cream. Unsweetened chocolate is a must to balance the sugar needed for cooking the egg whites into a meringue. When assembling, use an offset spatula to dome the mousse and the whipped cream as high as you can!

SKILL LEVEL: **Advanced**

PREP: **40 minutes**

BAKE: **10 minutes**

TOTAL: **5 hours, including chilling**

Crust

22 regular Oreo cookies (do not use Double Stuf) **(249g)**

5 tablespoons unsalted butter, melted **(71g)**

Chocolate Mousse Filling

8 ounces unsweetened chocolate, finely chopped **(226g)**

2 tablespoons unsalted butter **(28g)**

4 large egg whites **(120g)**

1 cup granulated sugar **(200g)**

¼ teaspoon cream of tartar

2 cups heavy cream, cold **(480g/ml)**

6 Oreo cookies, crushed into crumbs **(68g)**

Topping

Classic Whipped Cream (recipe follows)

Chocolate curls or mini chocolate chips, for garnish (optional)

TIP: A double boiler is necessary for the filling. Before you start, see Using a Double Boiler (and What to Do if You Don't Have One) on page 20.

1. Make the crust: Preheat the oven to 350°F (177°C). In a food processor or blender, pulse the whole cookies, including the filling, into fine crumbs. Transfer the crumbs to a medium bowl and stir in the melted butter. The mixture should be thick and quite wet. Pour the crumb mixture into a 9-inch pie dish and press in evenly to form a crust (see Crumb Crusts, page 150). Bake for 10 minutes. Place on a cooling rack to cool completely.

2. Make the chocolate mousse filling: Melt the chocolate with the butter (see Melting Chocolate, page 20). Set aside to cool slightly (1).

3. Set up a double boiler (see page 20). To the upper pot (or bowl), add the egg whites, sugar, and cream of tartar. Position the pot or bowl over, but not touching, the simmering water below. Whisking constantly, cook the egg white mixture until the sugar has dissolved and the mixture reaches 160°F (71°C) on an instant-read thermometer (2).

recipe continues >

Classic Whipped Cream

MAKES 2 CUPS

1 cup heavy cream, cold **(240g/ml)**

2 tablespoons granulated or powdered
   sugar

½ teaspoon vanilla extract

1. In a large bowl using a handheld or
stand mixer fitted with the whisk, whip
the heavy cream, sugar, and vanilla
on medium-high speed until medium
peaks form, about 3 minutes. Medium
peaks are between soft/loose peaks
and stiff peaks, and are the perfect
consistency for spreading and piping
on desserts. If you accidentally over-
whip the cream and it looks curdled
and heavy, pour in a little bit more cold
heavy cream and fold it in gently with
a spatula until it smooths out.

2. Use immediately or store covered
tightly in the refrigerator for up to
24 hours.

4. Transfer the egg white mixture to a large heat-safe bowl (if using a hand
mixer) or the bowl of a stand mixer fitted with the whisk. Beat on high speed
until soft, glossy peaks form, 5 to 6 minutes (3). Gently fold the melted chocolate into the whipped egg white mixture until combined (4, 5).

5. In another large bowl using a handheld or stand mixer fitted with the
whisk, whip the cream on medium-high speed until medium-to-stiff peaks
form, 3 to 4 minutes. Gently fold the whipped cream into the chocolate mixture (6). It will seem like a lot of whipped cream, but just keep folding and it
will eventually come together.

6. Using a small offset spatula, spread half of the mousse in the cooled pie
crust (7). Sprinkle the crushed cookie crumbs evenly over the top (8). Top
with the remaining chocolate mousse, mounding it in the center to create a
dome shape (9).

7. Make Classic Whipped Cream: See recipe, left (10).

8. Spread the whipped cream on top—keeping that dome shape in the center
(11). Top with chocolate curls or mini chocolate chips (if using). Refrigerate the pie, uncovered, for at least 4 hours and up to 1 day. Let it sit at room
temperature for 10 minutes before slicing and serving. Store covered tightly
in the refrigerator for up to 4 days.

Peanut Butter Baked Alaska Pie

SERVES 8 TO 10

SKILL LEVEL: **Intermediate**

PREP: **1 hour**

BAKE: **3 minutes**

TOTAL: **8 hours, including freezing**

This lofty treat is an homage to classic baked Alaska—a retro delight featuring cake, ice cream, and toasted meringue topping. Here, instead of using cake, the ice cream is spread in a salted pretzel crust that beautifully balances the sweet ice cream and meringue layers. While I have a soft spot for peanut butter ice cream, feel free to choose another flavor such as strawberry or chocolate. To conquer this impressive mountain of a pie, a 9-inch springform pan is key; the tall sides set and hold the shape.

Pretzel Crust

4 cups mini pretzel twists **(160g)**

¼ cup granulated sugar **(50g)**

8 tablespoons unsalted butter, melted **(113g)**

Filling

3 quarts (6 pints) peanut butter ice cream **(2.8L)**

Meringue Topping

4 large egg whites, at room temperature

1 cup granulated sugar **(200g)**

¼ teaspoon cream of tartar

1 teaspoon vanilla extract

TIP: A double boiler is necessary for the topping. Before you start, see Using a Double Boiler (and What to Do if You Don't Have One) on page 20.

1. **Make the pretzel crust:** In a food processor or blender, pulse the pretzels into a fine crumb. Pour the crumbs into a medium bowl and stir in the sugar. Add the melted butter and stir until uniformly mixed. Pour the mixture into a 9-inch springform pan. Using your hand, press the crumbs into the bottom and up the sides to make a compact crust. Freeze for 1 hour to set the crust.

2. **Make the filling:** About 10 minutes before the crust is ready, let the ice cream soften at room temperature until it is easily scoopable. Scoop half of the ice cream into the crust and use the back of a large spoon to spread it in an even layer. Scoop the remaining ice cream on top, mounding it in the center to create a dome shape. Cover tightly with plastic wrap and freeze for at least 6 hours or up to 2 days.

3. **Make the meringue topping:** Set up a double boiler (see page 20). To the upper pot (or bowl), add the egg whites, sugar, and cream of tartar. Position the pot or bowl over, but not touching, the simmering water below. Whisking constantly, cook the egg white mixture until the sugar has dissolved and the mixture reaches 160°F (71°C) on an instant-read thermometer.

4. Transfer the egg white mixture to a large heat-safe bowl (if using a hand mixer) or the bowl of a stand mixer fitted with the whisk. Add the vanilla. Beat on high speed until soft, glossy peaks form, 5 to 6 minutes.

5. Preheat the oven to 450°F (232°C). (Alternatively, you can skip the oven and toast the meringue with a kitchen torch.)

6. Uncover the pie and spread the meringue all over the ice cream, covering any exposed crust around the edges. Use the back of a spoon to create big peaks and swirls. Place the pie on a baking sheet and, watching closely so it doesn't burn, bake until lightly browned all over, 3 to 4 minutes. (If using a kitchen torch, toast the entire meringue topping.)

7. Remove the outer ring of the springform pan. Use a large sharp knife to slice and serve immediately. Store covered tightly in the freezer for up to 1 week.

Lemon Curd Tart

SERVES 8 TO 10

Lemon curd is a sweet yet tart silky-smooth spread used as a topping, garnish, or, as here, a brightly flavored filling. To ensure that the tart sets to a sliceable consistency, the curd is cooked on the stove, then added to the pastry crust and finished in the oven. The crust is a French pâte sucrée (sweet crust). Its shortbread-like texture strikes the perfect balance between crisp and tender and holds up even after chilling, making it an ideal companion for the filling. Prepare this luscious tart a day in advance so it has plenty of time to chill before serving.

SKILL LEVEL: **Advanced**

PREP: **1 hour 30 minutes, including crust**

BAKE: **35 minutes**

TOTAL: **8 hours 15 minutes, including chilling**

Crust

Nonstick spray or butter, for the pan

1½ cups all-purpose flour, plus more as needed **(188g)**

6 tablespoons powdered sugar **(45g)**

⅛ teaspoon salt

8 tablespoons unsalted butter, at room temperature and cut into 8 pieces **(113g)**

1 large egg, cold

Lemon Curd Filling

1 cup granulated sugar **(200g)**

3 large eggs, at room temperature

2 large egg yolks, at room temperature

½ cup fresh lemon juice **(120g/ml)**

⅛ teaspoon salt

8 tablespoons unsalted butter, at room temperature and cut into 8 pieces **(113g)**

1½ tablespoons lemon zest

1 tablespoon powdered sugar, for garnish

MAKE-AHEAD TIP: If you'd like to make this tart further in advance, once the tart has chilled after 4 hours, you can cover it and refrigerate it for up to 3 days.

1. Lightly grease a 9-inch tart pan with a removable base with nonstick spray.

2. **Make the crust:** In a food processor, combine the flour, powdered sugar, and salt and pulse or process on low speed to combine. Add the butter, 1 tablespoon at a time, pulsing a few times after each addition. Add the egg and pulse only until the dough comes together in a clump. The dough should be soft. Transfer it to a lightly floured surface and press it into a 1-inch-thick disc. Place the dough in the prepared pan (1) and use your hands to press it evenly into the pan and up the sides (2). It may seem like you don't have enough dough at first, but keep pressing. Use the bottom of a metal measuring cup to press the edges squarely. Flatten the top edge so it's even with the rim of the pan or use a paring knife to trim. Save the scraps to patch up any thin-looking areas. Prick the bottom of the crust all over with a fork. Cover and freeze for at least 30 minutes or up to 1 day.

3. Preheat the oven to 350°F (177°C). Remove the crust from the freezer and place the tart pan on a large baking sheet for easy handling.

4. Bake for 25 minutes or until the crust appears set. Place on a cooling rack to cool completely.

5. **Make the lemon curd filling:** Set up a double boiler (see page 20). To the upper pot (or bowl), add the sugar, eggs, egg yolks, lemon juice, and salt. Position the pot or bowl over, but not touching, the simmering water below. Whisking constantly, cook the mixture until it reaches 160°F (71°C) on an instant-read thermometer, about 10 minutes. It should be thick enough to coat a spoon without immediately dripping off (3). Remove from heat, then whisk in the butter. Strain the mixture through a fine-mesh sieve (4) and discard any solids. Whisk in the lemon zest. Pour the lemon curd into the cooled tart crust (5) and use a small offset spatula to spread it evenly.

6. Bake for 10 minutes. Cool the tart in the pan set on a cooling rack for 1 hour at room temperature. When fully cooled, transfer the tart to the refrigerator. Refrigerate, uncovered, for at least 4 hours.

7. Before serving, sift powdered sugar over the tart, then carefully remove the outer rim of the pan. Serve cold. Store covered tightly in the refrigerator for up to 3 days.

Chocolate Raspberry Tart

SERVES 8 TO 10

SKILL LEVEL: **Intermediate**

PREP: **1 hour 30 minutes, including crust**

BAKE: **25 minutes**

TOTAL: **6 hours, including chilling**

Between the tender chocolate crust, sweet raspberry preserves, velvety chocolate ganache, fresh raspberries, and fluffy whipped cream, this tastes like total dessert luxury! The crust is a cocoa version of the sweet crust used for Lemon Curd Tart (page 159). Most of the filling's flavor comes from the chocolate, so splurge on high-quality baking chocolate if you can.

Crust

Nonstick spray or butter, for the pan

1¼ cups all-purpose flour, plus more as needed **(156g)**

6 tablespoons powdered sugar **(45g)**

¼ cup unsweetened natural or Dutch-process cocoa powder **(21g)**

⅛ teaspoon salt

8 tablespoons unsalted butter, at room temperature and cut into 8 pieces **(113g)**

1 large egg, cold

Filling

⅓ cup thick raspberry preserves or jam, stirred until smooth **(100g)**

12 ounces semi-sweet or bittersweet chocolate, finely chopped **(340g)**

2 tablespoons unsalted butter, at room temperature

1⅓ cups heavy cream **(320g/ml)**

1 teaspoon vanilla extract

3 cups fresh raspberries **(350g)**

Optional Garnishes

Classic Whipped Cream (page 154)

Fresh mint sprigs

TIP: For a little extra raspberry flavor, replace 2 tablespoons of the heavy cream with a raspberry liqueur such as Chambord. You'll heat it with the rest of the cream.

1. Lightly grease a 9-inch tart pan with a removable base with nonstick spray.

2. **Make the crust:** In a food processor, combine the flour, powdered sugar, cocoa powder, and salt and pulse or process on low speed to combine. Add the butter, 1 tablespoon at a time, pulsing a few times after each addition. Add the egg and pulse until the dough comes together in a clump. The dough should be soft. Transfer to a lightly floured surface and press into a 1-inch-thick disc. Place the dough in the prepared pan and use your hands to press it evenly into the pan and up the sides. It may seem like you don't have enough dough at first, but keep pressing. Use the bottom of a metal measuring cup to press the edges squarely. Flatten the top edge so it's uniform with the rim of the pan or use a paring knife to trim. Save the scraps to patch up any thin-looking areas. Prick the bottom of the crust all over with a fork. Cover and freeze for at least 30 minutes or up to 1 day.

3. Preheat the oven to 350°F (177°C). Remove the crust from the freezer and place the tart pan on a large baking sheet for easy handling.

4. Bake the crust for 25 minutes or until it appears set. Place on a cooling rack to cool completely.

5. **Make the filling:** Spread the raspberry preserves evenly into the cooled crust. Set aside. Place the chocolate and butter in a medium heat-safe bowl. In a small saucepan over medium heat, heat the cream until it just begins to simmer. Do not let it come to a full boil—that's too hot! Remove from heat and stir in the vanilla. Pour over the chocolate and butter and let sit for 2 to 3 minutes. With a metal spoon or small spatula, slowly stir until the mixture is smooth.

6. Pour the chocolate ganache over the jam layer and use a small offset spatula to spread it evenly. Arrange the fresh raspberries on top in concentric circles. Refrigerate, uncovered, for at least 4 hours or up to 1 day. If refrigerating for longer than 4 hours, cover the tart.

7. Before serving, carefully remove the outer rim of the pan. Serve the tart cold with whipped cream and fresh mint sprigs (if using). Store covered tightly in the refrigerator for up to 3 days.

Ultimate Fruit Crisp: 4 Ways

SERVES 8

Introducing the ultimate fruit crisp recipe, the only one you'll ever need! With the sweet and crunchy brown sugar–oat crumble topping as the constant, you're free to indulge in any fruit or combination of fruits you love. Below, I have my top four favorites to get you started and to carry you through the seasons. If you prefer a topping without oats, use the topping from Simple Strawberry Rhubarb Crumble (page 164).

SKILL LEVEL: **Beginner**
PREP: **20 minutes**
BAKE: **40 minutes**
TOTAL: **1 hour 20 minutes, including some cooling**

Topping

⅔ cup all-purpose flour **(84g)**

½ cup brown sugar **(100g)**

1 teaspoon ground cinnamon

¼ teaspoon salt

8 tablespoons unsalted butter, cold and cubed **(113g)**

⅔ cup rolled oats or quick oats **(57g)**

⅔ cup chopped nuts such as pecans, walnuts, or almonds (optional) **(80g)**

Filling

Nonstick spray or butter, for the pan

6 cups chopped or sliced fresh fruit (see Fruit Options, right) **(700 to 800g)**

⅓ cup granulated sugar **(67g)**

¼ cup all-purpose flour **(31g)**

1 tablespoon fresh lemon juice

1 teaspoon vanilla extract

⅛ teaspoon salt

For Serving (Optional)

Vanilla ice cream

Classic Whipped Cream (page 154)

1. Make the topping: In a medium bowl, whisk the flour, brown sugar, cinnamon, and salt. Add the butter and use a pastry blender, two forks, or your fingers to blend until the mixture comes together in pea-sized crumbs. Stir in the oats and then the nuts (if using). Place in the refrigerator or freezer until needed.

2. Preheat the oven to 350°F (177°C). Grease a 9-inch square baking pan, 11 × 7-inch rectangular baking dish, 10-inch round baking dish, or cast-iron skillet with nonstick spray.

3. Make the filling: In a large bowl, stir the fruit, sugar, flour, lemon juice, vanilla, salt, and any other flavor additions used in the version you are making. Spread the filling in the prepared pan and sprinkle the cold topping evenly over the filling.

4. Bake for 40 to 50 minutes or until the filling is bubbling around the edges and the topping is golden brown. Check the crisp about halfway through baking—if the top is browning too quickly, tent with aluminum foil. Cool for at least 10 minutes before serving. Top with vanilla ice cream or whipped cream (if using). Store covered tightly in the refrigerator for up to 4 days.

Fruit Options

• **Stone Fruit:** Use a mix of peeled or unpeeled peaches, nectarines, plums, and/or apricots, sliced about ¼ inch thick, and pitted and halved dark cherries. Add ½ teaspoon almond extract to the filling.

• **Caramel Apple:** Use peeled or unpeeled apples chopped into 1-inch pieces. Add 1 teaspoon ground cinnamon and ¼ teaspoon ground nutmeg to the filling. After baking, drizzle with Salted Caramel Sauce (page 140).

• **Very Berry:** Use an equal mix of blueberries, chopped strawberries, and raspberries or blackberries. Add 1 teaspoon lemon zest to the filling.

• **Ginger Cardamom Pear:** Use peeled or unpeeled pears chopped into 1-inch pieces. Add 2 teaspoons minced fresh ginger and ¾ teaspoon ground cardamom to the filling.

Tips for Success
FRUIT CRISP

• Use fresh fruit—frozen fruit will result in a mushy topping, which is the exact opposite of crisp! And keep in mind that the juicier/riper the fruits, the juicier the baked filling will be.

• The volume and weight of fruit can vary depending on the size and ripeness. Use the measurement in the ingredient list as a guide, and don't be concerned if your fruit measurement is slightly different.

• Instead of a baking dish, the crisp can be baked in individual ovenproof ramekins. For ease of handling, place them on a baking sheet. The bake time and yield depend on their size, but bake until the topping is lightly browned and the filling bubbles up around the sides.

Simple Strawberry Rhubarb Crumble

SERVES 8

SKILL LEVEL: **Beginner**

PREP: **20 minutes**

BAKE: **40 minutes**

TOTAL: **1 hour 15 minutes, including some cooling**

One of my favorite ways to enjoy rhubarb is in this quick and easy crumble. Sweet strawberries balance rhubarb's tart flavor, and the two shine with a touch of orange juice and vanilla. The textural differences in each spoonful are unbelievable. You have the juicy fruit filling on the bottom, with a layer of soft and cakey crumb directly on top, and then the very top of the crumble is delightfully crisp. All this welcomes a big scoop of vanilla ice cream . . . and a little self-control!

Filling

Nonstick spray or butter, for the pan

3 cups chopped strawberries, about ¾-inch pieces **(465g)**

2½ cups sliced rhubarb, about ¼-inch-thick slices **(313g)**

½ cup granulated sugar **(100g)**

¼ cup all-purpose flour **(31g)**

2 teaspoons fresh orange juice

½ teaspoon vanilla extract

⅛ teaspoon salt

Topping

1 cup all-purpose flour **(125g)**

½ cup brown sugar **(100g)**

1 teaspoon baking powder

½ teaspoon ground cinnamon

⅛ teaspoon salt

6 tablespoons butter, melted **(85g)**

For Serving (Optional)

Vanilla ice cream

1. Preheat the oven to 375°F (191°C). Grease a 9-inch square baking pan or 9-inch deep-dish (that's at least 2 inches deep) pie dish with nonstick spray.

2. Make the filling: In a large bowl, gently stir the strawberries, rhubarb, sugar, flour, orange juice, vanilla, and salt. Pour into the prepared baking pan and use a spatula to spread it evenly.

3. Make the topping: In a medium bowl, whisk the flour, brown sugar, baking powder, cinnamon, and salt. Add the melted butter and mix with a fork until the topping is completely moistened and clumps together. Do not overmix; you want it to be crumbly. Spoon the topping evenly over the filling.

4. Bake for 40 to 50 minutes or until the filling is bubbling around the edges and the crumble topping is golden brown. Check on the crumble about half-way through baking—if the top is browning too quickly, tent with aluminum foil. Cool for at least 10 minutes before serving. Serve plain or with vanilla ice cream (if using). Store covered tightly in the refrigerator for up to 4 days.

Zucchini & Tomato Herbed Biscuit Cobbler

SERVES 6 TO 8

This garden-to-table dish takes advantage of the bountiful harvest during the warm months of the year. Think of it as a vegetable pot pie but with a tomato-based sauce. The Parmesan and herb–infused biscuit topping is flaky, fluffy, and holds its shape nicely because it's cold going into the oven. The star of the show is undoubtedly the vibrant vegetable filling, which benefits from a quick cook on the stove to help build flavor and reduce excess moisture.

SKILL LEVEL: **Beginner**
PREP: **35 minutes**
BAKE: **35 minutes**
TOTAL: **1 hour 20 minutes, including some cooling**

Biscuit Topping

1¾ cups all-purpose flour, plus more as needed **(219g)**

¾ cup (3 ounces) freshly grated Parmesan cheese **(85g)**

2 teaspoons baking powder

½ teaspoon dried basil

½ teaspoon dried oregano

¼ teaspoon salt

¼ teaspoon freshly ground black pepper

6 tablespoons unsalted butter, cold and cubed **(85g)**

¾ cup + 2 tablespoons buttermilk, divided **(210g/ml)**

Filling

3 tablespoons unsalted butter **(43g)**

1 tablespoon extra-virgin olive oil

1 cup diced yellow onion **(130g)**

2 tablespoons tomato paste

4 garlic cloves, minced

1 teaspoon salt

1 teaspoon granulated sugar

3 cups sliced zucchini, cut in ¼-inch half-moons **(400g)**

3 cups chopped tomatoes, cut in 1-inch chunks, or halved cherry/grape tomatoes **(450g)**

2 tablespoons all-purpose flour

2 tablespoons finely chopped fresh basil, or 2 teaspoons dried

1. Make the biscuit topping: In a large bowl or a food processor, combine the flour, Parmesan, baking powder, basil, oregano, salt, and pepper, and whisk or pulse until combined. Add the butter and cut it into the dry ingredients with a pastry blender or by pulsing several times in the processor, just until coarse crumbs form. If using a processor, transfer the mixture to a large bowl. Make a well in the center and pour in ¾ cup (180g/ml) of the buttermilk. Mix with a large spoon or spatula until the dough begins to come together. Do not overwork the dough. It should be shaggy and crumbly with some wet spots. With generously floured hands, shape and flatten the dough into 6 or 7 round biscuits, about ½ inch thick. The dough is sticky, so flour your hands as needed. Line a large plate or small baking sheet with parchment paper. Place the shaped biscuits on the parchment, cover loosely, and refrigerate until ready to use or for up to 2 days.

2. Preheat the oven to 400°F (204°C).

3. Make the filling: In a 10 × 2-inch cast-iron skillet, melt the butter with the olive oil over medium heat. Add the onion and cook, stirring occasionally, until they soften, about 5 minutes. Stir in the tomato paste, garlic, salt, and sugar and then add the zucchini and half of the tomatoes. Cook, stirring often, until the zucchini is fork-tender, 5 to 6 minutes. Stir in the flour and then the remaining tomatoes and the basil. Remove from heat.

4. Arrange the chilled biscuits in a single layer over the warm filling, pressing them down lightly to partially immerse them in the filling. Brush the remaining 2 tablespoons buttermilk on the biscuits.

5. Place a baking sheet on the bottom oven rack to catch any juices that may bubble over. Bake the cobbler on the center rack for 30 to 35 minutes or until the filling is bubbling around the edges and the biscuits are golden brown. Cool for at least 10 minutes before serving. Store covered tightly in the refrigerator for up to 5 days.

TIP: A 10 × 2-inch or slightly larger ovenproof skillet is handy for this recipe. If you don't have a skillet around this size, you can precook the filling in any large skillet and then transfer it to a greased 2½-quart baking dish.

Molten Chocolate Cobbler

SERVES 8

SKILL LEVEL: **Beginner**

PREP: **15 minutes**

BAKE: **35 minutes**

TOTAL: **1 hour 5 minutes, including some cooling**

Inspiration for this recipe came from an old issue of *Southern Living* magazine. I made some changes (because I can never leave things alone), and the outcome is like a warm chocolate cake with a molten center and a slightly crisp and crackled top. Taste-testing quickly became a group gathering, and by the end of the day, we were indulging straight from the pan. As for many other sweet treats in this chapter, make sure to grab some ice cream or make Classic Whipped Cream (page 154) to go with it. Mint chocolate chip ice cream is my favorite pairing!

Nonstick spray or butter, for the pan

Filling

1 cup all-purpose flour **(125g)**

¾ cup granulated sugar **(150g)**

¼ cup unsweetened Dutch-process cocoa powder **(21g)**

2 teaspoons baking powder

1 teaspoon instant espresso powder

½ teaspoon salt

1 cup semi-sweet chocolate chips **(180g)**

¾ cup chopped walnuts or pecans (optional) **(100g)**

½ cup milk, at room temperature **(120g/ml)**

6 tablespoons unsalted butter, melted and slightly cooled **(85g)**

2 large egg yolks, at room temperature

2 teaspoons vanilla extract

Topping

½ cup brown sugar **(100g)**

2 tablespoons granulated sugar

2 tablespoons unsweetened Dutch-process cocoa powder

1½ cups boiling water **(360g/ml)**

½ cup semi-sweet chocolate chips **(90g)**

For Serving (Optional)

Mint chocolate chip or vanilla ice cream

1. Preheat the oven to 350°F (177°C). Grease a 9-inch square baking pan, 11 × 7-inch rectangular baking dish, or 10-inch round baking dish with non-stick spray.

2. **Make the filling:** In a large bowl, whisk the flour, sugar, cocoa powder, baking powder, espresso powder, and salt. Stir in the chocolate chips and then the nuts (if using).

3. In a medium bowl, whisk the milk, melted butter, egg yolks, and vanilla. Pour into the flour mixture and stir gently to combine. Spread the batter evenly in the prepared pan.

4. **Make the topping:** In a medium bowl, whisk the brown sugar, granulated sugar, and cocoa powder. Sprinkle the mixture evenly over the chocolate batter, then pour the boiling water over the top without mixing it in. It will seem like a lot of water. Sprinkle the chocolate chips on top.

5. Bake for 35 to 38 minutes or until the top looks mostly set. Err on the side of underbaking. The top will be a little wobbly because of the rich molten pudding mixture underneath. Cool for at least 10 minutes before serving. Serve plain or with ice cream (if using). Store covered tightly in the refrigerator for up to 5 days.

Brunch Bakes

Spinach, Tomato & Feta Quiche

SERVES 8 TO 10

Quiche is a cornerstone brunch recipe and I've made it in a variety of flavors. A truly remarkable quiche is creamy and soft with textural contrast from the flaky pie crust. To avoid a soggy bottom (who wants that?!), be sure to parbake the crust before adding the filling. Most of the flavor in quiche comes from the add-ins, and here you'll use garlicky spinach, fresh tomatoes, and salty, tangy feta cheese. Even though it's common at the brunch and breakfast table, don't limit this dish to those morning hours! This quiche is a fantastic option for lunch or dinner.

SKILL LEVEL: **Intermediate**

PREP: **2 hours 40 minutes, including pie crust**

BAKE: **1 hour 7 minutes**

TOTAL: **4 hours 25 minutes, including chilling and cooling**

Crust

Double Pie Crust (page 136)

Egg wash: 1 large egg beaten with 1 tablespoon milk

Custard Filling

4 large eggs

½ cup whole milk **(120g/ml)**

½ cup heavy cream **(120g/ml)**

¼ teaspoon freshly ground black pepper

⅛ teaspoon salt

1 teaspoon extra-virgin olive oil

1 garlic clove, minced

3 cups chopped fresh spinach **(90g)**

1 cup (4 ounces) crumbled feta cheese **(113g)**

1 cup cherry tomatoes, halved **(115g)**

1. Make and chill the pie crust dough as directed. You will only need 1 disc for this (save the second disc for another use).

2. If you're new to working with pie dough, review Rolling Out Pie Dough (page 131). On a floured surface, roll out the dough to a 12-inch circle, giving the dough a quarter-turn after every few rolls to keep it even. Carefully place the dough into a 9-inch pie dish. Tuck and pat it in place with your fingers, making sure it is smooth. Crimp or flute the edges (see page 134). Lightly brush the edges of the crust with egg wash. Place the crust in the refrigerator for 20 minutes.

3. Preheat the oven to 375°F (191°C).

4. Parbake the crust (see page 135).

5. Remove the parbaked crust from the oven and **reduce the oven temperature to 350°F (177°C)**.

6. Make the custard filling: In a large bowl using a handheld or stand mixer fitted with the whisk, beat the eggs, milk, cream, pepper, and salt on high speed until combined, about 1 minute.

7. In a skillet, heat the olive oil over medium heat. Add the garlic and cook for 1 minute. Add the spinach and cook, stirring, until it has mostly wilted, about 1 minute. Remove from heat. Fold the warm spinach, feta, and tomatoes into the custard filling.

8. Pour the filling into the warm parbaked crust. Bake for 25 minutes. Add a pie crust shield (see page 132) to prevent the edges from browning too quickly. Bake for an additional 20 to 25 minutes or until the center is just about set. Let the quiche cool on a cooling rack for at least 15 minutes before slicing and serving. The quiche can be served warm or at room temperature. Store covered tightly in the refrigerator for up to 3 days.

Chocolate Chip Crumb Cake

SERVES 9 TO 12

SKILL LEVEL: **Beginner**

PREP: **20 minutes**

BAKE: **45 minutes**

TOTAL: **1 hour 20 minutes, including some cooling**

Crumb cakes are just an excuse to eat cake for breakfast. And, truly, is anyone mad about that? This buttery cake is easy to prepare and has a lot of patience, so feel free to make it hours in advance or even the night before. Sour cream adds delightful moisture while keeping the crumb light. I recommend using mini chocolate chips here so each bite has plenty! I also add mini chocolate chips to the cinnamon–brown sugar crumb topping, but if you want to scale back on the chocolate (it IS the morning after all!), replace them with chopped walnuts or pecans.

Cake

1¾ cups all-purpose flour **(219g)**

1½ teaspoons baking powder

½ teaspoon salt

¼ teaspoon baking soda

8 tablespoons unsalted butter, at room temperature **(113g)**

1 cup granulated sugar **(200g)**

2 large eggs, at room temperature

1 cup full-fat sour cream, at room temperature **(240g)**

2 teaspoons vanilla extract

¾ cup mini chocolate chips **(128g)** or 1 cup regular-size chocolate chips **(180g)**

Crumb Topping

⅔ cup all-purpose flour **(83g)**

½ cup brown sugar **(100g)**

2 teaspoons ground cinnamon

4 tablespoons unsalted butter, at room temperature **(56g)**

⅓ cup mini chocolate chips **(57g)** or ½ cup regular-size chocolate chips **(90g)**

1. Preheat the oven to 350°F (177°C). Line a 9-inch square baking pan with parchment paper, leaving a few inches of overhang on two opposite sides.

2. Make the cake: In a medium bowl, whisk the flour, baking powder, salt, and baking soda.

3. In a large bowl using a handheld or stand mixer fitted with the paddle, beat the butter and sugar on medium-high speed until the mixture is light and creamy, about 3 minutes. Scrape down the sides of the bowl as needed. Add the eggs and beat on medium-high speed until combined. Beat in the sour cream and vanilla until incorporated. Add the flour mixture and beat on low speed just until combined; do not overmix. Fold in the chocolate chips. The batter should be thick. Pour the batter into the prepared pan and smooth the top.

4. Make the crumb topping: In a small bowl, whisk the flour, brown sugar, and cinnamon. Add the butter, then use your hands or a fork to bring it together until large crumbles form. Stir in the chocolate chips. Sprinkle the topping evenly over the batter.

5. Bake for 45 to 50 minutes or until a toothpick inserted in the center comes out clean. If the top browns too quickly, loosely tent aluminum foil over the cake. Cool the cake in the pan set on a cooling rack for at least 20 minutes. Lift the cake out of the pan by gripping the parchment paper overhang; transfer to a cutting board and cut into squares. Store covered tightly at room temperature for up to 5 days or in the refrigerator for up to 1 week.

Tips for Success

PECAN STICKY BUN CAKE

- Pay attention to the order of the steps: Make the cake batter first, then the topping.
- We found in testing that if we let the caramel sauce sit for too long before baking, it solidified and wouldn't stick to the cake. Instead, you want it still fluid and warm as you spoon the cake batter on top of it.
- We also found that placing a baking sheet on a rack below the cake served two purposes: First, it caught any topping that might bubble over, and second, it blocked some direct heat on the bottom of the cake. In tests without the baking sheet, the brown sugar on the bottom (the eventual topping when inverted) burned.

Pecan Sticky Bun Cake

SERVES 12

You don't have to go another day without wondering what pecan sticky buns would taste like as a cake. (Because I'm sure that keeps you up at night.) Here you'll combine a simple brown sugar glaze with toasted pecans and a buttery-soft cake crumb. After inverting the warm Bundt cake, the glaze and pecans create an irresistible praline-like layer.

SKILL LEVEL: **Intermediate**
PREP: **30 minutes**
BAKE: **50 minutes**
TOTAL: **1 hour 50 minutes,** including some cooling

Cake

Nonstick spray or butter, for the pan

2½ cups all-purpose flour **(313g)**

1½ teaspoons baking powder

1 teaspoon ground cinnamon

¾ teaspoon salt

½ teaspoon baking soda

1 cup granulated sugar **(200g)**

12 tablespoons unsalted butter, at room temperature **(170g)**

½ cup brown sugar **(100g)**

1 cup full-fat sour cream, at room temperature **(240g)**

3 large eggs, at room temperature

2 tablespoons vegetable oil

1 teaspoon vanilla extract

⅓ cup milk, at room temperature **(80g/ml)**

Topping

½ cup brown sugar **(100g)**

6 tablespoons unsalted butter **(85g)**

2 tablespoons pure maple syrup or light corn syrup

2 tablespoons milk

Pinch of salt

½ teaspoon vanilla extract

1 cup chopped pecans, toasted (see Toasting Nuts, page 21) **(120g)**

1. Preheat the oven to 350°F (177°C). Grease a 10- to 12-cup Bundt pan with nonstick spray.

2. Make the cake: In a medium bowl, whisk the flour, baking powder, cinnamon, salt, and baking soda until combined.

3. In a large bowl using a handheld or stand mixer fitted with the paddle, beat the granulated sugar, butter, and brown sugar together on medium-high speed until the mixture is light and creamy, about 3 minutes. Scrape down the sides of the bowl as needed. Add the sour cream, eggs, oil, and vanilla and beat on high speed until combined, about 1 minute. Add the flour mixture and then the milk. Beat on low speed until combined. Whisk by hand a few times to be certain there are no lumps at the bottom of the bowl. The batter should be thick and creamy. Set aside while you make the topping.

4. Make the topping: In a medium saucepan, combine the brown sugar, butter, syrup, milk, and salt. Whisk constantly over medium heat until the butter is melted, then bring the mixture to a boil, whisking occasionally. Once it's bubbling, let it boil for 2 minutes. Watch closely; you may need to reduce the heat to prevent it from boiling over. Remove the topping from the heat and whisk in the vanilla.

5. Pour about half of the warm topping into the prepared pan (reserve the remaining half for step 7) and sprinkle with the pecans. Pour the cake batter over the pecans and topping and smooth the top.

6. Place the cake on the center oven rack, and place a baking sheet on the bottom oven rack to catch any liquid that may bubble over and protect the bottom of the cake (the eventual top, once inverted) from burning. Bake for 50 to 55 minutes or until a toothpick inserted in the center comes out clean. If the cake is browning too quickly, loosely tent it with foil. Cool the cake in the pan set on a cooling rack for 10 minutes. Invert the warm cake onto a large plate or cake stand. If some of the topping sticks to the inside of the pan, spoon it out and add it to the top of the cake. Cool for 20 minutes more.

7. Meanwhile, in the microwave at 50% power or on the stove over low heat, reheat the remaining topping, whisking to blend in any butter that may have separated out. Drizzle over the cake and serve warm or at room temperature. Store covered tightly at room temperature for up to 3 days or in the refrigerator for up to 1 week.

Rough Puff Pastry Dough

MAKES ABOUT 1 POUND (454G) OF PUFF PASTRY

SKILL LEVEL: **Advanced**

PREP: **3 hours, including chilling**

TOTAL: **3 hours**

Ready to become a domestic superhero? You're making homemade puff pastry! This pastry dough comes together using a "rough puff" method where you carefully work butter into the dry ingredients and then fold and flatten the dough many times to create countless flaky layers. I learned the process from cookbook author and chef Claire Saffitz. There are two stages of refrigeration that go up to 24 hours each, so this is a wonderful make-ahead dough with convenient options in terms of timing. Use the dough in recipes for Asparagus & Smoked Salmon Tart (page 181), Cream Cheese Puff Pastry Danishes (page 182), and Sausage, Egg & Cheese Turnovers (page 185)—or any recipe that calls for 1 pound puff pastry dough (or a store-bought package containing two puff pastry sheets). You know when you bite into golden-brown baked puff pastry and you hear that loud and glorious CRISP? That's exactly what you'll experience!

1⅓ cups all-purpose flour, plus more as needed **(167g)**

1 teaspoon granulated sugar

½ teaspoon salt

12 tablespoons unsalted butter, very cold and cubed **(170g)**

6 to 8 tablespoons ice-cold water **(90 to 120g/ml)**

TIP: Your hands are your best tool because they make it nearly impossible to overmix the dough (your hands would get too tired before reaching that point!). I do not recommend a food processor, electric mixer, or pastry blender here. These tools cut down the butter too much and you'll lose precious flaky layers.

1. In a large bowl, whisk the flour, sugar, and salt. Scatter the butter on top. Gently toss the flour and butter together with your hands and then briefly rub the butter into the flour to begin combining them (1). You do not want to break down the butter too much.

2. At this point, the butter is still in large cubes/chunks. Add the ice-cold water, 1 tablespoon at a time (2), using your hands to toss the mixture together after each addition. You can use a spatula or spoon for tossing, but I really do recommend your hands so you get a good feel for the dough. As the dough begins to hydrate after about 4 tablespoons of water, you can start lightly squeezing or clumping the dough together (3). The mixture should still be very shaggy. If your dough feels sticky and wet before adding 6 tablespoons of water, mix in 1 tablespoon of flour.

3. Pour the shaggy clump of dough out onto a lightly floured surface. There should still be large chunks of butter at this point. With lightly floured hands, begin patting the dough down until it's ¾ to 1 inch thick, about a 5 × 8-inch rectangle (4, 5). Fold the dough into thirds as if you were folding a business letter (6, 7). Use your hands to gently flatten and smooth out any cracks in the dough. Wrap it tightly in plastic wrap or parchment paper, or place it in an airtight container, and refrigerate for at least 2 hours and up to 24 hours.

4. If the dough has chilled for longer than about 3 hours, it's likely very stiff, so let it rest at room temperature for about 5 minutes before you begin rolling. On a lightly floured surface with lightly floured hands, gently flatten the dough. Using a rolling pin, roll the dough into a rectangle ½ inch thick and about 6 × 12 inches (8). The exact dimensions are not important, but the thickness is. As you roll, flip the dough over once or twice to make sure it's not sticking to the surface. Lightly flour the surface as needed. Fold the rectangle into thirds as if you were folding a business letter (9, 10). Turn it 90 degrees (11) and roll it out again into a ½-inch-thick 6 × 12-inch rectangle (12) and fold into thirds. Again turn it 90 degrees and roll out. Repeat the rolling, folding, and turning process four more times, for a total of six times.

5. Wrap the dough tightly and refrigerate for at least 15 minutes or up to 24 hours before using. (To freeze for later, see Freezing Baked Goods, page 23.)

Asparagus & Smoked Salmon Tart

SERVES 8 TO 12

Quiche and egg–based casseroles are brunch mainstays, but it's a nice change of pace to have a savory option that isn't centered around eggs! I love using rough puff pastry dough to make savory tarts, and I have several recipes on my website, including Butternut Squash Mushroom Tart and Cranberry Brie Tarts. Smoked salmon and asparagus came to mind when I was brainstorming my next great pairing, the flavors complemented by goat cheese, lemon, and fresh herbs.

SKILL LEVEL: **Advanced**

PREP: **3 hours 30 minutes, including Rough Puff Pastry Dough**

BAKE: **35 minutes**

TOTAL: **4 hours 10 minutes**

Dough & Assembly

Rough Puff Pastry Dough (page 178)

All-purpose flour, as needed for shaping

Egg wash: 1 large egg beaten with 1 tablespoon milk

Topping

4 ounces soft goat cheese **(113g)**

1 teaspoon fresh lemon juice

1 teaspoon chopped fresh dill

1 teaspoon chopped fresh chives

¼ teaspoon garlic powder

8 ounces slender asparagus spears, woody ends trimmed **(226g)**

2 teaspoons extra-virgin olive oil

Flaky sea salt and freshly ground black pepper

4 ounces smoked salmon, torn in pieces **(113g)**

Optional Garnishes

Lemon zest

Capers

Fresh dill sprigs

TIP: Use thin asparagus spears because thicker asparagus spears take longer to cook and weigh down the crust too much.

1. Prepare and chill the rough puff pastry dough as directed.

2. Preheat the oven to 400°F (204°C). Line a 13 × 18-inch baking sheet with parchment paper.

3. To assemble: On a lightly floured surface using a lightly floured rolling pin, roll the puff pastry dough to a 13 × 18-inch rectangle. The dough is thin, and that's what you want so it cooks through. Fold over a 1-inch border around the sides of the rectangle (into the center) and crimp the edges with a fork. Carefully transfer the dough to the prepared baking sheet. Lightly brush the pastry with egg wash and then prick the surface all over with a fork (not the crimped edges). Bake for 15 minutes; it will shrink a bit and that's okay.

4. Make the topping: In a medium bowl, use a fork to mix the goat cheese, lemon juice, dill, chives, and garlic powder until combined and crumbly.

5. Remove the parbaked crust from the oven. If there are any large air bubbles, prick them with a fork to release the steam. Dot the surface of the crust with spoonfuls of the cheese mixture. Lay the asparagus spears in a row across the top and drizzle with the olive oil. Return the tart to the oven and bake for 20 minutes or until the edges are golden brown and the asparagus is tender.

6. Cool the tart on the baking sheet for 5 minutes. Season with flaky sea salt and pepper and then top with smoked salmon. Garnish with lemon zest, capers, and dill sprigs (if using). Transfer the tart to a cutting board and use a sharp knife to cut into slices. Serve warm or at room temperature. Store covered tightly in the refrigerator for up to 5 days.

Cream Cheese Puff Pastry Danishes

MAKES 9 DANISHES

SKILL LEVEL: **Advanced**

PREP: **3 hours 40 minutes, including Rough Puff Pastry Dough**

BAKE: **22 minutes**

TOTAL: **4 hours 10 minutes**

With the help of rough puff pastry dough, you can put together über-flaky danishes that rival anything from a bakery! If I have free time the day before, I like to assemble and refrigerate the shaped pastries overnight so all I have to do is bake them in the morning. I love these with sweet cream cheese filling and fruity jam—raspberry and apricot are my top choices. You could also use cherry sauce topping (see Classic Cheesecake, page 123) or enjoy them as plain cheese danishes. Finished with a little vanilla icing, these are sure to bring a smile to any sleepyhead at the breakfast table.

Rough Puff Pastry Dough
(page 178)

Filling

5 ounces full-fat brick cream cheese, at room temperature **(141g)**

2 tablespoons granulated sugar

½ teaspoon fresh lemon juice

½ teaspoon vanilla extract

Assembly

All-purpose flour, as needed for shaping

Egg wash: 1 large egg beaten with 1 tablespoon milk

3 to 4 tablespoons fruit jam or preserves

Icing

½ cup powdered sugar, sifted **(60g)**

1 tablespoon milk

½ teaspoon vanilla extract

1. Prepare and chill the rough puff pastry dough as directed.

2. **Make the filling:** In a medium bowl using a handheld or stand mixer fitted with the paddle, beat the cream cheese and granulated sugar on medium-high speed until smooth, about 2 minutes. Add the lemon juice and vanilla and beat on medium-high speed until no lumps remain. Refrigerate the filling while you shape the dough.

3. **To assemble:** On a lightly floured surface using a lightly floured rolling pin, roll the puff pastry dough to a 12-inch square. Using a pizza cutter or a sharp knife, cut nine 4-inch squares. Working with 1 square at a time, fold the square in half to form a triangle (1). Using a sharp knife, cut along the inside of the triangle on two sides (not the folded side), about ½ inch from the edge, making sure not to cut all the way to the points (2). Unfold the triangle (3). Take the cut strip from the corner on one side and fold it over to line up with the corner point of the smaller square (4). Repeat with the other side to create a diamond-shaped pastry (5). Shape the remaining squares to make a total of 9 pastries. Place the shaped pastries on a parchment paper–lined baking sheet or large plate and refrigerate for at least 15 minutes or up to 1 day. If refrigerating for longer than 15 minutes, cover the pastries.

4. Preheat the oven to 400°F (204°C). Line two baking sheets with parchment paper.

5. **Finish assembling:** Remove the shaped pastries and cream cheese filling from the refrigerator. Arrange the pastries 3 inches apart on the prepared baking sheets. Lightly brush the edges with egg wash. Spoon a scant tablespoon of the cream cheese mixture in the center of each and top with 1 teaspoon of jam.

6. Bake for 20 to 22 minutes or until the edges of the pastries are golden brown. Cool the pastries on the baking sheets for 5 minutes before icing.

7. **Make the icing:** In a small bowl, whisk the powdered sugar, milk, and vanilla until smooth. Drizzle the icing over the warm danishes. They're best served the day they're baked. Store covered tightly in the refrigerator for up to 4 days.

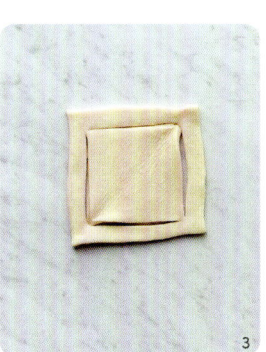

Sausage, Egg & Cheese Turnovers

MAKES 9 TURNOVERS

When thinking of breakfast pastries, our minds usually drift toward sweet and sugary, right? Yet I enjoy serving a savory option because it's a fun and flavorful switch-up! These turnovers feature sausage, egg, and cheese nestled inside crisp, buttery puff pastry. Diced green chilies really brighten the flavor; taste testers and I agreed the turnovers were missing a little something without them.

SKILL LEVEL: **Advanced**

PREP: **3 hours 35 minutes, including Rough Puff Pastry Dough**

BAKE: **23 minutes**

TOTAL: **4 hours 55 minutes**

Rough Puff Pastry Dough
(page 178)

Filling

4 ounces bulk Italian sausage **(113g)**

2 tablespoons canned diced green chilies

3 large eggs

¼ teaspoon onion powder

¼ teaspoon salt

⅛ teaspoon freshly ground black pepper

Assembly

All-purpose flour, as needed for shaping

½ cup (2 ounces) freshly shredded Cheddar cheese **(57g)**

Egg wash: 1 large egg beaten with 1 tablespoon milk

Everything Bagel Seasoning (page 194), for topping (optional)

1. Prepare and chill the rough puff pastry dough as directed.

2. **Make the filling:** In a medium skillet, cook the sausage and green chilies over medium heat, stirring, until the sausage is cooked through and crumbled, 8 to 10 minutes. Transfer to a paper towel–lined plate and set aside to cool. Keep the skillet (no need to clean it) near the stove.

3. In a small bowl, whisk the eggs, onion powder, salt, and pepper. Add the egg mixture to the skillet and cook, scrambling the eggs, until almost but not quite set, 3 to 4 minutes. Return the sausage mixture to the skillet and stir to combine. Remove from heat and set aside.

4. **To assemble:** On a lightly floured surface using a lightly floured rolling pin, roll the puff pastry dough to a 12-inch square. Using a pizza cutter or a sharp knife, cut nine 4-inch squares (1). Spoon about 2 tablespoons of the sausage-and-egg mixture into the center of each pastry square and top with a scant tablespoon of cheese (2). Fold one corner of the square over the filling to make a triangle (3). Using a fork, crimp the edges of the turnover to seal. Place the shaped turnovers on a parchment paper–lined baking sheet or large plate and refrigerate for at least 15 minutes or up to 1 day. If refrigerating for longer than 15 minutes, cover the turnovers.

5. Preheat the oven to 400°F (204°C). Line two baking sheets with parchment paper.

6. Remove the turnovers from the refrigerator and arrange 3 inches apart on the prepared baking sheets. Lightly brush with the egg wash. Cut two or three vents into the top of each to allow steam to escape. Sprinkle with everything bagel seasoning (if using, 4).

7. Bake for 23 to 25 minutes or until the turnovers are golden brown. Cool the turnovers on the baking sheets for 5 minutes before serving. Store covered tightly in the refrigerator for up to 3 days.

The Crowd's Favorite Cinnamon Rolls

MAKES 12 ROLLS

SKILL LEVEL: **Intermediate**

PREP: **3 hours 30 minutes, including rises**

BAKE: **25 minutes**

TOTAL: **4 hours or overnight**

It took me ten years to carefully fine-tune this recipe and process so we could all enjoy the softest, most buttery homestyle cinnamon rolls. These are big and satisfying, and my go-to when I need a crowd-pleasing brunch dish. They're loaded with cinnamon and brown sugar, are extra gooey served warm out of the oven, and I wouldn't dare to serve these without icing on top. I have my cream cheese icing here, but you could instead try vanilla icing (see Cinnamon Swirl Quick Bread, page 214). To get a head start on the morning, use the overnight option, page 188.

Dough

1 cup warm whole milk (about 110°F/43°C), plus more as needed **(240g/ml)**

⅔ cup granulated sugar, divided **(133g)**

1½ tablespoons instant or active dry yeast (2 standard packets) **(14g)**

8 tablespoons unsalted butter, at room temperature, cut into 4 pieces **(113g)**

4½ cups all-purpose flour or bread flour, plus more as needed **(563g)**

2 large eggs, at room temperature

½ teaspoon salt

Nonstick spray or butter, for the bowl and pan

Filling

8 tablespoons unsalted butter, softened **(113g)**

⅔ cup brown sugar **(133g)**

1½ tablespoons ground cinnamon

Cream Cheese Icing

4 ounces full-fat brick cream cheese, at room temperature **(113g)**

1 cup powdered sugar **(120g)**

1 tablespoon heavy cream or milk

½ teaspoon vanilla extract

1. Make the dough: In the bowl of a stand mixer fitted with the dough hook, whisk the warm milk, 2 tablespoons of sugar, and the yeast. Cover and let sit for 5 to 10 minutes or until foamy and frothy on the surface. (If you don't have a stand mixer, simply use a large mixing bowl and mix the dough with a wooden spoon or spatula in the next step.)

2. Add the remaining sugar and the butter and beat on medium speed until the butter is slightly broken up. Add 1 cup (125g) of the flour, the eggs, and salt. Beat on low speed for 30 seconds, scrape down the sides of the bowl, then add the remaining flour. Beat on medium speed until the dough comes together and pulls away from the sides of the bowl, about 2 minutes. If it seems too sticky and clings to the sides of the bowl instead of forming a rough mass around the dough hook or spoon, add more flour, 1 tablespoon at a time, and continue to mix until the dough pulls away from the sides of the bowl but is still moist and tacky. If it feels dry and crumbly, add more milk, 1 teaspoon at a time, mixing well after each addition.

3. When the dough reaches the proper consistency, beat on low speed for 5 minutes more or until it is smooth, supple, and elastic. (Or knead by hand on a lightly floured surface for 5 minutes. Keep a small bowl of flour nearby to lightly flour your hands and/or the dough as needed, as it can be quite sticky.) To see if the dough is ready, use the poke test or the windowpane test (see page 241). If it's not ready, keep kneading.

4. Lightly grease a large bowl with nonstick spray. Place the dough in the bowl, turning it to coat. Cover the bowl with a tea towel or plastic wrap and let the dough rise at room temperature for 1½ to 2 hours or until doubled in size.

5. Add the filling: Grease a metal or glass 9 × 13-inch baking pan with nonstick spray or line it with parchment paper. When the dough is risen, punch it down to release the air. Place the dough on a lightly floured surface and, with a floured rolling pin, roll the dough to a 12 × 18-inch rectangle (1). If the dough shrinks as you try to roll it out, cover it loosely and let the dough rest for 10 minutes before trying again. Spread the softened butter all over the dough (2). (The softer the butter is, the easier it is to spread in this step. Heat it in the microwave for a few seconds to soften if needed.) In a small bowl, mix the brown sugar and cinnamon; sprinkle this evenly over the butter (3).

recipe continues >

OVERNIGHT OPTION: After shaping the rolls and arranging in the baking pan, cover loosely with plastic wrap and place in the refrigerator for up to 16 hours. Remove from the refrigerator, keep covered, and allow to rise for 1 to 2 hours at room temperature, then bake as directed.

Tightly roll up the dough to form an 18-inch-long log (4). If some filling spills out, sprinkle it on top of the roll. With an extra-sharp knife or bench scraper, cut 12 even rolls, each about 1½ inches thick (5).

6. Arrange the rolls in the prepared pan, cut side up (6). Cover the pan with a tea towel or plastic wrap and let the rolls rise at room temperature until puffy, about 1 hour. (Or use the overnight option, left.)

7. Preheat the oven to 350°F (177°C).

8. Bake the rolls for 25 to 28 minutes or until golden brown on top, rotating the pan halfway through. If the tops are browning too quickly, loosely tent aluminum foil over the rolls. Let the rolls cool in the pan set on a cooling rack for about 10 minutes while you make the icing.

9. Make the cream cheese icing: In a large bowl using a handheld or stand mixer fitted with the paddle, beat the cream cheese on medium speed until smooth and creamy. Add the powdered sugar, cream, and vanilla. Beat on low speed for 30 seconds, then increase to high speed and beat for 1 minute. Using a knife or icing spatula, spread the icing on the warm rolls and serve immediately. Store covered tightly at room temperature for up to 2 days or in the refrigerator for up to 5 days.

Bacon & Cheddar Biscuits with Spicy Honey Butter

MAKES 8 TO 10 BISCUITS

SKILL LEVEL: **Beginner**
PREP: **35 minutes**
BAKE: **20 minutes**
TOTAL: **55 minutes**

These flaky, extra-flavorful biscuits are not only perfect for breakfast alongside eggs and fresh fruit but are also a delicious accompaniment to many dinner entrées. My crew DEVOURED these, and just wait until you taste the spicy-sweet butter topping!

Biscuits

6 slices uncooked bacon

2½ cups all-purpose flour, plus more as needed **(313g)**

1 tablespoon baking powder

¾ teaspoon salt

½ teaspoon baking soda

8 tablespoons unsalted butter, cold and cubed **(113g)**

1 cup + 2 tablespoons buttermilk, cold and divided **(270g/ml)**

1 tablespoon honey

1 cup (4 ounces) freshly shredded Cheddar cheese **(113g)**

3 tablespoons chopped fresh chives

Spicy Honey Butter

2 tablespoons unsalted butter, melted **(28g)**

2 teaspoons honey

¼ teaspoon crushed red pepper flakes

TIPS: The butter needs to be very cold to create lots of flaky biscuit layers. I usually cube the butter first, then place it in the freezer for about 15 minutes while I cook the bacon.

Do not twist the biscuit cutter when pressing down into the dough; this seals off the edges of the biscuits, which prevents them from fully rising.

1. Make the biscuits: In a 10-inch ovenproof skillet, preferably cast-iron, cook the bacon over medium heat until crisp. Remove from heat and transfer the bacon to a paper towel–lined plate to drain. Leave about 1 to 2 tablespoons of bacon fat in the skillet for baking the biscuits. When the bacon is cool enough to handle, crumble it into small pieces.

2. Preheat the oven to 425°F (218°C).

3. In a large bowl or food processor, combine the flour, baking powder, salt, and baking soda, and whisk or pulse until incorporated. Add the cold cubed butter and cut it into the dry ingredients with a pastry blender (1; see visuals, page 192) or by pulsing several times in the processor until coarse crumbs form. If you used a food processor, transfer the mixture to a large bowl. Make a well in the center of the flour mixture. Pour in 1 cup (240g/ml) of the buttermilk and drizzle the honey on top. Mix with a large spoon or spatula until the dough begins to come together. Fold in the crumbled bacon, cheese, and chives. Do not overwork the dough. The dough should be shaggy and crumbly with some wet spots.

4. Pour the dough and any dough crumbles onto a floured surface and gently bring it together with generously floured hands (2). The dough will be sticky; have extra flour nearby and use it often to flour your hands and surface in this step. Using your hands or a floured rolling pin, flatten the dough into a ¾-inch-thick rectangle. Fold one side into the center (3), then the other side (4). Turn the dough horizontally. Gently flatten into a ¾-inch-thick rectangle again (5). Repeat the folding again (6, 7). Turn the dough horizontally one more time. Gently flatten into a ¾-inch-thick rectangle. Repeat the folding one last time, for a total of three turns. Flatten into the fourth and final ¾-inch-thick rectangle.

5. Cut into 3-inch rounds with a biscuit cutter (8). Gather the scraps, re-roll, and cut more biscuits until all the dough is used. You should have 8 to 10 biscuits. Arrange the biscuits in the skillet. Brush the tops with the remaining 2 tablespoons buttermilk (9).

6. Bake for 20 to 22 minutes or until the tops are golden brown. Cool the biscuits in the pan set on a cooling rack for 5 minutes before topping.

recipe continues >

7. Make the spicy honey butter: In a small bowl, stir the melted butter, honey, and red pepper flakes until combined. Brush on the biscuits and serve warm. The biscuits are best the day they are made, but they can be stored covered tightly at room temperature for up to 2 days or in the refrigerator for up to 5 days.

Hot 'n' Fresh Bagels

MAKES 8 BAGELS

Ready for some bragging rights? You're making homemade bagels! I make these often and have learned a couple of non-negotiables. First, bread flour is essential. It has a higher protein content than all-purpose; using all-purpose would produce bagels that are a bit flimsy and not nearly as chewy. Boiling the bagels in water and a little barley malt syrup or honey also is crucial. It helps set the bagels' shape and gives them their signature chewy crust. If you skip this step, you'll be eating a bagel-shaped roll . . . something entirely different! Whether you prefer them fresh out of the oven, plain, topped, toasted, or cream cheese–schmeared, the satisfying taste and texture of homemade bagels is unparalleled.

SKILL LEVEL: Intermediate

PREP: **2 hours 20 minutes, including rises and boiling**

BAKE: **20 minutes**

TOTAL: **3 hours, including some cooling**

Dough

1½ cups warm water (about 110°F/43°C) **(360g/ml)**

1 tablespoon barley malt syrup, granulated sugar, or brown sugar

2¾ teaspoons instant or active dry yeast **(8g)**

4 cups bread flour, plus more as needed **(520g)**

2 teaspoons salt

Nonstick spray or butter, for the bowl

Boiling & Topping

2 quarts water **(1.9L)**

¼ cup barley malt syrup or honey **(85g)**

Egg wash: 1 egg white beaten with 1 tablespoon water

Optional toppings (see Bagel Toppings, page 194)

OVERNIGHT OPTION: Prepare the dough through most of step 4, allowing the dough to rise in the refrigerator for up to 16 hours instead of at room temperature. Remove the dough from the refrigerator and let the dough come to room temperature, about 1 hour. Then shape, boil, and bake as directed.

TIP: Barley malt syrup can be a little hard to find, but it gives the bagels a distinctive malty flavor. Most natural foods stores carry it or you can order it online.

1. Make the dough: In the bowl of a stand mixer fitted with the dough hook, whisk the warm water, barley malt syrup, and yeast. Cover and let sit for 5 to 10 minutes or until foamy and frothy on the surface. (If you don't have a stand mixer, use a large bowl and mix the dough with a wooden spoon or spatula in the next step.)

2. Add the flour and salt and beat on medium speed until the dough comes together and pulls away from the sides of the bowl, about 2 minutes. If it seems too sticky and clings to the sides of the bowl instead of forming a rough mass around the dough hook or spoon, add more flour, 1 tablespoon at a time, and continue to mix until the dough pulls away from the sides of the bowl. The dough should be stiff and somewhat dry. If it is crumbly and breaks off in pieces, add more water, 1 teaspoon at a time, mixing well after each addition.

3. When the dough has reached the proper consistency, beat on low speed for 6 to 7 minutes more or until it is smooth, supple, and elastic. (Or knead by hand on a lightly floured surface for 6 to 7 minutes.) To see if the dough is ready, use the poke test or the windowpane test (see page 241). If it's not ready, keep kneading.

4. Lightly grease a large bowl with nonstick spray. Place the dough in the bowl, turning it to coat. Cover the bowl with a tea towel or plastic wrap and let the dough rise at room temperature for 1½ to 2 hours or until doubled in size.

5. Line two large baking sheets with parchment paper or silicone baking mats.

6. When the dough is risen, punch it down to release the air. On a lightly floured surface, divide the dough into 8 equal portions, about 4 ounces (113g) each. Shape each piece of dough into a ball. Press your index finger through the center of each ball (1) to make a hole 1½ to 2 inches in diameter. Arrange the shaped bagels on the prepared baking sheets. Cover the shaped bagels loosely with a tea towel or plastic wrap and let them rest for 5 to 10 minutes.

7. Preheat the oven to 425°F (218°C).

recipe continues >

Bagel Toppings

• **Everything Bagel Seasoning:** Use a mix of 2 tablespoons poppy seeds, 2 tablespoons sesame seeds, 1 tablespoon dried minced onion, 1 tablespoon dried garlic flakes, and 1 tablespoon coarse salt.

• **Sesame Seed Topping:** Use ⅓ cup (40g) sesame seeds.

• **Poppy Seed Topping:** Use ⅓ cup (45g) poppy seeds.

8. Boil the bagels: In a large pot, whisk the water and barley malt syrup and bring to a boil over high heat. Reduce to medium-high heat. Drop 2 to 3 bagels into the boiling water and boil for 1 minute. Use a spatula to flip each bagel and boil for 1 minute more. Using a slotted metal spatula, lift the bagels out of the water, letting excess water drain off (2). Place the bagels back on the prepared baking sheets. Repeat with the remaining bagels.

9. Top the bagels: If you're adding toppings, place each topping in a shallow bowl or on a plate. Brush the egg wash on top and around the sides of each bagel. Dip the tops of the bagels into the toppings immediately after applying the egg wash. Return the bagels to the baking sheets, leaving at least 2 inches between them (3).

10. Bake for 20 to 25 minutes, rotating the pans halfway through, until the bagels are dark golden brown. Allow the bagels to cool on the baking sheets for 20 minutes before transferring to a cooling rack to cool completely. Store covered tightly at room temperature for up to 4 days or in the refrigerator for up to 1 week.

Maple Brown Sugar Oatmeal Brûlée

SERVES 6 TO 8

Oatmeal may seem like a relatively boring breakfast option, but I'm here to convince you that it deserves the shiny spotlight at your next brunch. By mixing oats with eggs, maple syrup, milk, and flavorings (all in one bowl!) and baking it, you'll be rewarded with an easy, satisfying breakfast option that provides all the cozy feels. And while we're at it, let's take it to the next level with a brûléed brown sugar topping. This is actually very easy and gives the soft, chewy baked oatmeal a crisp, caramelized top. You'll use your oven's broil setting, but if you have a kitchen torch, use that instead. Serve warm, either plain or topped with yogurt and/or fresh berries.

SKILL LEVEL: **Beginner**
PREP: **15 minutes**
BAKE: **35 minutes for pan, 25 minutes for ramekins**
TOTAL: **55 minutes**

Nonstick spray or butter, for the pan

2 cups milk, at room temperature **(480g/ml)**

⅔ cup brown sugar, divided **(133g)**

2 large eggs, at room temperature

¼ cup pure maple syrup **(85g)**

4 tablespoons unsalted butter, melted and slightly cooled **(56g)**

1 teaspoon vanilla extract

½ teaspoon maple extract

2¾ cups rolled oats **(234g)**

1 teaspoon baking powder

1 teaspoon ground cinnamon

¼ teaspoon salt

1. Preheat the oven to 350°F (177°C). Grease a 9-inch square baking pan or six 8-ounce (240ml) ramekins with nonstick spray. If using ramekins, place them on a baking sheet.

2. In a large bowl, whisk the milk, ⅓ cup (67g) of the brown sugar, the eggs, maple syrup, melted butter, vanilla, and maple extract. Whisk in the oats, baking powder, cinnamon, and salt. The mixture should be very liquid-y.

3. Pour the mixture into the prepared baking pan or ramekins. Use a spoon to ensure the mixture is evenly distributed, as most of the oats sink to the bottom of the bowl.

4. Bake until the center appears almost set, 35 minutes for the baking pan or 25 minutes for the ramekins.

5. Remove from the oven and sprinkle the remaining ⅓ cup (67g) brown sugar evenly over the top.

6. Adjust the oven to high broil and return the baked oatmeal to the oven. Watching closely so it doesn't burn, broil for 1 to 1½ minutes or until the sugar begins bubbling all over the surface. A kitchen torch also can be used to caramelize the sugar.

7. Cool for 5 minutes before serving. For the baking pan version, you can use a knife to slice or a serving spoon to dish out servings. For the ramekins, serve with spoons. Store covered tightly in the refrigerator for up to 4 days.

Lemon Blueberry Scones

MAKES 8 LARGE SCONES

SKILL LEVEL: **Beginner**

PREP: **30 minutes**

BAKE: **22 minutes**

TOTAL: **1 hour**

Brimming with juicy blueberries and a dose of lemon zing, these buttery scones are tender and soft inside with crisp, crumbly edges. It's important to keep the ingredients cold so the scones turn out wonderfully flaky and hold a neat, well-defined shape after baking. To finish them off, I have an easy two-ingredient lemon glaze that's also tasty on the lemon poppy seed Ultimate Muffins (page 227).

2 cups all-purpose flour, plus more as needed **(250g)**

6 tablespoons granulated sugar **(75g)**

1 tablespoon lemon zest

2½ teaspoons baking powder

½ teaspoon salt

8 tablespoons unsalted butter, frozen **(113g)**

½ cup + 1 tablespoon heavy cream, cold and divided **(135g/ml)**

1 large egg

1½ teaspoons vanilla extract

1 cup fresh blueberries (do not use frozen) **(140g)**

1 tablespoon water

2 tablespoons coarse sugar, for topping (optional)

Icing

1 cup powdered sugar **(120g)**

3 tablespoons fresh lemon juice

TIPS: When I make scones, I like to freeze the stick of butter and then use a box grater to shred it into the dry ingredients. If you don't have a box grater, you can simply cut cold butter into small cubes and freeze the cubes for 15 minutes before starting. Another quick tip that helps the scones maintain their shape is to refrigerate the shaped dough as the oven preheats.

1. In a large bowl, whisk the flour, sugar, lemon zest, baking powder, and salt. Using the large holes of a box grater, shred the frozen butter. Add the butter to the flour mixture (1) and use a pastry blender, two forks, or your fingers to blend until the mixture comes together in pea-sized crumbs (2). Place the bowl in the freezer for 5 minutes before continuing.

2. In a small bowl, whisk ½ cup (120g/ml) of the cream, the egg, and vanilla. Remove the flour mixture from the freezer. Drizzle the cream mixture over the flour mixture and add the blueberries. Gently mix with a spatula or wooden spoon until everything appears moistened and the ingredients are just combined (3).

3. Pour the crumbly mixture onto a lightly floured surface and, with lightly floured hands, work the dough into a ball as best you can. The dough should be sticky and shaggy. If it's too sticky, sprinkle a little more flour on top. Press the dough into an 8-inch disc, about 1 inch thick. Use a sharp knife or a bench scraper to cut the disc into 8 wedges (4).

4. In a small bowl, mix the remaining 1 tablespoon cream with the water. Using a pastry brush, brush the cream mixture over the scones. Sprinkle the tops evenly with coarse sugar (if using, 5). Place the scones on a plate or a parchment paper–lined baking sheet, cover lightly, and refrigerate for at least 15 minutes or up to 24 hours.

5. Preheat the oven to 400°F (204°C). Line a large baking sheet with parchment paper or a silicone baking mat. Arrange the chilled scones 2 to 3 inches apart on the prepared baking sheet.

6. Bake for 22 to 25 minutes or until lightly browned on top and golden around the edges. Cool the scones on the baking sheet for 5 minutes before icing.

7. Make the icing: In a small bowl or liquid measuring cup, whisk the powdered sugar and lemon juice until combined. Drizzle the icing over the scones. Store covered tightly at room temperature for up to 2 days or in the refrigerator for up to 5 days.

Variations

Three of the most popular scone recipes on my website include the lemon blueberry (pictured) and these variations:

Cranberry Orange: Replace the lemon zest with orange zest and the blueberries with fresh cranberries. In the glaze, replace the lemon juice with orange juice.

Chocolate Chip: Skip the lemon zest. Add 1 teaspoon ground cinnamon to the flour mixture. Replace the granulated sugar with brown sugar. Replace the blueberries with 1¼ cups (225g) mini chocolate chips. Skip the icing and dust the baked scones lightly with powdered sugar.

Tips for Success

POPOVERS

Even though they look complex, popovers are one of the easiest baked goods. If you're new to popovers, I have some tips that will help:

1. Use a blender. It breaks up the flour and helps create a smooth, frothy batter.

2. Preheat your pan in the oven so it's extra hot when you pour in the batter. This helps ensure a nice crisp crust while keeping the centers moist.

3. Start the popovers in an extra-hot oven and then lower the temperature. An initial burst of very hot air helps form the shape.

4. To get the tallest popover tops possible, do not open the oven door while the popovers bake. Popovers do not like to be interrupted!

Gruyère & Thyme Popovers

MAKES 6 LARGE OR 10 SMALL POPOVERS

If you've never had them, popovers are light, airy rolls similar to English Yorkshire pudding. I love serving them at brunch or breakfast, and they're equally welcome at the dinner table. The impressive rise comes from the eggs and careful preparation—no yeast or chemical leavening is required. There are dedicated popover pans that usually have 6 cups to yield six large popovers. However, a standard muffin pan works just as well to make ten smaller popovers. I love adding flavor, and my overall favorite is this Gruyère and thyme version. Feel free to switch up the cheese and herbs or leave them plain. If desired, for some sweetness in the plain version, add 2 tablespoons of sugar with the flour.

SKILL LEVEL: **Beginner**

PREP: **25 minutes**

BAKE: **20 minutes for small and 30 minutes for large popovers**

TOTAL: **50 to 60 minutes**

1¼ cups lukewarm whole milk (about 90°F/32°C) **(300g/ml)**

1¼ cups all-purpose flour **(156g)**

3 large eggs, at room temperature

1 teaspoon fresh thyme leaves

½ teaspoon salt

3 tablespoons unsalted butter, melted and divided **(43g)**

½ cup (2 ounces) freshly shredded Gruyère cheese **(57g)**

1. Adjust the oven rack to the lowest or second-lowest position and preheat the oven to 425°F (218°C).

2. In a blender, combine the warm milk, flour, eggs, thyme, and salt. Blend until combined, stopping to scrape down the sides as needed. Add 2 tablespoons of the melted butter and blend until frothy (1). The batter should be thin. Cover the batter and let it rest at room temperature for 15 minutes.

3. While the batter rests, place a popover pan or muffin pan in the oven and allow it to preheat for 15 minutes.

4. Carefully remove the hot pan from the oven and use a pastry brush to coat the wells with the remaining 1 tablespoon melted butter. If using a 12-cup muffin pan, leave the two middle wells empty.

5. Pour the batter evenly into the prepared wells; they should be about three-quarters full. Top each with an equal portion of the cheese and use the tip of a knife to gently swirl the cheese into the batter (2).

6. Bake for 20 minutes for the popover pan and 15 minutes for the muffin pan. Without opening the oven door, **reduce the oven temperature to 350°F (177°C)** and continue baking until the popovers are puffed, golden brown, and crisp around the edges, about 10 minutes more for the popover pan and 5 minutes more for the muffin pan.

7. Remove from the oven and immediately prick the top of each popover with the tip of a sharp knife, to allow steam to escape. Cool the popovers in the pan for about 5 minutes. They will deflate slightly. Remove the popovers from the pan and serve warm. Store covered tightly at room temperature for up to 4 days or in the refrigerator for up to 1 week.

Eggs Benedict Breakfast Casserole

SERVES 12

SKILL LEVEL: **Beginner**

PREP: **25 minutes, plus 1 to 24 hours chilling time before baking**

BAKE: **50 minutes**

TOTAL: **2 hours 25 minutes**

If you're entertaining and looking for a savory brunch option beyond quiche, this is a lavish special-occasion casserole. I've taken the scrumptious flavors of eggs Benedict—eggs typically served on English muffins and topped with rich hollandaise sauce—and combined them in a casserole. Be sure to let the English muffins get a bit stale before using. You can assemble the dish the night before and bake it in the morning, which is what I usually do!

Casserole

Nonstick spray or butter, for the pan

5 slightly stale English muffins, cut into pieces (about 5 cups) **(305g)**

1 heaping cup (6 ounces) chopped Canadian bacon **(170g)**

1 cup (4 ounces) freshly shredded white Cheddar cheese (or use pepper Jack cheese for a spicy kick!) **(113g)**

1½ cups whole milk **(360g/ml)**

9 large eggs

3 large egg whites

2 teaspoons chopped fresh parsley

2 teaspoons chopped fresh chives

1 teaspoon onion powder

½ teaspoon garlic powder

½ teaspoon ground mustard

½ teaspoon smoked paprika

½ teaspoon salt

¼ teaspoon freshly ground black pepper

Chopped fresh parsley, chives, or dill, for garnish (optional)

Hollandaise Sauce

3 large egg yolks, at room temperature

2 teaspoons fresh lemon juice, plus more to taste

½ teaspoon Dijon mustard

⅛ teaspoon smoked paprika

⅛ teaspoon salt

8 tablespoons unsalted butter, melted and slightly cooled **(113g)**

Pinch of cayenne pepper, dash of hot sauce, or freshly ground black pepper

1. Make the casserole: Grease a 9 × 13-inch baking pan with nonstick spray. Spread the English muffin pieces across the bottom, and top with the Canadian bacon and cheese.

2. In a large bowl, whisk the milk, eggs, egg whites (set aside the egg yolks for the sauce), parsley, chives, onion powder, garlic powder, ground mustard, paprika, salt, and pepper until combined. Pour the egg mixture over the English muffins. Cover the pan tightly and refrigerate for at least 1 hour or up to 1 day.

3. Let the casserole sit at room temperature for 10 to 15 minutes while you preheat the oven to 375°F (191°C).

4. Bake the casserole, uncovered, for 40 minutes. Cover loosely with aluminum foil and bake for about 10 more minutes or until the center of the casserole is set. It will puff up and then settle as it cools.

5. Make the hollandaise sauce: In a blender, combine the egg yolks, lemon juice, Dijon mustard, paprika, and salt and blend on high speed for 30 seconds or until the mixture is fully combined and pale yellow in color. Remove the lid insert from the blender top. Working quickly and with the blender running on medium speed, slowly add the melted butter in a thin stream. Blend until a creamy sauce forms. Season with cayenne pepper and add more lemon juice if desired. (Alternatively, do this by hand with a whisk, making sure to vigorously whisk the sauce.)

6. Just before serving, drizzle the warm baked casserole with hollandaise sauce, adding it either to the whole casserole or individual servings. Garnish with fresh herbs (if using). Store covered tightly in the refrigerator for up to 3 days.

TIP: I created this recipe to conveniently use exactly one dozen eggs. You'll save three of the egg yolks to whip up a velvety-smooth hollandaise sauce to drizzle over the casserole at serving time.

Baked Chocolate Cake Donuts

MAKES 16 TO 18 DONUTS

I have young children and a love for rainbow sprinkles, so you can imagine that donuts are often on the menu when we want a special treat. Donuts baked in a donut pan are my prime choice. Unlike their fried counterparts, baked donuts are quick, simple, and don't require messing with hot oil on the stove. This recipe is the best chocolate version I know. They're inherently moist, thanks to the buttermilk, and have a soft sponge-like crumb that's a little denser than, say, a chocolate cupcake. The crowning glory undoubtedly is the glossy chocolate glaze. Because there's a little butter in it, the glaze slightly sets on the donuts, just like those from a bakery. This makes them a little less messy when arranging on a serving platter, but I can't promise a completely mess-free experience!

SKILL LEVEL: **Beginner**

PREP: **30 minutes**

BAKE: **12 minutes per batch**

TOTAL: **45 minutes**

Donuts

Nonstick spray or butter, for the pan(s)

2 cups all-purpose flour **(250g)**

½ cup unsweetened natural cocoa powder **(43g)**

1 teaspoon baking powder

1 teaspoon baking soda

½ teaspoon salt

2 large eggs, at room temperature

1 cup granulated sugar **(200g)**

1 cup buttermilk, at room temperature **(240g/ml)**

2 teaspoons vanilla extract

8 tablespoons unsalted butter, melted and slightly cooled **(113g)**

Chocolate Glaze

1½ cups powdered sugar **(180g)**

¼ cup unsweetened natural or Dutch-process cocoa powder **(21g)**

3 tablespoons heavy cream

1 tablespoon unsalted butter **(14g)**

1 tablespoon light corn syrup

1 teaspoon vanilla extract

Sprinkles (optional)

1. Preheat the oven to 350°F (177°C). Grease three donut pans with nonstick spray (or bake in batches).

2. Make the donuts: In a large bowl, whisk the flour, cocoa powder, baking powder, baking soda, and salt.

3. In a medium bowl, lightly whisk the eggs. Add the sugar, buttermilk, and vanilla and whisk to combine. Pour the egg mixture into the flour mixture and mix until combined. Stir in the melted butter until incorporated. The batter should be slightly thick.

4. Transfer the donut batter to a gallon-size zip-top plastic bag and use scissors to snip off the tip of one bottom corner. Pipe the batter into the donut pan cavities, filling each about halfway (1).

5. Bake for 12 to 13 minutes or until the donuts bounce back when lightly pressed. Cool the donuts in the pan set on a cooling rack for 2 minutes, then remove them from the pan and place on the rack to cool for 15 minutes before glazing.

6. Make the chocolate glaze: In a heat-safe medium bowl, whisk the powdered sugar and cocoa powder. In a microwave-safe bowl or glass liquid measuring cup, or in a small saucepan over medium-low heat, heat the cream and butter until the butter has melted. Whisk in the corn syrup and vanilla. Slowly pour the cream mixture into the cocoa mixture, whisking constantly as you pour. Whisk until a smooth, thick glaze forms.

7. Dip the warm tops of the donuts in the glaze (2), then decorate with sprinkles (if using, 3). Enjoy immediately or wait for the glaze to set, about 2 hours. Store covered tightly in the refrigerator for up to 5 days.

TIP: Make the chocolate glaze while the donuts are cooling. If you make it too early, it will thicken up too much to dip the donuts. If the glaze does thicken, you can warm it up in the microwave at 50% power for 10 seconds and whisk to smooth it out.

French Toast Casserole: 3 Ways

SERVES 12

SKILL LEVEL: **Beginner**

PREP: **25 minutes, plus 3 to 24 hours chilling time before baking**

BAKE: **45 minutes**

TOTAL: **4 hours 20 minutes**

When it comes to serving a special breakfast, French toast casserole is always a hit. I offer three flavor options here including classic, blueberry, and holiday-ready gingerbread spice. No matter which you choose, use sturdy bread such as a French loaf, challah, or even Brioche-Style Sandwich Rolls (page 258). Flimsy, thin sandwich bread won't adequately absorb the liquid, resulting in a soggy casserole. You can assemble this the night before and refrigerate, then bake it in the morning.

Casserole

Nonstick spray or butter, for the pan

12-ounce loaf of sturdy day-old bread, such as French bread or challah, cut in 1-inch cubes **(340g)**

2 cups whole milk **(480g/ml)**

8 large eggs

½ cup heavy cream **(120g/ml)**

½ cup brown sugar **(100g)**

2 teaspoons vanilla extract

2 teaspoons ground cinnamon

Pinch of salt

Crumb Topping

⅓ cup brown sugar **(67g)**

⅓ cup all-purpose flour **(42g)**

½ teaspoon ground cinnamon

6 tablespoons unsalted butter, cold and cubed **(85g)**

Optional Garnishes

Powdered sugar

Pure maple syrup

Sugared Cranberries (recipe follows)

TIP: The bread should be slightly stale to absorb a good portion of the liquid. If you don't have time to let it sit out, spread fresh bread cubes on a baking sheet and bake in a 300°F (149°C) oven for 10 minutes.

1. Make the casserole: Grease a 9 × 13-inch baking pan or a 3½- to 4-quart baking dish with nonstick spray. Spread the cubed bread in the pan.

2. In a large bowl, whisk the milk, eggs, cream, brown sugar, vanilla, cinnamon, and salt until combined. Pour over the bread. Cover the pan tightly and refrigerate for at least 3 hours or up to 1 day. This gives the bread a chance to soak up the custard, a key step in the recipe.

3. Make the crumb topping: In a medium bowl, mix the brown sugar, flour, and cinnamon. Add the cold butter. Using a pastry blender or two forks, cut the butter into the brown sugar mixture until pea-sized crumbles form. Cover and refrigerate the topping for at least 15 minutes or up to 1 day. Chilling it helps ensure that it won't sink into the casserole.

4. Remove the casserole from the refrigerator and let it sit at room temperature for 10 to 15 minutes while you preheat the oven to 350°F (177°C).

5. Sprinkle the crumb topping evenly over the casserole. Bake uncovered for 20 minutes. Cover loosely with aluminum foil and continue to bake until the center appears set, 25 to 35 minutes more.

6. Cool the casserole for 5 minutes before serving. If desired, sift powdered sugar lightly over the top and serve warm with maple syrup and sugared cranberries. Store covered tightly in the refrigerator for up to 3 days.

recipe continues >

Variations

Blueberry French Toast Casserole: After placing the bread in the baking dish, sprinkle with 1 cup (140g) fresh or frozen blueberries. When whisking the egg mixture, add 1 teaspoon lemon zest.

Gingerbread French Toast Casserole: When whisking the egg mixture, add 3 tablespoons unsulfured molasses, 1 teaspoon ground ginger, ½ teaspoon ground allspice, ¼ teaspoon ground nutmeg, ¼ teaspoon ground cloves, and ¼ teaspoon orange zest. Before serving, garnish with sugared cranberries.

Sugared Cranberries

MAKES ½ CUP

½ cup fresh cranberries (do not use frozen) **(60g)**

1 cup granulated sugar, divided **(200g)**

½ cup water **(120g/ml)**

1. Place the cranberries in a medium heat-safe bowl.

2. In a medium saucepan, bring ½ cup (100g) of the sugar and the water to a boil over medium heat, whisking until the sugar has dissolved. Remove from heat and let cool for 5 minutes.

3. Pour the sugar syrup over the cranberries, stir, and let them sit at room temperature or in the refrigerator for at least 6 hours and up to 24 hours. The syrup should thickly coat the cranberries.

4. Line a baking sheet with parchment paper or a silicone mat. Drain off the syrup from the cranberries. Add the remaining ½ cup (100g) sugar to the berries and toss gently until they are evenly coated. Pour them onto the prepared baking sheet, separating any that are stuck together. Let them dry for at least 2 hours at room temperature or 1 hour in the refrigerator. They can be used immediately or covered tightly and stored in the refrigerator for up to 3 days.

Quick Breads

& Muffins

Apple Cider Spice Bread

MAKES 1 LOAF

I'll go ahead and call this quick bread a big ol' hug from an apple orchard. There's no better way to describe the sweet, warming flavors of cinnamon, nutmeg, allspice, and cloves. The recipe starts by reducing apple cider to a flavorful, concentrated liquid that's used in both the bread and the glaze. Orange zest adds a bright note, but don't go overboard; more than ½ teaspoon will overpower the cider and spices. Shredded apple in the bread brings even more flavor to each bite and keeps the loaf moist for days. A slice makes a wonderful dessert, afternoon snack, or a special treat on a fall morning . . . or anytime you feel like a hug!

SKILL LEVEL: **Beginner**
PREP: **30 minutes**
BAKE: **55 minutes**
TOTAL: **2 hours 25 minutes, including some cooling**

Bread

1 cup fresh apple cider **(240g/ml)**

Nonstick spray or butter, for the pan

1¾ cups all-purpose flour **(219g)**

2 teaspoons ground cinnamon

1 teaspoon baking soda

¾ teaspoon salt

¼ teaspoon ground allspice

¼ teaspoon ground cloves

¼ teaspoon ground nutmeg

½ cup vegetable oil or melted coconut oil **(113g/120ml)**

½ cup brown sugar **(100g)**

½ cup granulated sugar **(100g)**

2 large eggs, at room temperature

¼ cup unsweetened applesauce **(60g)**

½ teaspoon orange zest

1½ cups peeled and shredded apple (from 1 large apple) **(210g)**

Apple Cider Glaze

3 tablespoons reduced apple cider (from above)

2 tablespoons unsalted butter **(28g)**

1 cup powdered sugar, sifted **(120g)**

⅛ teaspoon ground cinnamon

Pinch of salt

1. Reduce the apple cider: In a small saucepan, bring the apple cider to a simmer over medium heat. Simmer until it has reduced to ½ cup (120g/ml), about 20 minutes. Set aside to cool. It will be used for the bread and the glaze.

2. Preheat the oven to 350°F (177°C). Grease a 9 × 5-inch or 8 × 4-inch loaf pan with nonstick spray.

3. Make the bread: In a large bowl, whisk the flour, cinnamon, baking soda, salt, allspice, cloves, and nutmeg.

4. In a medium bowl, whisk the oil, brown sugar, granulated sugar, eggs, applesauce, orange zest, and ¼ cup (60g/ml) of the reduced apple cider until well combined. Pour the oil mixture into the flour mixture and whisk until combined. Fold in the shredded apple. The batter should be thin.

5. Pour the batter into the prepared pan and smooth the top. Bake until a toothpick inserted in the center comes out clean, 55 to 65 minutes, tenting with aluminum foil after about 30 minutes to prevent the top from becoming too brown. Cool the bread in the pan set on a cooling rack for 1 hour. Remove the bread from the pan and return it to the rack to cool completely before glazing.

6. Make the apple cider glaze: In a small saucepan over medium heat, combine the reduced apple cider and butter. Whisking constantly, bring to a boil. Once boiling, stop whisking and let boil for 1 minute. Remove from heat and whisk in the powdered sugar, cinnamon, and salt. Let the glaze cool for 10 to 15 minutes to slightly thicken.

7. Pour the warm glaze over the bread. It will thicken and set as it cools. Slice and serve. Store covered tightly at room temperature for up to 2 days or in the refrigerator for up to 1 week.

Cinnamon Swirl Quick Bread

MAKES 1 LOAF

SKILL LEVEL: **Beginner**
PREP: **20 minutes**
BAKE: **50 minutes**
TOTAL: **2 hours 10 minutes, including some cooling**

Don't blink or you'll miss it! As a reader of my website put it: "This is a quick bread in every way." It's "quick to put together" and "quick to disappear from your kitchen counter." With its thick ribbon of cinnamon-sugar cutting through a soft, moist crumb, and a crackly crust underneath all that glorious vanilla icing, a slice is nearly impossible to resist. As if you need more convincing to preheat the oven, the ingredient list is super basic and no mixer is required. Cue the excitement when you first cut into it . . . what will the swirl inside look like? You're going to have A LOT of fun with this one.

Cinnamon Swirl

½ cup granulated sugar **(100g)**

1 tablespoon ground cinnamon

Bread

Nonstick spray or butter, for the pan

2 cups all-purpose flour **(250g)**

1 teaspoon baking soda

½ teaspoon salt

¾ cup granulated sugar **(150g)**

⅔ cup milk, at room temperature **(160g/ml)**

⅓ cup vegetable oil **(75g/80ml)**

⅓ cup full-fat sour cream or plain 2% Greek yogurt, at room temperature **(80g)**

1 large egg, at room temperature

1½ teaspoons vanilla extract

Vanilla Icing

1 cup powdered sugar, sifted **(120g)**

2 to 3 tablespoons milk, half-and-half, or heavy cream

½ teaspoon vanilla extract

Pinch of salt (optional)

1. Make the cinnamon swirl: In a small bowl, mix the sugar and cinnamon. Set aside.

2. Preheat the oven to 350°F (177°C). Grease a 9 × 5-inch or 8 × 4-inch loaf pan with nonstick spray.

3. Make the bread: In a large bowl, whisk the flour, baking soda, and salt. In a medium bowl, whisk the sugar, milk, oil, sour cream, egg, and vanilla. Pour this mixture into the flour mixture and whisk just until combined. Avoid overmixing. The batter should be thick and creamy.

4. Pour about half of the batter into the prepared pan, spreading it evenly over the bottom. Reserving 2 tablespoons to be used for the top, sprinkle the cinnamon swirl mixture evenly over the batter. Add the remaining batter and spread it as evenly as you can. Don't worry if it sticks a bit to the cinnamon swirl; just do your best to have an even layer. Sprinkle the remaining 2 tablespoons of cinnamon swirl mixture on top. Use a knife to gently swirl the layers together, taking care not to overmix (1).

5. Bake until a toothpick inserted in the center comes out clean, 50 to 65 minutes, tenting with aluminum foil after about 30 minutes to prevent the top from becoming too brown. Cool the bread in the pan set on a cooling rack for 1 hour. Remove the bread from the pan and return it to the rack to cool completely before icing.

6. Make the vanilla icing: In a small bowl, whisk the powdered sugar, 2 tablespoons of the milk, and the vanilla. For thinner icing, whisk in another tablespoon of milk. Taste; add a pinch of salt, if desired.

7. Drizzle the icing over the cooled bread. Slice and serve. Store covered tightly at room temperature for up to 3 days or in the refrigerator for up to 1 week.

Easy Beer Bread

MAKES 1 LOAF

Requiring very little effort after cracking open the beer, this one-bowl batter comes together with just six ingredients. Honey adds lovely flavor without making the bread particularly sweet. I use melted butter both *in* and *on* the batter. The butter poured on top before baking transforms the crust into a crumbly-crisp, biscuit-like texture. Beer bread makes an excellent snack and an even better accompaniment to hearty soups and stews.

SKILL LEVEL: **Beginner**

PREP: **10 minutes**

BAKE: **45 minutes**

TOTAL: **1 hour 5 minutes, including some cooling**

Nonstick spray or butter, for the pan

3 cups all-purpose flour **(375g)**

1 tablespoon baking powder

1 teaspoon salt

1 (12-ounce) bottle of beer **(355ml)**

¼ cup honey **(85g)**

8 tablespoons butter, melted and slightly cooled, divided **(113g)**

Flaky sea salt, for sprinkling

TIP: The type of beer used makes a big difference in flavor. Unless you don't mind a bitter edge to the bread, avoid IPA styles. Instead, choose a beer with malty sweetness. Classic lager works well, as do ale and stout. My team and I especially love it with seasonal pumpkin ale. Although the alcohol bakes off, the bread can be made with nonalcoholic beer if preferred. You will lose some flavor, though, and the finished texture will be more cake-like.

1. Preheat the oven to 375°F (191°C). Grease a 9 × 5-inch loaf pan with non-stick spray.

2. In a large bowl, whisk the flour, baking powder, and salt. Add the beer, honey, and 4 tablespoons of the melted butter and mix with a spatula or wooden spoon until well combined. The batter should be thick.

3. Transfer the batter to the prepared pan and smooth the top. Pour the remaining 4 tablespoons melted butter over the top and sprinkle with flaky sea salt.

4. Bake until the bread is lightly browned and a toothpick inserted in the center comes out clean, 45 to 50 minutes. Cool the bread in the pan set on a cooling rack for 10 minutes. Remove the bread from the pan, slice, and serve warm. Store wrapped tightly at room temperature for up to 3 days or in the refrigerator for up to 1 week.

Date & Walnut Soda Bread

MAKES 1 LOAF

SKILL LEVEL: **Beginner**

PREP: **15 minutes**

BAKE: **50 minutes**

TOTAL: **1 hour 15 minutes, including some cooling**

This recipe uses the core ingredients of Irish soda bread, including buttermilk, flour, baking soda, and salt. I add an egg, sugar, butter, dates, and walnuts, the mix of ingredients leading to a rich, subtly sweet quick bread with a dense interior and rustic, craggy crust. Much like the simplicity of Easy Beer Bread (page 217), the dough comes together in a single bowl with minimal shaping. The best part of all? You can indulge in warm, fresh bread in just over an hour. Be sure to use Medjool dates, which are extra soft with a sweet, caramel-like flavor.

1⅓ cups buttermilk, cold **(320g/ml)**

1 large egg, cold

1 packed cup (6 ounces) chopped Medjool dates **(170g)**

⅔ cup chopped walnuts **(80g)**

3⅔ cups all-purpose flour, plus more as needed **(458g)**

¼ cup granulated sugar **(50g)**

1 teaspoon baking soda

1 teaspoon salt

4 tablespoons butter, cold and cubed **(56g)**

TIP: Instead of a baking sheet, you can use a 6-quart (or similar-size) Dutch oven lined with parchment paper. The baking instructions are the same, and when it's time to cover the bread with foil to prevent it from browning too much, you can just use the Dutch oven's lid.

1. Preheat the oven to 400°F (204°C). Line a large baking sheet with parchment paper or a silicone baking mat.

2. In a liquid measuring cup or small bowl, whisk the buttermilk and egg. Refrigerate until needed.

3. In a medium bowl, combine the dates and walnuts, stirring to break up any dates that clump together. The fine bits of chopped nuts will coat the dates so they don't stick together as much.

4. In a large bowl, whisk the flour, sugar, baking soda, and salt. Add the cubed butter and use a pastry blender, two forks, or your fingers to mix and blend until the butter breaks down into pea-sized crumbs. The mixture should be floury and dry. Stir in the dates and walnuts and then pour in the buttermilk mixture. Gently mix with a spatula or wooden spoon until the dough is too stiff to stir.

5. Pour the dough onto a lightly floured surface and, with lightly floured hands, work it into a ball as best you can (1). Knead the dough for about 30 seconds or until all the flour is moistened. If the dough is too sticky, add a little more flour. Shape into a smooth ball about 3 inches high and 6 inches in diameter. Transfer the shaped dough to the prepared baking sheet. Using a very sharp knife or bread lame, score the dough with an X about ½ inch deep (2).

6. Bake until the bread is golden brown and the center is cooked through and reads 195°F (90°C) on an instant-read thermometer, 50 to 55 minutes. Loosely tent the bread with aluminum foil if the top is browning too quickly.

7. Cool the bread on the baking sheet for 10 minutes, then transfer to a cooling rack. Slice and serve warm or at room temperature. Store wrapped tightly at room temperature for up to 5 days or in the refrigerator for up to 1 week.

The Banana Bread Loved Around the World

MAKES 1 LOAF

Banana bread is a staple in American home baking, and many families have their own special recipe. This is mine, and I will be thrilled if it becomes yours, too! As the most popular recipe on my website, millions of bakers have tried and loved it. The cinnamon-kissed bread has a soft, pleasantly dense texture, and I credit the yogurt for that. Either white or brown sugar works here, so use what's on hand. You need about three or four ripe bananas—the browner and spottier, the better.

SKILL LEVEL: **Beginner**
PREP: **15 minutes**
BAKE: **60 minutes**
TOTAL: **2 hours 15 minutes, including some cooling**

Nonstick spray or butter, for the pan

2 cups all-purpose flour **(250g)**

1 teaspoon baking soda

½ teaspoon ground cinnamon

¼ teaspoon salt

8 tablespoons unsalted butter, at room temperature **(113g)**

¾ cup granulated sugar or brown sugar **(150g)**

2 large eggs, at room temperature

1½ cups mashed bananas (about 3 to 4 large ripe bananas) **(345g)**

⅓ cup plain 2% Greek yogurt or full-fat sour cream, at room temperature **(80g)**

1 teaspoon vanilla extract

¾ cup chopped pecans or walnuts **(90g)**, or 1 cup semi-sweet chocolate chips **(180g)** (optional)

1. Preheat the oven to 350°F (177°C). Grease a 9 × 5-inch loaf pan with non-stick spray.

2. In a medium bowl, whisk the flour, baking soda, cinnamon, and salt.

3. In a large bowl using a handheld or stand mixer fitted with the paddle, beat the butter and sugar on medium-high speed until the mixture is light and creamy, about 3 minutes. With the mixer on medium speed, add the eggs one at a time, beating well after each addition. Scrape down the sides of the bowl as needed. Beat in the mashed bananas, yogurt, and vanilla. It's okay if the mixture looks separated; it will come together when the flour is added.

4. Add the flour mixture to the banana mixture and beat on low speed just until combined. Do not overmix. Fold in the nuts or chocolate chips (if using). The batter should be thick.

5. Pour the batter into the prepared pan and smooth the top. Bake until a toothpick inserted in the center comes out clean with only a few moist crumbs, 60 to 65 minutes, tenting with aluminum foil after about 30 minutes to prevent the top from becoming too brown. Cool the bread in the pan set on a cooling rack for 1 hour. Remove the bread from the pan and return it to the rack to cool completely before slicing and serving. Store wrapped tightly at room temperature for up to 3 days or in the refrigerator for up to 1 week.

Tips for Success

FREEZING BANANAS FOR BAKING
If you have spotty-brown, extra-ripe bananas that you aren't ready to use, they can be frozen and used for baking recipes at a later time.

- You can freeze bananas with or without the peel. The peel will darken or turn black, but the fruit inside is fine.
- Bananas keep in a freezer-friendly container for up to 3 months. Thaw at room temperature for 2 hours or in the refrigerator overnight.
- You can also thaw bananas in the microwave. Timing varies, but thawing 4 bananas takes about 3 minutes at 50% power.
- Bananas release liquid as they thaw. For best success in baking recipes, pour most of this liquid out because it could add too much liquid to the batter.
- Gently mash thawed, drained bananas with a fork to use in the recipe. For best results, do not mash to a thin liquid; you still want some chunks.

Banana Nutella Muffins

MAKES 12 MUFFINS

SKILL LEVEL: **Beginner**

PREP: **20 minutes**

BAKE: **24 minutes**

TOTAL: **55 minutes,** including some cooling

Every bit as delicious and moist as The Banana Bread Loved Around the World (page 221), these muffins are quicker to bake and easily portable. Plus, there's a surprise Nutella filling inside and a crunchy-sweet hazelnut streusel on top. Quick, easy, Nutella, AND streusel? You better start preheating your oven now.

Hazelnut Streusel Topping

¼ cup finely chopped hazelnuts **(35g)**

¼ cup brown sugar **(50g)**

½ teaspoon ground cinnamon

Muffins

1⅔ cups all-purpose flour **(208g)**

1 teaspoon baking powder

1 teaspoon baking soda

1 teaspoon ground cinnamon

½ teaspoon salt

1½ cups mashed bananas (3 to 4 large ripe bananas) **(345g)**

¾ cup granulated sugar **(150g)**

6 tablespoons unsalted butter, melted **(85g)**

1 large egg, at room temperature

1 teaspoon vanilla extract

¼ cup buttermilk, at room temperature **(60g/ml)**

½ cup Nutella **(150g)**

1. Preheat the oven to 425°F (218°C). Line a 12-count muffin pan with cupcake liners.

2. **Make the hazelnut streusel topping:** In a small bowl, mix the hazelnuts, brown sugar, and cinnamon. Set aside.

3. **Make the muffins:** In a medium bowl, whisk the flour, baking powder, baking soda, cinnamon, and salt.

4. In a large bowl using a handheld or stand mixer fitted with the paddle, beat the mashed bananas, sugar, melted butter, egg, and vanilla until well combined. Scrape down the sides of the bowl as needed. Add the flour mixture, then the buttermilk. Whisk or beat until combined. The batter should be thick.

5. Spoon the muffin batter into the prepared muffin cups, filling them about halfway. Drop a heaping teaspoonful of Nutella in the center of each, then top with the remaining batter. Sprinkle the streusel evenly over each muffin.

6. Bake for 5 minutes at 425°F. **Reduce the oven temperature to 350°F (177°C).** Continue to bake until a toothpick inserted in the center comes out clean, 19 to 20 minutes more. Cool the muffins in the pan set on a cooling rack for 10 minutes, then transfer the muffins from the pan to the rack to cool completely. Store covered tightly at room temperature for up to 5 days or in the refrigerator for up to 1 week.

Ultimate Muffins: 5 Ways

LEFT TO RIGHT

Apple Cinnamon Muffins

Lemon Poppy Seed Muffins

Blueberry Muffins

Birthday Cake Muffins

Chocolate Chip Muffins

Recipe follows

Ultimate Muffins: 5 Ways

MAKES 12 MUFFINS

SKILL LEVEL: **Beginner**

PREP: **20 minutes**

BAKE: **20 minutes**

TOTAL: **50 minutes, including some cooling**

How can I write a muffins chapter without including this website-favorite recipe? It starts with a delightfully soft, buttery base muffin that is endlessly customizable. I detail five flavor variations here to give you the idea, and then you can run with it. Create your own muffin masterpiece, swapping in different berries, other fresh citrus zest such as orange or lime, different baking chips such as peanut butter or butterscotch morsels, and so on. Mix in your desired add-ins, then top with either crunchy coarse sugar or the crumb topping below. Have fun mixing and matching!

Optional Crumb Topping

⅓ cup brown sugar **(67g)**

1 tablespoon granulated sugar

½ teaspoon ground cinnamon

4 tablespoons unsalted butter, melted **(56g)**

⅔ cup all-purpose flour **(83g)**

Muffins

1¾ cups all-purpose flour **(219g)**

1 teaspoon baking powder

1 teaspoon baking soda

½ teaspoon salt

8 tablespoons unsalted butter, at room temperature **(113g)**

½ cup granulated sugar **(100g)**

¼ cup brown sugar **(50g)**

½ cup full-fat sour cream or plain 2% Greek yogurt, at room temperature **(120g)**

2 large eggs, at room temperature

1½ teaspoons vanilla extract

¼ cup milk, at room temperature **(60g/ml)**

Add-ins (see Flavor Variations, page 227)

2 tablespoons coarse sugar, for sprinkling (if not using the crumb topping)

1. Preheat the oven to 425°F (218°C). Line a 12-count muffin pan with cupcake liners.

2. **Make the crumb topping (if using):** In a medium bowl, mix the brown sugar, granulated sugar, and cinnamon. Stir in the melted butter. Using a fork, gently work in the flour just enough to combine. Do not overmix; the mixture should have large crumbles. If overmixed, the topping will turn into a thick paste. Set the topping aside.

3. **Make the muffins:** In a medium bowl, whisk the flour, baking powder, baking soda, and salt.

4. In a large bowl using a handheld or stand mixer fitted with the paddle, beat the butter, granulated sugar, and brown sugar on high speed until smooth and creamy, about 2 minutes. Scrape down the sides of the bowl as needed. Add the sour cream, eggs, and vanilla. Beat on medium speed for 1 minute, then increase to high speed and beat until the mixture is combined. If it looks curdled and lumpy, that's okay. Add the flour mixture and beat on low speed until almost combined. Add the milk and continue to beat on low speed until combined. Fold in the chosen add-ins (1). The batter should be very thick.

5. Spoon the batter into the prepared muffin cups, filling them to the top. Sprinkle the tops with coarse sugar *or* spoon on the crumb topping (2) and lightly press the crumbles so they stick to the batter.

6. Bake for 5 minutes at 425°F. **Reduce the oven temperature to 350°F (177°C).** Continue to bake until a toothpick inserted in the center comes out clean, 15 to 16 minutes more. Cool the muffins in the pan set on a cooling rack for 10 minutes, then transfer the muffins from the pan to the rack to cool completely. Store covered tightly at room temperature for up to 5 days or in the refrigerator for up to 1 week.

TIP: If you want even more room to play with this base recipe, try topping the muffins with vanilla icing (see Cinnamon Swirl Quick Bread, page 214) or lemon icing (see Lemon Blueberry Scones, page 198).

Flavor Variations

- **Apple Cinnamon Muffins:** 1½ cups (180g) peeled and chopped apples (½-inch chunks, about 2 medium apples), 1½ teaspoons ground cinnamon

- **Lemon Poppy Seed Muffins:** 3 tablespoons fresh lemon juice, 2 tablespoons poppy seeds, 1½ tablespoons lemon zest

- **Blueberry Muffins:** 1½ cups (210g) fresh or frozen blueberries, 1 teaspoon lemon zest

- **Birthday Cake Muffins:** 1 cup (180g) white chocolate chips, ⅓ cup (65g) rainbow sprinkles (jimmies-style strands or disc-shaped quins), ½ teaspoon almond extract

- **Chocolate Chip Muffins:** 1½ cups (270g) semi-sweet chocolate chips, ½ teaspoon ground cinnamon

Spiced Carrot Oat Muffins

MAKES 12 MUFFINS

SKILL LEVEL: **Beginner**

PREP: **20 minutes**

BAKE: **22 minutes**

TOTAL: **55 minutes,** including some cooling

Coconut oil and applesauce create a tender, moist crumb, while oats, carrots, and walnuts add substance and a satisfying texture. Don't let the nutritious ingredients fool you, though; each bite of these wholesome muffins is like a sweet and spiced bite of The Only Carrot Cake Recipe You Need (page 93), only heartier. If you want to skip the raisins, chopped dried apricots are a tasty substitute.

1½ cups whole-wheat flour **(195g)**

¾ cup rolled oats **(64g)** + 1 tablespoon for topping

1½ teaspoons baking powder

1½ teaspoons ground cinnamon

½ teaspoon salt

¼ teaspoon baking soda

¼ teaspoon ground ginger

¼ teaspoon ground nutmeg

¾ cup unsweetened applesauce **(180g)**

½ cup coconut oil, melted **(113g)**

½ cup brown sugar **(100g)**

2 large eggs, at room temperature

¼ cup pure maple syrup **(85g)**

1½ cups freshly grated peeled carrots (about 3 large carrots) **(200g)**

½ cup raisins **(75g)**

½ cup chopped walnuts **(60g)**

1. Preheat the oven to 425°F (218°C). Line a 12-count muffin pan with cupcake liners.

2. In a large bowl, whisk the flour, ¾ cup (64g) of the oats, the baking powder, cinnamon, salt, baking soda, ginger, and nutmeg.

3. In a medium bowl, whisk the applesauce, oil, brown sugar, eggs, and maple syrup. Stir in the carrots. Pour this mixture into the flour mixture and whisk just until combined. Avoid overmixing. Fold in the raisins and walnuts. The batter should be very thick.

4. Spoon the batter into the prepared muffin cups, filling them to the top. Sprinkle evenly with the remaining 1 tablespoon oats.

5. Bake for 5 minutes at 425°F. **Reduce the oven temperature to 350°F (177°C).** Continue to bake until a toothpick inserted in the center comes out clean, 17 to 19 minutes more. Cool the muffins in the pan set on a cooling rack for 10 minutes, then transfer the muffins from the pan to the rack to cool completely. Store covered tightly at room temperature for up to 5 days or in the refrigerator for up to 1 week.

Tips for Success

FOR TALL, PERFECTLY ROUNDED MUFFIN TOPS
Every muffin recipe in this book instructs you to bake muffins at 425°F (218°C) for the first 5 minutes and then reduce the temperature to 350°F (177°C) for the remaining bake time. Why? This initial burst of heat lifts the muffin straight up, creating a high muffin top with a rounded dome. Baking at a lower temperature for the rest of the time cooks the center of the muffin.

FOR MINI OR JUMBO MUFFINS
For every muffin recipe in this book, you can replace the standard 12-count muffin pan with a 24-count mini muffin pan or 6-count jumbo muffin pan.

- **For mini muffins,** bake at 350°F (177°C) for 12 to 14 minutes.
- **For jumbo muffins,** bake for 5 minutes at 425°F (218°C), then reduce the oven temperature to 350°F (177°C) and bake for an additional 22 to 25 minutes.

Chocolate Zucchini Muffins

MAKES 12 MUFFINS

Why mix chocolate and zucchini? I say . . . why not?! Zucchini is a magical ingredient in the baking world, adding moisture and bulk and virtually zero flavor. The combination of zucchini, banana, and Greek yogurt gives these double-chocolate muffins a slight nutritional boost, while chocolate chips make the kids (and, let's be honest, adults) happy. Plus, it never hurts to have a zucchini recipe on hand for when summer crops are extra bountiful. If desired, you can omit the banana and use unsweetened applesauce instead. Feel free to peel the zucchini or leave it unpeeled; and be sure to shred it on the large holes of a box grater.

SKILL LEVEL: **Beginner**
PREP: **15 minutes**
BAKE: **20 minutes**
TOTAL: **50 minutes, including some cooling**

1¼ cups all-purpose flour **(156g)**

½ cup unsweetened natural cocoa powder **(43g)**

1 teaspoon baking powder

1 teaspoon baking soda

¼ teaspoon salt

¾ cup granulated sugar **(150g)**

½ cup mashed banana (about 1 large ripe banana) **(115g)**

½ cup plain 2% Greek yogurt, at room temperature **(120g)**

2 large eggs, at room temperature

¼ cup vegetable oil or avocado oil **(56g/60ml)**

1 teaspoon vanilla extract

1½ cups shredded zucchini **(180g)**

¾ cup semi-sweet chocolate chips **(135g)**

1. Preheat the oven to 425°F (218°C). Line a 12-count muffin pan with cupcake liners.

2. In a large bowl, whisk the flour, cocoa powder, baking powder, baking soda, and salt.

3. In a medium bowl, whisk the sugar, banana, yogurt, eggs, oil, and vanilla just until combined. Pour this mixture into the flour mixture and whisk to combine. Fold in the zucchini and chocolate chips. The batter should be thick.

4. Spoon the batter into the prepared muffin cups; it may seem like too much batter for 12 muffins, but trust me, just fill those cups up to the very top!

5. Bake for 5 minutes at 425°F. **Reduce the oven temperature to 350°F (177°C).** Continue to bake until a toothpick inserted in the center comes out clean, 15 to 17 minutes more. Cool the muffins in the pan set on a cooling rack for 10 minutes, then transfer the muffins from the pan to the rack to cool completely. Store covered tightly at room temperature for up to 5 days or in the refrigerator for up to 1 week.

Jam-Swirled Donut Muffins

MAKES 12 MUFFINS

SKILL LEVEL: **Beginner**

PREP: **20 minutes**

BAKE: **20 minutes**

TOTAL: **1 hour, including some cooling**

I have a weak spot for jelly-filled donuts from the bakery. When the craving hits and I want a quick homemade alternative, I have this recipe on speed dial. They're denser than fluffy Ultimate Muffins (page 226) and will remind you of a soft cake-style donut. One thing to note is that the sweetness level really depends on how much sugar is in your jam/preserves. I like these best with raspberry jam, but feel free to use your favorite. If you want more of a classic jelly donut experience, skip the swirling.

1¾ cups all-purpose flour **(219g)**

2 teaspoons baking powder

¾ teaspoon salt

½ teaspoon ground cinnamon

¼ teaspoon ground nutmeg

8 tablespoons unsalted butter, at room temperature **(113g)**

⅔ cup granulated sugar **(133g)**

2 large eggs, at room temperature

1½ teaspoons vanilla extract

⅔ cup milk **(160g/ml)**

½ cup raspberry jam or preserves **(150g)**

¼ cup powdered sugar **(30g)**, for dusting

1. Preheat the oven to 425°F (218°C). Line a 12-count muffin pan with cupcake liners.

2. In a medium bowl, whisk the flour, baking powder, salt, cinnamon, and nutmeg.

3. In a large bowl using a handheld or stand mixer fitted with the paddle, beat the butter and sugar on medium-high speed until the mixture is light and creamy, about 3 minutes. Add the eggs and vanilla and beat until combined. Scrape down the sides of the bowl as needed. Pour the flour mixture and then the milk into the bowl and beat on low speed just until combined. The batter should be creamy and slightly thick. Avoid overmixing.

4. Spoon about 1½ tablespoons of batter into each muffin cup. Top with a heaping teaspoonful of jam, followed by a spoonful of the remaining batter. Use a table knife to lightly swirl the jam and the batter together in each muffin (1).

5. Bake for 5 minutes at 425°F. **Reduce the oven temperature to 350°F (177°C).** Continue to bake until a toothpick inserted in the center comes out clean, 15 to 17 minutes more. Cool the muffins in the pan set on a cooling rack for 20 minutes, then transfer the muffins from the pan to the rack to cool completely.

6. Just before serving, use a small sieve to dust the muffins with powdered sugar. Store covered tightly at room temperature for up to 2 days or in the refrigerator for up to 5 days.

Pumpkin Spice Latte Muffins

MAKES 12 MUFFINS

I've given my favorite pumpkin muffin recipe a coffeehouse twist, inspired by the fall season's quintessential drink. The result is completely irresistible: a soft, spiced muffin with an espresso-hinted creamy center that pairs with it seamlessly, like a crisp fall morning and your favorite sweater.

SKILL LEVEL: **Beginner**
PREP: **30 minutes**
BAKE: **22 minutes**
TOTAL: **1 hour 40 minutes, including cooling**

Muffins

- 1¾ cups all-purpose flour **(219g)**
- 2 teaspoons pumpkin pie spice, homemade (page 47) or store-bought
- 1 teaspoon baking powder
- 1 teaspoon baking soda
- 1 teaspoon ground cinnamon
- ½ teaspoon salt
- ¼ teaspoon ground ginger
- 1½ cups canned pumpkin puree **(340g)**
- ½ cup vegetable oil **(113g/120ml)**
- ½ cup brown sugar **(100g)**
- ½ cup granulated sugar **(100g)**
- 2 large eggs, at room temperature
- ¼ cup milk **(60g/ml)**
- 2½ teaspoons espresso powder
- 1 tablespoon coarse sugar, for topping

Whipped Cream Filling

- 4 ounces full-fat brick cream cheese, at room temperature **(113g)**
- ½ cup powdered sugar **(60g)**
- ½ teaspoon espresso powder
- ½ teaspoon vanilla extract
- ⅔ cup heavy cream, cold **(160g/ml)**

Pumpkin pie spice, for sprinkling

1. Preheat the oven to 425°F (218°C). Line a 12-count muffin pan with cupcake liners.

2. **Make the muffins:** In a large bowl, whisk the flour, pumpkin pie spice, baking powder, baking soda, cinnamon, salt, and ginger.

3. In a medium bowl, whisk the pumpkin, oil, brown sugar, granulated sugar, and eggs until combined. Pour this mixture into the flour mixture and whisk just until combined. The batter should be thick. Heat the milk until warm to the touch and stir in the espresso powder. Pour the espresso milk into the batter and whisk just until combined.

4. Spoon the batter into the prepared muffin cups. Sprinkle coarse sugar on top of each.

5. Bake for 5 minutes at 425°F. **Reduce the oven temperature to 350°F (177°C).** Continue to bake until a toothpick inserted in the center comes out clean, 17 to 18 minutes more. Cool the muffins in the pan set on a cooling rack for 10 minutes, then transfer the muffins from the pan to the rack to cool for at least 30 minutes more.

6. **Make the whipped cream filling:** In a large bowl using a handheld or stand mixer fitted with the whisk, beat the cream cheese until smooth. Scrape down the sides of the bowl as needed. Add the powdered sugar, espresso powder, and vanilla, and beat on low speed just until combined. Scrape down the sides of the bowl again. With the mixer on low speed, slowly pour in the cream, then increase to high speed and beat for 1 full minute, or until the filling is light and creamy.

7. Using a sharp knife, cut a circle into the center of the cooled muffins to create a little cone-shaped pocket about 1 inch deep. Spoon or pipe the cream filling inside each carved-out muffin, letting it mound slightly higher than the muffin top. Crumble some of the cone-shaped pieces you cut out of the muffins over top of the cream filling. Use a small sieve to dust the tops with pumpkin pie spice. Store covered tightly in the refrigerator for up to 3 days.

Cranberry Cornbread Muffins

MAKES 12 MUFFINS

SKILL LEVEL: **Beginner**

PREP: **15 minutes**

BAKE: **21 minutes**

TOTAL: **50 minutes,**
including some cooling

These buttery, cranberry-studded cornbread muffins are my top choice when I need a quick, easy side dish that will satisfy adults and kids alike. Sugar and honey provide subtle sweetness that balances the tart cranberries, but the muffins aren't particularly sweet. The texture is the real star of the show here—moist and tender with a pleasant grittiness from the cornmeal. If you don't have buttermilk, use my substitute (see DIY Buttermilk, page 17).

1 cup fine stone-ground yellow cornmeal **(125g)**

1 cup all-purpose flour **(125g)**

1 teaspoon baking powder

½ teaspoon baking soda

⅛ teaspoon salt

1 cup buttermilk, at room temperature **(240g/ml)**

8 tablespoons unsalted butter, melted and slightly cooled **(113g)**

2 large eggs, at room temperature

¼ cup granulated sugar **(50g)**

3 tablespoons honey

1⅓ cups fresh or unthawed frozen cranberries **(150g)**

1. Preheat the oven to 425°F (218°C). Line a 12-count muffin pan with cupcake liners.

2. In a large bowl, whisk the cornmeal, flour, baking powder, baking soda, and salt.

3. In a medium bowl, whisk the buttermilk, melted butter, eggs, sugar, and honey until smooth. Pour this mixture into the cornmeal mixture and whisk until combined. The batter should be slightly thick. Avoid overmixing. Fold in the cranberries.

4. Spoon the batter into the prepared muffin cups, filling them to the top.

5. Bake for 5 minutes at 425°F. **Reduce the oven temperature to 350°F (177°C).** Continue to bake until a toothpick inserted in the center comes out clean, 16 to 18 minutes more. Cool the muffins in the pan set on a cooling rack for 20 minutes, then transfer the muffins from the pan to the rack to cool completely. Store covered tightly at room temperature for up to 5 days or in the refrigerator for up to 1 week.

TIP: To make plain cornbread muffins, omit the cranberries and fold in ¾ cup (130g) fresh, canned/drained, or frozen corn kernels. For extra flavor with a hint of heat, serve them with the Spicy Honey Butter on page 190.

Yeast Breads

& Pizza

Yeast Bread Basics

Kneading Dough

Kneading incorporates air into the dough and also stretches out the gluten strands to build structure and strength in the baked bread. You can knead dough with your hands (see below) or with a stand mixer. If you *don't* knead, your baked bread won't rise as high and the texture will be dense. Since kneading times vary, here are two ways to check to see if your dough has been kneaded long enough:

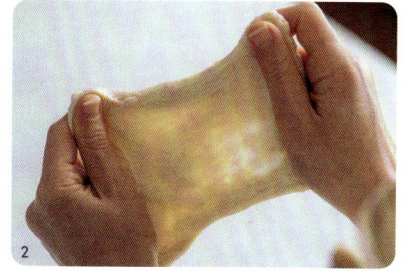

1. The poke test: Poke the dough with your finger. If the dough bounces back without sticking to your finger, it's been kneaded enough. If it doesn't bounce back, keep kneading.

2. The windowpane test: Tear off a small piece of the dough and stretch it out until you can see some light coming through it. (Just hold it up to a light or a window.) If the dough tears before that point, keep kneading.

How to Knead Dough by Hand

Place the dough on a lightly floured surface and lightly flour your hands. Using the heels of your hands, gently push the dough away from you in a rocking motion, alternating hands as you go. You want to put some energy into it, to really stretch out the dough. Keep a small bowl of flour nearby to lightly re-flour your hands and/or the surface as needed.

Baking with Yeast Cheat Sheet

☐ **Always check the expiration date of your yeast** before using it. Do not use it if the expiration date has passed.

☐ **Bring the yeast to room temperature** before using. If it has been stored in the freezer, measure the amount you need and let it sit out at room temperature for 45 to 60 minutes before using.

☐ In nearly all of my yeasted dough recipes, I instruct you to **"proof" the yeast,** regardless of whether you are using active dry or instant yeast. This step proves that the yeast is alive and active. Mix the yeast with warm liquid, such as milk or water, and a small amount of sugar. After 5 to 10 minutes, the mixture should be foamy and frothy on top. If it's not, the yeast is dead and should be tossed. This step isn't absolutely necessary, but it's still good practice, especially if your yeast is nearing its expiration date.

☐ **Yeast thrives in warm temperatures,** which is why warm liquid is typically added to dough. However, yeast will begin to die in temperatures of 135°F (57°C) or higher. A good rule of thumb: If the liquid is too hot to comfortably touch, it's too hot for the yeast.

☐ **Active dry yeast has a moderate rate of rising, and instant yeast has a faster rate of rising.** Active dry and instant yeast can be used interchangeably in recipes (1:1); just keep an eye on your dough so it doesn't rise too much.

☐ **With yeasted doughs, consider the specified amount of flour as a baseline.** Flour can absorb moisture differently depending on factors like humidity levels, kitchen temperature, composition of other ingredients in the dough, and even the brand of flour used. Generally, you may need to add more flour to produce a less sticky dough. If the dough seems dry and isn't absorbing all the flour, add more liquid than the recipe calls for (milk or water), 1 teaspoon at a time.

How/Where to Let Dough Rise

- Unless otherwise instructed, cover and place the dough in a draft-free location for as long as the recipe instructs. The warmer your kitchen, the quicker the rise.

- A 70°F (21°C) kitchen is fine, but if you're pressed for time, you can speed it up by placing the dough in the oven. Preheat to 150°F (65°C), then immediately turn the oven off. Wait a few minutes, then place the dough in the bowl inside the oven with the oven door cracked open. After about 30 minutes, close the oven door to trap the air inside with the rising dough.

- Dough can also rise in cooler temperatures, but the yeast activity slows down and the rise time extends.

- Many yeasted dough recipes require two rises. The first is right after kneading the dough, and the second rise is after shaping the dough. After the first rise and before shaping, you typically punch down the dough to release the air. Doing so redistributes yeast, sugars, and moisture back into one cohesive form. Use gentle force when punching the dough.

Pizza Dough (& Homemade Pizza)

MAKES TWO 12-INCH PIZZAS

This easy 6-ingredient pizza dough recipe is made for beginners because it's straightforward without any fancy ingredients or techniques. You don't have to be a dough novice to appreciate it, though—the ingredients and unfussy method produce a delightfully chewy base for your choice of toppings. This is a popular recipe on my website, and readers have described the crust as "consistently perfect" and "better than delivery." Here's the best part: You can use this dough to make more than just pizza! Try the homemade Stromboli (page 248) and the Calzones (page 250).

SKILL LEVEL: **Beginner**
PREP: **2 hours 15 minutes, including rises**
BAKE: **13 minutes**
TOTAL: **2 hours 30 minutes**

Dough

1⅓ cups warm water (about 110°F/43°C) **(320g/ml)**

1 tablespoon granulated sugar

2¼ teaspoons instant or active dry yeast (1 standard packet) **(7g)**

3½ to 4 cups all-purpose flour, plus more as needed **(438 to 500g)**

2 tablespoons extra-virgin olive oil, plus more for the bowl and pan

1 teaspoon salt

Yellow cornmeal, for the pan

Toppings

Extra-virgin olive oil, for brushing

2 garlic cloves, minced

1 cup store-bought pizza sauce **(250g)**

4 cups (1 pound) shredded mozzarella cheese **(454g)**

Optional Garnishes

Fresh basil leaves

Freshly grated Parmesan cheese

Dried basil and oregano

Crushed red pepper flakes

TIP: If making only one pizza, halve the topping amounts and freeze the extra dough.

1. Make the dough: In the bowl of a stand mixer fitted with the dough hook, whisk the warm water, sugar, and yeast. Cover and let sit for 5 to 10 minutes or until foamy and frothy on the surface (1; see visuals, page 247). (If you don't have a stand mixer, use a large mixing bowl and mix the dough with a wooden spoon or spatula in the next step.)

2. Add the flour, olive oil, and salt and beat on medium speed until the dough comes together and pulls away from the sides of the bowl, about 2 minutes (2). If it seems too sticky and clings to the sides of the bowl instead of forming a rough mass around the dough hook or spoon, add more flour, 1 tablespoon at a time, until the dough pulls away from the sides of the bowl but is still a little tacky. If it feels dry and crumbly, add more water, 1 teaspoon at a time, mixing well after each addition.

3. When the dough reaches the proper consistency, beat on low speed for 5 minutes more or until it is smooth, supple, and elastic. (Or knead by hand on a lightly floured surface for 5 minutes (3). Keep a small bowl of flour nearby to lightly flour your hands and/or the dough as needed, as it can be quite sticky.) To see if the dough is ready, use the poke test or the windowpane test (see page 241). If it's not ready, keep kneading.

4. Lightly grease a large bowl with olive oil. Place the dough in the bowl, turning it to coat all sides with the oil. Cover the bowl with a tea towel or plastic wrap and let the dough rise at room temperature for 60 to 90 minutes or until doubled in size (4).

5. Preheat the oven to 475°F (246°C). Lightly grease a 13 × 18-inch baking sheet or round pizza pan with olive oil. Lightly sprinkle with cornmeal, which gives the crust extra crunch and flavor.

6. Punch the dough down to release the air (5). Divide the dough in half (6). (If you are making only one pizza, refrigerate 1 of the dough halves for up to 3 days or freeze. See Freezing Pizza Dough, page 246.) On a lightly floured surface using lightly floured hands or a floured rolling pin, gently flatten each portion of dough into a disc (7). Place on the prepared pan and stretch, flatten, and shape the disc into a 12-inch circle about ½ inch thick. If the dough shrinks back as you try to shape it, cover it loosely and let it rest for 10 minutes before trying again. Once shaped, lift up and pinch the edge of the dough to create a lip around the perimeter (8).

recipe continues >

OVERNIGHT OR ALL-DAY OPTION:
Prepare the dough through covering the bowl in step 4, but let it rise for 8 to 12 hours in the refrigerator. (If it needs to be in the refrigerator longer, use cooler water in the dough, which will slow the dough's rise and allow for more time.) When ready, shape, top, and bake as directed. If the dough didn't quite double in size in the refrigerator, let it sit at room temperature for 30 to 45 minutes before punching down and shaping.

Freezing Pizza Dough

The pizza dough recipe yields enough dough for two 12-inch pizzas, a little less than 2 pounds (900g) total. After the risen dough is divided in half in step 6, you can freeze one or both portions to make pizza, stromboli, or calzones another time.

- Lightly coat all sides of the dough ball(s) with olive oil. Place in individual zip-top bag(s), squeeze out all the air, and seal tightly.

- Freeze for up to 3 months.

- Thaw the frozen dough in the refrigerator for about 8 hours or until thawed, then let it rest for 1 hour at room temperature. Prepare and bake as directed in the recipe.

7. Cover the dough loosely and let it rest as you prepare your pizza toppings.

8. Top the pizza: Using your fingers, press dimples in the surface of the dough to prevent bubbling. Lightly brush the surface with olive oil. Sprinkle half of the minced garlic on each pizza crust, followed by half of the pizza sauce, spreading it to the lip of the dough. Sprinkle 2 cups (226g) of the cheese on each (9).

9. Bake for 13 to 15 minutes or until the crust is golden brown.

10. Sprinkle the baked pizza with fresh basil, Parmesan, dried basil, dried oregano, and red pepper flakes (if using). Slice and serve immediately. Store covered tightly in the refrigerator for up to 3 days.

Stromboli

MAKES 2 STROMBOLIS; SERVES 20

SKILL LEVEL: **Intermediate**

PREP: **2 hours, including rises**

BAKE: **25 minutes**

TOTAL: **2 hours 30 minutes**

Stromboli is a pizzeria menu staple around Philadelphia, where I grew up, and this homemade version tastes just as good, and *maaaybe* even better. (Not trying to put any restaurants out of business here!) It starts with pizza dough and includes a variety of meats and cheeses, such as Genoa salami, pepperoni, ham, prosciutto, provolone, and mozzarella. I love that this recipe makes two strombolis so you can use different fillings for each or freeze half of the dough for another time. Stromboli makes a wonderful main dish but also works as an appetizer for a party (and never lasts long . . . thank goodness the recipe makes two!).

Pizza Dough (page 245)

3 tablespoons unsalted butter **(43g)**

2 garlic cloves, minced, or ½ teaspoon garlic powder

2 teaspoons chopped fresh parsley or 1 teaspoon dried parsley

1 pound thinly sliced meats such as Italian cold cuts, deli ham, or large pepperoni slices **(454g)**

¾ to 1 pound cheese (3 to 4 cups shredded or 16 to 20 thin slices deli cheese) **(340 to 454g)**

Egg wash: 1 large egg beaten with 1 tablespoon water

Optional Toppings

Chopped fresh or dried parsley

Coarse or flaky sea salt

Freshly ground black pepper

Italian seasoning

Freshly grated Parmesan cheese

Warm marinara sauce or pizza sauce, for serving

MAKE-AHEAD TIP: After shaping the strombolis, cover tightly and refrigerate for up to 12 hours before baking.

1. Make the pizza dough and let rise until doubled as directed.

2. Preheat the oven to 400°F (204°C). Line two large baking sheets with parchment paper or silicone baking mats.

3. When the dough is risen, punch it down to release the air and divide it in half. (If you are making only one stromboli, refrigerate 1 of the dough halves for up to 3 days or freeze for up to 3 months. See Freezing Pizza Dough, page 246.)

4. On a lightly floured surface using a lightly floured rolling pin, roll each portion of dough into a 10 × 16-inch rectangle. Use your hands to square off the edges. If the dough shrinks back as you try to roll it out, cover it loosely and let the dough rest for 10 minutes before trying again.

5. In a small saucepan, melt the butter. Remove from heat and stir in the minced garlic. Using a pastry brush or the back of a spoon, spread the garlic butter evenly over each rectangle. Sprinkle each with parsley (1). Set one of the rectangles with a long side facing you. Leaving an uncovered 1-inch border on the bottom and sides, and a 3-inch border at the top, arrange a layer of sliced meats onto each dough rectangle, usually 8 to 10 overlapping slices on each, depending on the size of your slices. Add a layer of cheese. Repeat with more meat and cheese until all has been used—about 8 ounces (226g) meat and 6 to 8 ounces (170 to 226g) cheese per stromboli.

6. Brush the edges with egg wash, including the entire 3-inch border at the top (2). Slowly and carefully roll each stromboli into a tight 16-inch log (3), folding in the two ends as you roll.

7. Carefully transfer each stromboli to a prepared baking sheet. Pinch or tuck in the ends to seal. Brush the top of each stromboli with egg wash and sprinkle on the parsley, sea salt, pepper, Italian seasoning, and Parmesan cheese (if using). Using a sharp knife, cut a few vents into the top (4).

8. Bake for 25 minutes or until golden brown. If you have an instant-read thermometer, the center of the stromboli should be at least 200°F (93°C). If baking both strombolis at the same time, swap the pans between racks and rotate them 180 degrees halfway through baking. Cool the stromboli on the baking sheet for 5 minutes before transferring to a cutting board and slicing. Serve with warm marinara sauce for dipping. Store wrapped tightly in the refrigerator for up to 3 days.

TIP: When assembling the stromboli, the 1-inch border is left on the bottom so you have dough to start rolling and on the sides for pinching the dough to seal the rolled shape. At the top, the 3-inch border won't end up as empty space; the fillings will be pushed forward as you roll the stromboli.

Calzones

MAKES 8 CALZONES

SKILL LEVEL: **Intermediate**

PREP: **2 hours 20 minutes,** including rises

BAKE: **25 minutes**

TOTAL: **2 hours 45 minutes**

Though both use the same dough, calzones take a bit more effort than pizza. However, when you bite into these filled pockets, your work will be graciously rewarded. Calzones are traditionally filled with various meats, vegetables, and cheeses, but what distinguishes this Naples original is that it almost always includes ricotta cheese. I make mine with sausage, onions, and peppers, and add herbs, seasonings, and chopped spinach to the ricotta. The result is a massively flavorful, creamy filling tucked inside a crisp and chewy crust . . . a pocket of perfection, if you will.

Pizza Dough (page 245)

½ pound (8 ounces) bulk Italian sausage **(226g)**

1 cup diced bell peppers **(150g)**

½ cup diced onions **(60g)**

1 cup chopped fresh spinach **(40g)**

1 cup ricotta cheese **(250g)**

½ cup (2 ounces) freshly grated Parmesan cheese **(57g)**

1 teaspoon dried basil

1 teaspoon dried oregano

¾ teaspoon garlic powder

½ teaspoon salt

¼ teaspoon freshly ground black pepper

2 cups (8 ounces) shredded mozzarella cheese **(226g)**

Topping

2 tablespoons extra-virgin olive oil or egg wash (1 large egg beaten with 1 tablespoon water)

2 tablespoons freshly grated Parmesan cheese

½ teaspoon dried oregano

Warm marinara sauce or pizza sauce, for serving

1. Make the pizza dough and let rise until doubled as directed.

2. In a medium skillet over medium heat, cook the sausage, bell peppers, and onions, stirring, until the sausage is cooked through and evenly crumbled, 10 to 12 minutes. Transfer to a paper towel–lined plate and set aside to cool.

3. Preheat the oven to 400°F (204°C). Line two baking sheets with parchment paper or silicone baking mats.

4. In a medium bowl, mix the spinach, ricotta, Parmesan, basil, oregano, garlic powder, salt, and pepper.

5. When the dough is risen, punch it down to release the air. On a lightly floured surface, divide the dough into 8 portions of about 4 ounces (113g) each. Using a floured rolling pin or lightly floured hands, roll or stretch each portion into a circle about 8 inches in diameter (1).

6. Leaving a ½-inch border around the edge, spread ¼ cup (35g) of the ricotta mixture over half of the circle. Sprinkle ¼ cup (35g) of the sausage mixture over the ricotta mixture, then top with ¼ cup (28g) of the mozzarella (2). Fold the uncovered dough over the filling to make a half-moon shape. Pinch the edges to seal, and crimp with a fork. Repeat with the remaining dough and filling.

7. **Top the calzones:** Place 4 calzones on each prepared baking sheet. Lightly brush the tops and sides with olive oil or egg wash and sprinkle with Parmesan and oregano. Using a sharp knife, cut a 1-inch vent into the top of each calzone (3).

8. Bake for 25 minutes or until golden brown. Some of the filling may seep out of the vent on top; that's okay. Cool the calzones on the baking sheets for 10 minutes before serving. Serve with warm marinara sauce on the side for dipping. Store wrapped tightly in the refrigerator for up to 3 days.

TIP: To make vegetarian calzones, skip the sausage and substitute more bell peppers, or try a mix of quartered artichoke hearts, sliced olives, and sliced mushrooms. If not using sausage, cook the vegetables with 1 tablespoon olive oil.

MAKE-AHEAD TIP: After shaping the calzones, cover with plastic wrap or aluminum foil and refrigerate them on the baking sheet for up to 12 hours. If refrigerated for several hours, the dough has time to absorb a lot of the filling, which results in a crispier crust after baking. Calzones that are baked right away, in contrast, have a chewier crust.

The Focaccia of Your Dreams

SERVES 10 TO 12

As anyone with kids knows, sometimes they're the toughest critics. My six-year-old gives this recipe "10 stars out of 5!" and for me there's no better testimonial! I dream about this bread, and you will too, as it needs a rest in the refrigerator overnight. There certainly are a few steps, but the dough uses just five simple ingredients, and the hands-on time is only about twenty minutes (if it's more than that, you're overworking the dough!). Give this sticky, highly hydrated dough the time that it needs to rest, and you'll be rewarded with a salty, crispy golden crust and a chewy crumb that's as fluffy as a pillow.

SKILL LEVEL: **Intermediate**

PREP: **15 hours 20 minutes, including rises**

BAKE: **22 minutes**

TOTAL: **16 hours, including some cooling**

Dough

1½ cups warm water (110°F/43°C) **(360g/ml)**

2 teaspoons instant or active dry yeast **(6g)**

3¼ cups bread flour **(423g)**

3 tablespoons extra-virgin olive oil, divided, plus more as needed

2 teaspoons coarse or flaky sea salt, plus more for topping

Optional Topping

¾ cup halved cherry tomatoes **(85g)**

2 garlic cloves, minced

2 teaspoons minced fresh herbs such as oregano, rosemary, or thyme

1. Make the dough: In a large bowl, whisk the warm water and yeast. Cover and let sit for 10 minutes to dissolve the yeast. Add the flour, 1 tablespoon of the olive oil, and the salt. Gently mix with a wooden spoon or spatula until combined. The dough should be sticky and wet. Working in the bowl, shape it into a ball as best you can. Drizzle lightly with olive oil and rub it over the dough.

2. Cover the bowl with plastic wrap and refrigerate it for at least 12 hours or up to 48 hours. The dough will expand to the sides of the bowl and have a slick, bubbly surface.

3. When you're ready to bake the focaccia, pour the remaining 2 tablespoons olive oil into a 9 × 13-inch baking pan. Use a pastry brush to spread it over the bottom and up the sides; you want a very generous coating.

4. Remove the dough from the refrigerator. Using a wooden spoon or spatula and starting on the side of the bowl farthest from you, gently pull the edge of the dough into the center, which will release some of the air (1). Turn the bowl and repeat 3 more times, for a total of 4 folds (2). Place the dough into the prepared pan, then gently flip it over so both sides are coated with oil (3). Cover the pan and let the dough rest at room temperature for at least 3 hours or up to 5 hours. The dough won't really rise, but it will stretch toward the edges of the pan.

5. Preheat the oven to 450°F (232°C). Coat your fingers with olive oil and press them into the surface of the dough, creating dimples and deep depressions all over the top (4). Stretch the dough as you do this so it fills the pan. Sprinkle generously with coarse salt. If using the optional topping, press the halved tomatoes into the surface of the dough and sprinkle evenly with the minced garlic and herbs (5).

6. Bake for 22 to 25 minutes or until golden brown. Cool the focaccia in the pan set on a cooling rack for at least 10 minutes before slicing and serving. Store covered tightly at room temperature for up to 3 days or in the refrigerator for up to 4 days.

Soft Dinner Rolls: 3 Ways

MAKES 15 ROUND ROLLS, 18 CLOVERLEAF ROLLS, OR 24 CRESCENT ROLLS

Perfect for soaking up sauces, soups, and gravies, dinner rolls are your main dish's best friend. These are buttery and mildly sweet with a golden crust and fluffy interior. In fact, one recipe tester said the rolls were "super soft—I wanted to float on them!" Though the classic round shape is undoubtedly timeless, I use the same dough to make pull-apart cloverleaf rolls and crescent-shaped rolls, too. Before the rolls join your dinner feast, brush them with honey butter and sprinkle with flaky sea salt. The best!

SKILL LEVEL: **Beginner**

PREP: **3 hours 25 minutes, including rises**

BAKE: **20 minutes**

TOTAL: **3 hours 50 minutes**

Dough

1 cup warm whole milk (about 110°F/43°C) **(240g/ml)**

2¼ teaspoons instant or active dry yeast (1 standard packet) **(7g)**

2 tablespoons granulated sugar, divided

3 cups bread flour or all-purpose flour, plus more as needed **(390g)**

4 tablespoons unsalted butter, at room temperature and cut into 4 pieces **(56g)**

1 large egg, at room temperature

1 teaspoon salt

Nonstick spray or butter, for the bowl and pan

Honey Butter Topping

2 tablespoons unsalted butter, melted **(28g)**

1 tablespoon honey

Flaky or coarse sea salt

OVERNIGHT OPTION: Prepare the dough through the shaping in step 5. Cover the shaped rolls and place in the refrigerator for up to 16 hours. Remove from the refrigerator and let the dough rise at room temperature for 1 to 2 more hours or until puffy, then bake as directed.

TIP: While bread flour, with its higher protein content, is a must for chewier, sturdier bread, if you use all-purpose flour in these smaller, softer rolls, you won't notice a huge difference.

1. Make the dough: In the bowl of a stand mixer fitted with the dough hook, whisk the warm milk, yeast, and 1 tablespoon of the sugar. Cover and let sit for 5 to 10 minutes or until foamy and frothy on the surface. (If you don't have a stand mixer, use a large mixing bowl and mix the dough with a wooden spoon or spatula in the next step.)

2. Add the remaining 1 tablespoon sugar, 1 cup (130g) of the flour, the butter, egg, and salt, and mix on low speed for 30 seconds. Scrape down the sides of the bowl, then add the remaining 2 cups (260g) flour. Beat on medium speed until the dough comes together and pulls away from the sides of the bowl, about 2 minutes. If it seems too sticky and clings to the sides of the bowl instead of forming a rough mass around the dough hook or spoon, add more flour, 1 tablespoon at a time, and continue to mix until the dough pulls away from the sides of the bowl but is still moist and tacky. If it feels dry and crumbly, add more milk, 1 teaspoon at a time, mixing well after each addition.

3. When the dough reaches the proper consistency, beat on low speed for 5 minutes more or until it is smooth, supple, and elastic. (Or knead by hand on a lightly floured surface for 5 minutes. Keep a small bowl of flour nearby to lightly flour your hands and/or the dough as needed, as it can be quite sticky.) To see if the dough is ready, use the poke test or the windowpane test (see page 241). If it's not ready, keep kneading.

4. Lightly grease a large bowl with nonstick spray. Place the dough in the bowl, turning it to coat. Cover the bowl with a tea towel or plastic wrap and let the dough rise at room temperature for 1 to 2 hours or until doubled in size.

5. Shape the rolls: When the dough is risen, punch it down to release the air.

Classic Round Dinner Rolls: Grease a 9 × 13-inch baking pan with nonstick spray. Divide the dough into 15 equal pieces. Take one piece and stretch the top of the dough while pinching and sealing the bottom to make a smooth ball. Repeat with the remaining dough. Arrange the shaped rolls in the prepared pan, leaving a bit of space between them (1).

recipe continues >

Classic Round Dinner Rolls

Cloverleaf Rolls

Crescent Rolls

Cloverleaf Rolls: Grease a 12-count muffin pan with nonstick spray, and grease 6 cups in a second muffin pan (or bake in batches). Divide the dough into 18 equal pieces, then divide each piece again into 3 equal pieces. Shape each piece into a smooth ball, and place 3 dough balls side by side in each muffin cup (2).

Crescent Rolls: Line two baking sheets with parchment paper or silicone baking mats. Divide the dough in half and lightly cover one piece of the dough. With a lightly floured rolling pin on a lightly floured surface, roll the other piece of dough to a 14-inch circle. With a pizza cutter or sharp knife, cut the circle into 12 wedges (3). Starting from the wide bottom of a wedge, tightly roll it in toward its point (4). Place the roll on a prepared baking sheet with the point tucked underneath; curl the two ends inward to create a crescent shape (5). Roll the remaining wedges, and repeat with the second half of the dough and the second baking sheet.

6. Cover the shaped rolls and let rise at room temperature until puffy, about 1 hour for the classic round rolls, and 30 minutes for the cloverleaf or crescent rolls.

7. Preheat the oven to 350°F (177°C).

8. Bake the rolls for 20 to 25 minutes or until golden brown on top, rotating the pan(s) halfway through. If the tops are browning too quickly, loosely tent aluminum foil over the rolls. Set the pan on a cooling rack to cool for 10 minutes.

9. **Make the topping:** In a small bowl, mix the melted butter and honey. Brush the honey butter over the warm rolls and sprinkle lightly with sea salt. Store covered tightly at room temperature for up to 3 days or in the refrigerator for up to 5 days.

Brioche-Style Sandwich Rolls

MAKES 8 LARGE ROLLS

SKILL LEVEL: **Intermediate**

PREP: **3 hours 35 minutes, including rises**

BAKE: **25 minutes**

TOTAL: **4 hours**

Golden brown with a hint of sweetness, these big buttery rolls are ready for all your sandwich and burger fixings. I wanted a roll that was a bit sturdier than Soft Dinner Rolls (page 255) but still puffy and tender. Brioche came to mind; it's a type of bread that's rich with eggs and butter and holds its shape quite nicely. While these rolls may not precisely mirror traditional brioche with its elevated butter-to-flour ratio, they come remarkably close! Though you can get away without a mixer for some of the yeasted dough recipes in this book, I strongly recommend using one for this. (Your arms will thank you.) The rolls can be enjoyed warm, but for sandwiches and burgers, I recommend cooling completely before slicing and using.

Dough

½ cup warm whole milk (about 110°F/43°C) **(120g/ml)**

¼ cup warm water (about 110°F/43°C) **(60g/ml)**

¼ cup granulated sugar, divided **(50g)**

2¼ teaspoons instant or active dry yeast (1 standard packet) **(7g)**

3¾ cups bread flour, divided, plus more as needed **(488g)**

2 large eggs, at room temperature

1 large egg yolk, at room temperature (reserve egg white for the egg wash)

1½ teaspoons salt

8 tablespoons unsalted butter, at room temperature and cut into 8 pieces **(113g)**

Nonstick spray or butter, for the bowl and pan

Topping

Egg wash: 1 egg white (from above) beaten with 1 tablespoon water

2 tablespoons sesame seeds (optional)

OVERNIGHT OPTION: Prepare the dough through the shaping in step 6. Cover the shaped rolls and place in the refrigerator for up to 16 hours. Remove from the refrigerator and let the dough rise at room temperature for 1 to 2 more hours or until puffy, then bake as directed.

1. Make the dough: In the bowl of a stand mixer fitted with the dough hook, whisk the warm milk, warm water, 2 tablespoons of the sugar, and the yeast. Cover and let sit for 5 to 10 minutes or until foamy and frothy on the surface.

2. Add the remaining 2 tablespoons sugar, 1 cup (130g) of the flour, the eggs, egg yolk, and salt and mix on low speed for 30 seconds. Scrape down the sides of the bowl, then add the remaining flour. With the mixer running on medium speed, add the butter, 1 tablespoon at a time. When all the butter has been added, continue to beat until the butter has been fully incorporated and the dough pulls away from the sides of the bowl, 4 to 5 minutes. The dough should feel tacky. If it seems wet and sticks to the sides of the bowl instead of forming a rough mass around the dough hook, add more flour, 1 tablespoon at a time, and continue to mix until the dough pulls away from the sides of the bowl. If it feels dry and crumbly, add more water, 1 teaspoon at a time, mixing well after each addition.

3. When the dough reaches the proper consistency, beat on low speed for 10 minutes more or until it is smooth, supple, and elastic. Keep a small bowl of flour nearby to lightly flour the dough if it begins to stick to the sides of the bowl again. To see if the dough is ready, use the poke test or the windowpane test (see page 241). If it's not ready, keep kneading.

4. Lightly grease a large bowl with nonstick spray. Place the dough in the bowl, turning it to coat. Cover the bowl with a tea towel or plastic wrap and let the dough rise at room temperature for 2 hours or until doubled in size.

5. Line a baking sheet with parchment paper or a silicone baking mat.

6. When the dough is risen, punch it down to release the air. Divide the dough into 8 equal pieces. Take 1 piece and stretch the top of the dough while pinching and sealing the bottom to make a smooth ball. Repeat with the remaining dough. Arrange the rolls 3 inches apart on the prepared baking sheet.

7. Cover the shaped rolls and let rise at room temperature until puffy, about 1 hour.

8. Preheat the oven to 350°F (177°C).

9. Top the rolls: Brush the tops of the rolls with egg wash and sprinkle with sesame seeds (if using). Bake the rolls for 25 minutes or until golden brown on top, rotating the pan halfway through. If the tops are browning too quickly, loosely tent aluminum foil over the rolls. Cool the rolls on the baking sheet for 10 minutes, then transfer to a cooling rack to cool completely. Once cooled, slice in half horizontally to use as sandwich rolls. Store wrapped tightly at room temperature for up to 4 days or in the refrigerator for up to 1 week.

Buttermilk Chive Fantail Rolls

MAKES 12 ROLLS

When you want to add a little pizzazz to your dinner rolls—I'm talking tangy buttermilk, flavorful seasonings, fragrant chives, and an ornate shape—this recipe delivers. Shaping requires rolling out the dough, covering it in butter and seasonings, and cutting it into strips that are then layered together. As the rolls bake, the bottoms stay plush and soft, while the fanned-out tops develop a chewier, crispier texture. We love peeling away the layers and eating them one by one!

SKILL LEVEL: **Intermediate**
PREP: **3 hours, including rises**
BAKE: **20 minutes**
TOTAL: **3 hours 20 minutes**

Dough

¾ cup warm buttermilk (about 110°F/43°C) **(180g/ml)**

2 teaspoons instant or active dry yeast **(6g)**

2 teaspoons granulated sugar

3 cups bread flour or all-purpose flour, plus more as needed **(390g)**

4 tablespoons unsalted butter, melted **(56g)**

1 large egg, at room temperature

1 teaspoon salt

½ teaspoon garlic powder

½ teaspoon onion powder

Nonstick spray or butter, for the bowl and pan

Shaping & Brushing

4 tablespoons unsalted butter, melted and divided **(56g)**

3 tablespoons chopped fresh chives, plus more for garnish

½ teaspoon garlic powder

½ teaspoon onion powder

Coarse or flaky sea salt

OVERNIGHT OPTION: Prepare the dough through covering the shaped rolls in step 7, and place the muffin pan in the refrigerator for up to 16 hours. Remove from the refrigerator and let the dough rise at room temperature for 1 hour or until slightly puffy, then bake as directed.

1. Make the dough: In the bowl of a stand mixer fitted with the dough hook, whisk the warm buttermilk, yeast, and sugar. Cover and let sit for 5 to 10 minutes or until foamy and frothy on the surface. (If you don't have a stand mixer, use a large mixing bowl and mix the dough with a wooden spoon or spatula in the next step.)

2. Add 1 cup (130g) of the flour, the melted butter, egg, salt, garlic powder, and onion powder and mix on low speed for 30 seconds. Scrape down the sides of the bowl, then add the remaining flour. Beat on medium speed until the dough comes together and pulls away from the sides of the bowl, about 2 minutes. If it seems too sticky and clings to the sides of the bowl instead of forming a rough mass around the dough hook, add more flour, 1 tablespoon at a time, and continue to mix until the dough pulls away from the sides of the bowl but is still moist and tacky. If it feels dry and crumbly, add more buttermilk, 1 teaspoon at a time, mixing well after each addition.

3. When the dough reaches the proper consistency, beat on low speed for 5 minutes more, or until the dough is smooth, supple, and elastic. (Or knead by hand on a lightly floured surface for 5 minutes. Keep a small bowl of flour nearby to lightly flour your hands and/or the dough as needed, as it can be quite sticky.) To see if the dough is ready, use the poke test or the windowpane test (see page 241). If it's not ready, keep kneading.

4. Lightly grease a large bowl with nonstick spray. Place the dough in the bowl, turning it to coat. Cover the bowl with a tea towel or plastic wrap and let the dough rise at room temperature for 1 to 2 hours or until doubled in size.

5. Generously grease a 12-cup muffin pan with nonstick spray.

6. Shape and brush the rolls: When the dough is risen, punch it down to release the air and divide it in half. With a lightly floured rolling pin on a lightly floured surface, roll each piece of dough to a 12-inch square. Brush each square with 1 tablespoon of the melted butter (reserve the rest for the topping), then sprinkle each evenly with chives, garlic powder, and onion powder. With a pizza cutter or sharp knife, cut 1 of the dough squares into six 2-inch-wide strips (1). Layer the strips on top of each other to make a tall 6-layer stack of dough (2). Using a sharp knife, cut it into 6 equal squares (3). If the layers slide around because of the melted butter, do your best to keep them neatly stacked. Repeat with the second square of dough, so that you have 12 layered squares.

recipe continues >

Turn each on its side so the cut layers face up, and place in the prepared muffin pan (4). Slightly separate the layers so they fan outward.

7. Cover the shaped rolls and let rise at room temperature until slightly puffy, about 30 minutes. You do not want the rolls to puff up too much during this second rise or they won't hold the fantail shape.

8. Preheat the oven to 375°F (191°C).

9. Bake the rolls for 20 minutes or until golden brown on top, rotating the pan halfway through. If the tops are browning too quickly, loosely tent aluminum foil over the rolls.

10. Brush the remaining 2 tablespoons melted butter over the hot rolls and sprinkle lightly with sea salt and more chives. Cool in the pan for 10 minutes before serving. Store wrapped tightly at room temperature for up to 3 days or in the refrigerator for up to 1 week.

Oatmeal Wheat Sandwich Bread

MAKES 1 LOAF

This is my top choice when I make homemade sandwich bread because my whole family loves it, and most of the prep time is hands-off. My special trick is to soak the oats in the liquid used for the dough so they're extra plump before the dough even rises. The result is an extraordinarily soft, chewy, and wholesome bread that we love using for toast, PB&Js, and grilled cheese sandwiches.

SKILL LEVEL: **Beginner**

PREP: **3 hours 40 minutes, including rises**

BAKE: **40 minutes**

TOTAL: **4 hours 45 minutes, including some cooling**

Dough

⅔ cup rolled oats **(57g)**

1¾ cups boiling water **(420g/ml)**

3 tablespoons brown sugar **(37g)**

2¼ teaspoons instant or active dry yeast (1 standard packet) **(7g)**

1 cup whole-wheat flour **(130g)**

3 tablespoons unsalted butter, at room temperature **(43g)**

1½ teaspoons salt

2⅓ cups bread flour, divided, plus more as needed **(303g)**

Nonstick spray or butter, for the bowl and pan

Topping

Egg wash: 1 egg white beaten with 1 tablespoon water

1 to 2 tablespoons rolled oats

TIP: If you do not own a stand mixer, you can mix this dough with a large wooden spoon or spatula, but it will take a bit of arm muscle!

1. Make the dough: Place the oats in a large heat-safe bowl or the bowl of a stand mixer and pour the boiling water over them. Let the mixture cool until a thermometer reads 110°F (43°C), about 20 minutes. Don't rush this step; you don't want to kill the yeast in the next step with an oat mixture that's too hot.

2. In the bowl of a stand mixer fitted with the dough hook, whisk the warm oat mixture, brown sugar, and yeast. Cover and let sit for 5 to 10 minutes or until foamy and frothy on the surface.

3. Add the whole-wheat flour, butter, and salt. Beat on low speed for 30 seconds. Scrape down the sides of the bowl, then add about half of the bread flour. Beat on medium speed until mostly incorporated; it's okay if there are small chunks of butter. Add the remaining bread flour, then beat on medium speed until the dough comes together and pulls away from the sides of the bowl, about 2 minutes. If it seems too sticky and clings to the sides of the bowl instead of forming a rough mass around the dough hook or spoon, add more bread flour, 1 tablespoon at a time, and continue to mix until the dough pulls away from the sides of the bowl. The dough should be heavy, dense, and a little sticky. If it feels dry and crumbly, add more water, 1 teaspoon at a time, mixing well after each addition.

4. When the dough reaches the proper consistency, beat on low speed for 5 minutes more or until the dough is smooth, supple, and elastic. (Or knead by hand on a lightly floured surface for 5 minutes. Keep a small bowl of flour nearby to lightly flour your hands and/or the dough as needed, as it can be quite sticky.) To see if the dough is ready, use the poke test or the windowpane test (see page 241). If it's not ready, keep kneading.

5. Lightly grease a large bowl with nonstick spray. Place the dough in the bowl, turning it to coat. Cover the bowl with a tea towel or plastic wrap and let the dough rise at room temperature for 1 to 2 hours or until doubled in size.

6. Grease a 9 × 5-inch loaf pan with nonstick spray. When the dough is risen, punch it down to release the air. Place the dough on a lightly floured surface and, with a floured rolling pin, roll the dough to an 8 × 15-inch rectangle. It does not have to be perfect; the corners can be rounded. Roll the dough into an 8-inch log and place the loaf, seam side down, in the prepared pan.

recipe continues >

OVERNIGHT OPTIONS:

OPTION 1: Make and knead the dough and let the dough have its first rise in the refrigerator overnight. Cover the dough tightly and place in the refrigerator for up to 12 hours. Remove from the refrigerator and let the dough come to room temperature, then shape the loaf, let rise, and bake as directed.

OPTION 2: Prepare the recipe through shaping the loaf and putting it in the pan in step 6. Cover the shaped loaf tightly and refrigerate for up to 15 hours. Remove from the refrigerator and let the loaf rise at room temperature for about 1 hour before baking.

7. Cover the shaped loaf and let rise at room temperature for 1 hour or until it's about 1 inch above the top of the pan.

8. Adjust the oven rack to the lower-third position and preheat the oven to 350°F (177°C).

9. Top the loaf: Lightly brush the top of the loaf with egg wash, then sprinkle with the oats.

10. Bake for 40 to 45 minutes or until golden brown on top. If you give the top a gentle tap, a fully baked loaf should sound hollow. For a more accurate test, the bread is done when an instant-read thermometer reads the center of the loaf as 195°F (91°C). Check on the bread about halfway through baking; if the top is browning too quickly, tent with aluminum foil.

11. Cool for 10 minutes in the pan set on a cooling rack, then remove the loaf from the pan and carefully place it upright on the rack to cool completely before slicing. Store wrapped tightly at room temperature for up to 5 days or in the refrigerator for up to 10 days.

Cinnamon Raisin Swirl Bread

MAKES 1 LOAF

I'm quite certain nothing rivals homemade cinnamon swirl bread with sticky-sweet raisins speckled throughout. The aroma wafting from the oven is enough to weaken the knees, let alone that first soft and flaky slice. (My mouth is watering as I write this.) A version of this is on my website, but here I've replaced some of the butter with an egg yolk. The yolk adds a bit of richness, and I use melted butter instead of softened. As for most of the yeast bread recipes in this chapter, an instant-read thermometer takes out the guesswork so you know exactly when your loaf is done . . . and, more importantly, when you can dig in!

SKILL LEVEL: **Intermediate**

PREP: **3 hours 30 minutes,** including rises

BAKE: **40 minutes**

TOTAL: **4 hours 30 minutes,** including some cooling

Dough

½ cup warm water (about 110°F/43°C) **(120g/ml)**

½ cup warm whole milk (about 110°F/43°C) **(120g/ml)**

¼ cup granulated sugar **(50g)**

2¼ teaspoons instant or active dry yeast (1 standard packet) **(7g)**

4 tablespoons unsalted butter, melted and slightly cooled **(56g)**

1 large egg yolk, at room temperature (reserve egg white for the egg wash)

3⅓ cups bread flour, plus more as needed **(433g)**

¾ cup raisins **(113g)**

1 teaspoon salt

Nonstick spray or butter, for the bowl and pan

Filling

⅓ cup brown sugar **(67g)**

1 tablespoon ground cinnamon

Egg wash: 1 egg white (from above) beaten with 1 tablespoon water

Topping

1 tablespoon unsalted butter, melted **(14g)**

TIP: The egg wash helps the cinnamon–sugar swirl adhere to the dough and reduces the risk of air gaps in the bread.

1. Make the dough: In the bowl of a stand mixer fitted with the dough hook, whisk the warm water, warm milk, sugar, and yeast. Cover and let sit for 5 to 10 minutes or until foamy and frothy on the surface. (If you don't have a stand mixer, use a large mixing bowl and mix the dough with a wooden spoon or spatula in the next step.)

2. Add the melted butter and egg yolk and mix on low speed until combined. Add the flour, raisins, and salt, and beat on low speed until the dough pulls away from the sides of the bowl, about 2 minutes. It should feel tacky. If it seems too sticky and clings to the sides of the bowl instead of forming a rough mass around the dough hook or spoon, add more flour, 1 tablespoon at a time, and continue to mix until the dough pulls away from the sides of the bowl but is still moist and tacky. If it feels dry and crumbly, add more water, 1 teaspoon at a time, mixing well after each addition.

3. When the dough reaches the proper consistency, beat on low speed for 5 minutes more or until it is smooth, supple, and elastic. (Or knead by hand on a lightly floured surface for 5 minutes. If some of the raisins fall out of the dough as you knead, just press them back in. Keep a small bowl of flour nearby to lightly flour your hands and/or the dough as needed, as it can be quite sticky.) To see if the dough is ready, use the poke test or the windowpane test (see page 241). If it's not ready, keep kneading.

4. Lightly grease a large bowl with nonstick spray. Place the dough in the bowl, turning it to coat. Cover the bowl with a tea towel or plastic wrap and let the dough rise at room temperature for 1 to 2 hours or until doubled in size.

5. Fill the bread: In a small bowl, mix the brown sugar and cinnamon. Grease a 9 × 5-inch loaf pan with nonstick spray.

6. When the dough is risen, punch it down to release the air. Place the dough on a lightly floured surface and, with a floured rolling pin, roll the dough to an 8 × 20-inch rectangle. Leaving a 1-inch border uncovered, lightly brush the dough with the egg wash (1), then sprinkle with the cinnamon-sugar (2). Roll the dough into an 8-inch log (3) and pinch the ends to seal. Place the loaf, seam side down, in the prepared pan.

recipe continues >

OVERNIGHT OPTION: Make and knead the dough and let the dough have its first rise in the refrigerator overnight. Cover the dough tightly and place in the refrigerator for up to 12 hours. Remove from the refrigerator and let the dough rise at room temperature for 1 more hour, then continue with step 5.

7. Cover the shaped loaf and let rise at room temperature for 1 hour or until it's about 1 inch above the top of the pan.

8. Adjust the oven rack to the lower-third position and preheat the oven to 350°F (177°C).

9. Top the loaf: Drizzle or lightly brush the melted butter on top of the shaped loaf before baking (4).

10. Bake for 40 to 45 minutes or until golden brown on top. If you give the top a gentle tap, a fully baked loaf should sound hollow. For a more accurate test, the bread is done when an instant-read thermometer reads the center of the loaf as 195°F (91°C). Check on the bread about halfway through baking; if the top of the loaf is browning too quickly, tent it with aluminum foil.

11. Cool for 10 minutes in the pan set on a cooling rack, then remove the loaf from the pan and carefully place it upright on the rack to cool completely before slicing. Store wrapped tightly at room temperature for up to 5 days or in the refrigerator for up to 10 days.

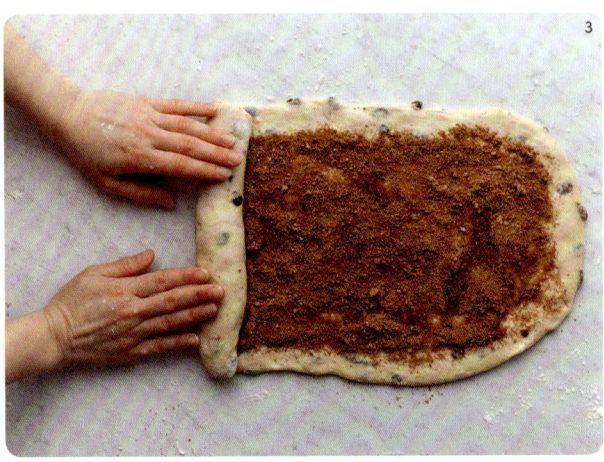

Maple Walnut Pull-Apart Bread

MAKES 1 LOAF

I speak from experience: After you tear off and taste that first bite, you will not be able to think about anything besides this bread. Whether you're faced with a sink of dishes, a pile of laundry, or a looming cookbook deadline (again, I've been there), this bread has the magical ability to make all other concerns vanish. The pull-apart pieces are stuffed with maple-flavored brown sugar and walnuts, and after baking, every nook and cranny is drizzled with warm maple icing. If you're a fan of all things maple flavored, consider this bread a must-try. Now, excuse me while I attempt to re-enter reality!

SKILL LEVEL: **Intermediate**
PREP: **3 hours, including rises**
BAKE: **50 minutes**
TOTAL: **4 hours**

Dough

¾ cup warm whole milk (about 110°F/43°C) **(180g/ml)**

¼ cup granulated sugar, divided **(50g)**

2¼ teaspoons instant or active dry yeast (1 standard packet) **(7g)**

2½ cups bread flour, plus more as needed **(325g)**

3 tablespoons unsalted butter, at room temperature **(43g)**

1 large egg, at room temperature

½ teaspoon salt

Nonstick spray or butter, for the bowl and pan

Filling

½ cup brown sugar **(100g)**

6 tablespoons unsalted butter, softened **(85g)**

1 teaspoon ground cinnamon

½ teaspoon maple extract

¾ cup chopped walnuts **(90g)**

Maple Icing

2 tablespoons unsalted butter **(28g)**

⅓ cup pure maple syrup **(113g)**

1 cup sifted powdered sugar **(112g)**

Pinch of salt

1. Make the dough: In the bowl of a stand mixer fitted with the dough hook, whisk the warm milk, 1 tablespoon of sugar, and the yeast. Cover and let sit until foamy and frothy on the surface, 5 to 10 minutes. (If you don't have a stand mixer, use a large mixing bowl and mix the dough with a wooden spoon or spatula in the next step.)

2. Add the remaining sugar, the flour, butter, egg, and salt. Beat on low speed for 1 minute, until the flour is mostly incorporated, then beat on medium speed until the dough comes together and pulls away from the sides of the bowl, about 2 minutes. If it seems too sticky and clings to the sides of the bowl instead of forming a rough mass around the dough hook, add more flour, 1 tablespoon at a time, and continue to mix until the dough pulls away from the sides of the bowl but is still moist and tacky. If it feels dry and crumbly, add more milk, 1 teaspoon at a time, mixing well after each addition.

3. When the dough reaches the proper consistency, beat on low speed for 5 minutes more or until it is smooth, supple, and elastic. (Or knead by hand on a lightly floured surface for 5 minutes. Keep a small bowl of flour nearby to lightly flour your hands and/or the dough as needed, as it can be quite sticky.) To see if the dough is ready, use the poke test or the windowpane test (see page 241). If it's not ready, keep kneading.

4. Lightly grease a large bowl with nonstick spray. Place the dough in the bowl, turning it to coat. Cover the bowl with a tea towel or plastic wrap and let the dough rise at room temperature for 1 to 2 hours or until doubled in size.

5. Make the filling: The softer the butter is, the easier it is to mix in this step. Heat it in the microwave for a few seconds to soften if needed. In a small bowl, mix the brown sugar, butter, cinnamon, and maple extract.

6. Grease a 9 × 5-inch loaf pan. Punch the dough down to release the air. Place the dough on a lightly floured surface. Divide it into 12 equal pieces, about ¼ cup (55g) of dough each. With lightly floured hands, flatten each piece of dough into a 4-inch circle. They don't have to be perfect circles. Leaving a ¼-inch border around the edges, spread 2 heaping teaspoons of filling over each circle (1). Sprinkle 1 tablespoon of walnuts on top. Fold the rounds in half to make half-moon shapes (like a taco), and place in a row in the prepared pan, open side up (2). The filling may squeeze out as you arrange the half-moons in the pan; that's okay.

recipe continues >

OVERNIGHT OPTION: Make and knead the dough and let the dough have its first rise in the refrigerator overnight. Cover the dough tightly and place in the refrigerator for up to 12 hours. Remove from the refrigerator and let the dough rise at room temperature for 1 more hour, then continue with step 5.

7. Cover the shaped loaf and let rise at room temperature until puffy, about 45 minutes.

8. Adjust the oven rack to the lower-third position and preheat the oven to 350°F (177°C). Place a baking sheet on the bottom rack to catch any drips.

9. Bake the bread for 50 minutes or until golden brown on top. For a more accurate test, the bread is done when an instant-read thermometer reads the center of the loaf as 195°F (91°C). Check on the bread about halfway through baking; if the top is browning too quickly, tent with aluminum foil.

10. Cool for 10 minutes in the pan set on a cooling rack, then remove the bread from the pan and carefully place upright on a cooling rack set over a piece of parchment paper.

11. Make the maple icing: In a small saucepan over low heat, melt the butter with the maple syrup, whisking occasionally. Remove from heat and whisk in the powdered sugar and salt. Drizzle over the warm bread. Pull apart the pieces to serve. Store iced bread loosely wrapped at room temperature for up to 2 days or in the refrigerator for up to 1 week.

Rustic Rosemary Garlic Bread

MAKES 1 LOAF

This no-knead recipe proves that some homemade breads don't require a ton of effort but instead go easy with some hands-off time. I think I can muster up enough patience if the reward is fresh-baked, chewy-crisp rosemary bread! Letting this dough sit at room temperature to rise and then refrigerating it helps develop extraordinary flavor and texture. Since the dough can rest in the refrigerator for up to two days, this is a wonderful recipe to begin ahead of time.

SKILL LEVEL: **Beginner**
PREP: **6 hours, including rises**
BAKE: **35 minutes**
TOTAL: **6 hours 50 minutes, including some cooling**

3¼ cups bread flour, plus more as needed **(430g)**

2 tablespoons finely chopped fresh rosemary leaves

2¼ teaspoons instant or active dry yeast (1 standard packet) **(7g)**

3 garlic cloves, minced

2 teaspoons coarse sea salt

¼ teaspoon freshly ground black pepper

1½ cups water, at room temperature (about 70°F/21°C) **(360g/ml)**

TIP: An interesting step you'll find here, and one I swear by, is creating a steamy oven with boiling water. A humid environment lets the free-form bread expand to its full potential, and once it does, it helps set the crispy crust.

1. In a large bowl, whisk the flour, rosemary, yeast, garlic, salt, and pepper. (Note: This dough is too sticky for a mixer.) Pour in the water and gently mix with a wooden spoon or spatula. The dough will seem dry and shaggy, but keep working it, with your hands if necessary, until all the flour is moistened. The dough should be sticky. Working in the bowl, shape it into a ball as best you can.

2. Cover the bowl tightly with plastic wrap and let the dough rise at room temperature for 2 to 3 hours. The dough will just about double in size, stick to the sides of the bowl, and have a lot of air bubbles.

3. Using a wooden spoon or spatula and starting on the side of the bowl farthest from you, gently pull the edge of the dough into the center, which will release some of the air. Turn the bowl and repeat 3 more times, for a total of 4 folds. Cover the bowl tightly again and place it in the refrigerator for at least 3 hours and up to 48 hours.

4. Turn the dough out onto a lightly floured surface. Using generously floured hands, shape it into a ball as best you can. Lightly dust a baking sheet with flour. Transfer the dough to the prepared sheet, cover with a tea towel or plastic wrap, and let the dough rest at room temperature for 45 minutes.

5. Preheat the oven to 425°F (218°C). Boil a kettle of water and have ready a large, shallow metal or cast-iron baking pan or skillet.

6. Use a very sharp knife or bread lame to score the dough with a slash or an X, about ½ inch deep. If the shaped loaf has flattened during the 45-minute rest, use floured hands to reshape it into a ball.

7. When the oven is preheated, put the baking pan on the bottom oven rack. Carefully and quickly pour about 1 inch of boiling water into the pan. Place the baking sheet with the bread dough on the rack above the pan and quickly shut the oven door, trapping the steam inside.

8. Bake for 35 to 40 minutes or until golden brown. If you give the top a gentle tap, a fully baked loaf should sound hollow. For a more accurate test, the bread is done when an instant-read thermometer reads the center of the loaf as 195°F (91°C).

9. Transfer the bread to a cooling rack and let cool for at least 30 minutes before slicing and serving. Store wrapped tightly at room temperature for up to 5 days or in the refrigerator for up to 10 days.

Soft Pretzels

MAKES 12 PRETZELS

As my older daughter likes to say, "Mom, you have to save the best for last." And so I did! These soft pretzels are an absolute treasure in our family. I've been making them this exact way for a decade, and you'll find this recipe (and hundreds of glowing reviews!) on my website. It's one of the easiest, quickest methods for pretzels I've come across, because the dough is manageable to mix by hand and only needs about 10 minutes to rest. A quick baking soda bath gives the pretzels their traditional flavor and signature chewy texture, so don't skip it. The cheese dip, with its sharp, balanced flavor and mustard undertones, seals the deal: You won't want to share this gold!

SKILL LEVEL: **Beginner**

PREP: **50 minutes, including boiling**

BAKE: **12 minutes**

TOTAL: **1 hour 10 minutes**

Dough

1½ cups warm water (about 100°F/38°C) **(360g/ml)**

1 tablespoon brown or granulated sugar

2¼ teaspoons instant or active dry yeast (1 standard packet) **(7g)**

1 tablespoon unsalted butter, melted and slightly cooled **(14g)**

1 teaspoon salt

3¾ to 4 cups all-purpose flour, plus more as needed **(469 to 500g)**

Nonstick spray, for the baking sheets

Baking Soda Bath

½ cup baking soda **(120g)**

9 cups water **(2.13L)**

Coarse salt, for topping

White Cheddar Cheese Dip (recipe follows), for serving

TIP: Shaping pretzels may seem tricky, but it gets easier once you get going. Don't use too much flour on your surface; the dough needs a little stickiness to roll into long ropes without shrinking.

1. Make the dough: In a large bowl or the bowl of a stand mixer fitted with the dough hook, whisk the warm water, sugar, and yeast. Cover and let sit for 1 minute to dissolve the yeast.

2. Whisk or mix in the melted butter and salt. Add 3 cups (375g) of the flour, then mix on low speed or with a wooden spoon until combined. Add ¾ cup (94g) more flour and mix until the dough is slightly tacky but not overly wet and sticky. If it seems too sticky and clings to the sides of the bowl instead of forming a rough mass around the dough hook, add up to ¼ cup (31g) more flour, 1 tablespoon at a time, and continue to mix until the dough pulls away from the sides of the bowl but is still moist and tacky. If it feels dry and crumbly, add more water, 1 teaspoon at a time, mixing well after each addition.

3. When the dough reaches the proper consistency, beat on low speed for 3 to 5 minutes more or until it is smooth, supple, and elastic. (Or knead by hand on a lightly floured surface for 3 to 5 minutes. Keep a small bowl of flour nearby to lightly flour your hands and/or the dough as needed, as it can be quite sticky.) To see if the dough is ready, use the poke test or the windowpane test (see page 241). If it's not ready, keep kneading.

4. Shape the dough into a ball. Cover with a tea towel or plastic wrap and let the dough rest at room temperature for at least 10 minutes or up to 30 minutes, or cover tightly and refrigerate for up to 1 day.

5. Preheat the oven to 400°F (204°C). Line two baking sheets with parchment paper or silicone baking mats and lightly grease with nonstick spray.

6. Using a sharp knife, bench scraper, or pizza cutter, cut the dough into sections, each about ⅓ cup (75g); you should have about 12, depending on how much flour was added to the dough (1). On a lightly floured surface, roll each dough section into a 20- to 22-inch rope (2). Form a circle with a dough rope by bringing the 2 ends together at the top of the circle (3). Twist the ends together (4). Bring the twisted ends back down toward you and press them down to form a pretzel shape (5). Repeat with the remaining dough. See visuals on page 276.

7. Make the baking soda bath: In a large pot, stir the baking soda into the water and bring to a boil.

recipe continues >

8. Carefully drop 1 or 2 pretzels into the boiling water and boil for 20 to 30 seconds. Any longer than that and the pretzels will taste metallic. Using a slotted metal spatula, lift the pretzels out of the water and let the excess water drain off. Place the pretzels on the prepared baking sheets and sprinkle with coarse salt (6). Repeat with the remaining pretzels. If desired, cover the boiled, unbaked pretzels with lightly oiled plastic wrap and refrigerate for up to 24 hours before baking.

9. Bake the pretzels for 12 to 15 minutes or until dark golden brown.

10. Serve warm with white Cheddar cheese dip. Store wrapped tightly at room temperature for up to 2 days.

White Cheddar Cheese Dip

MAKES 3 CUPS

3 tablespoons unsalted butter **(43g)**

3 tablespoons all-purpose flour **(23g)**

2 cups whole milk **(480g/ml)**

2 cups (8 ounces) freshly shredded sharp white
Cheddar cheese **(226g)**

1 teaspoon apple cider vinegar

1 teaspoon Dijon mustard

½ teaspoon Worcestershire sauce

½ teaspoon garlic powder

¼ teaspoon smoked paprika

¼ teaspoon salt

⅛ teaspoon freshly ground black pepper

1. Melt the butter in a medium saucepan over medium heat.
Add the flour and whisk constantly until a thick paste forms,
1 to 2 minutes.

2. Whisking constantly as you do so, pour the milk into the
saucepan in a slow, steady stream. Continue whisking until the
mixture thickens, about 5 minutes. It should be thick but still
pourable.

3. Add the cheese and continue to cook, whisking constantly,
until it is melted and smooth. Add the vinegar, mustard,
Worcestershire sauce, garlic powder, paprika, salt, and pepper
and whisk until combined.

4. Transfer the cheese dip to a heat-safe serving dish. The dip
is thin right off the stove but thickens after a few minutes.
Store covered tightly in the refrigerator for up to 3 days.

Acknowledgments

You wouldn't be holding this book if not for the invaluable contributions from the incredible people named on this page. First and foremost, thank you to Kevin, my biggest supporter, most willing taste tester, and the driving force who kept me going, even when I faced overwhelming challenges (like a broken oven and eight recipe fails in a row). Thank you to our children, who consistently remind me why I do this: to have fun!

To my parents, Bruce and Jeanne, and sisters, Saundra and Sarah, for believing in me my entire life and taste-testing my creations (even the bizarre ones!) far more than anyone else.

To my fabulous team at Sally's Baking—Stephanie, Lexi, Trina, and Erin—for their daily support and for keeping the website running as I poured myself into this project. This also includes Allie, James, and my tremendous kitchen team leader and recipe co-writer, Beth, who meticulously analyzed, baked, and tasted every single recipe in this book and carefully made sure we've shared all the information you may need. Her precision, enthusiasm, and unwavering determination are irreplaceable, and I could not have done this without her. Beth, I am so grateful for you and for our friendship.

Deep-felt gratitude to Alison Fargis, my literary agent, who championed my vision from the start and guided me every step of the way.

Thank you to the incredible team at Clarkson Potter. I am extremely lucky to have collaborated with the best of the best, and this includes my encouraging editor, Susan Roxborough, and creative mastermind/art director, Marysarah Quinn. Thank you to Francis Lam for welcoming me into the Clarkson Potter author family!

To my deeply talented, creative, and hardworking prop and food stylists, Giulietta Pinna and Diana Jeffra, aka my Dream Team Extreme, for elevating my photography skills and helping me create my most beautiful book yet. To Danielle Wood and Allison Pynn, for making me look and feel my best on set, even after I got frosting in my freshly styled hair.

To Stronz Vanderploeg and David Flores, my exceptional lifestyle photography team, for capturing my kitchen moments in the best light (literally and figuratively!). Your artistic talents are truly remarkable, and I am grateful for the fundamental photography lessons you have taught me over the years. Working with you both is a dream.

To my talented friends in the food blogging industry, whose invaluable advice and encouragement has kept me inspired and determined.

In addition to my team members, I'd like to thank the following individuals for testing these recipes and providing crucial feedback so everyone can have recipe success: Amanda Yee, Sarah McDoniel, Saundra Reed, Ellie Miller, Amy and Lily Robinson, Ashley McGuirk, Marie Busta, Michelle Bode, Erin Fitzpatrick, Amanda Sabo, Sarah Travers, Jessica Dunn, Patty Koestner, Anna Gavin, Lael Grigg, Meredith Lustig, Caity Lozinak, and Maddy Nilsson.

And finally, to my incredible readers and "Sally's Squad." I would not have the opportunity to do what I do without you. Your support, enthusiasm, and feedback influence and motivate me every day, and together we have built an incredibly special worldwide baking community. Thank you for welcoming me into your kitchens, sharing my recipes, and taking this (delicious!) journey with me. I am forever appreciative. This cookbook is FOR YOU!

COOKIE CREW
COOKIE CREW

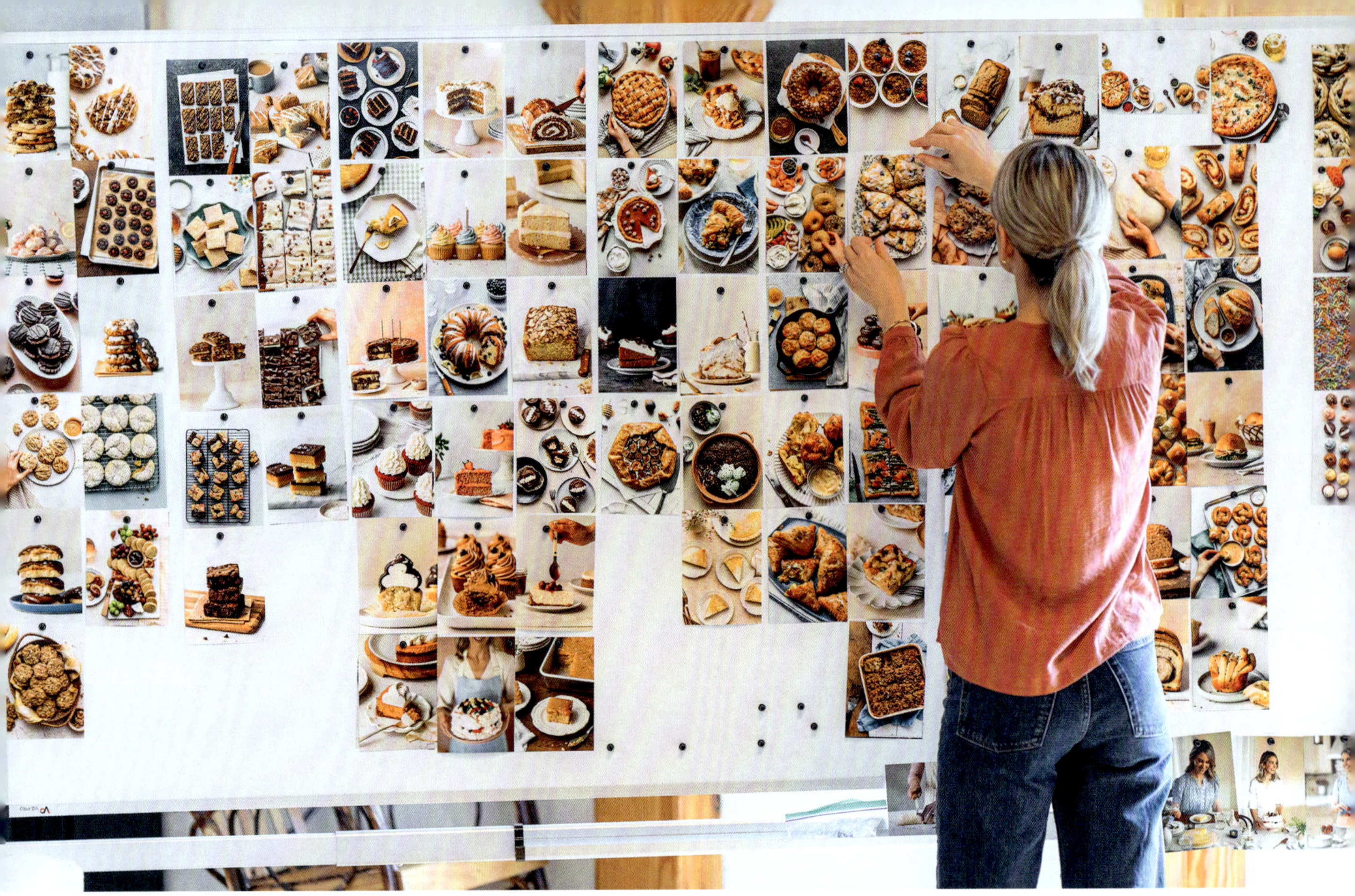

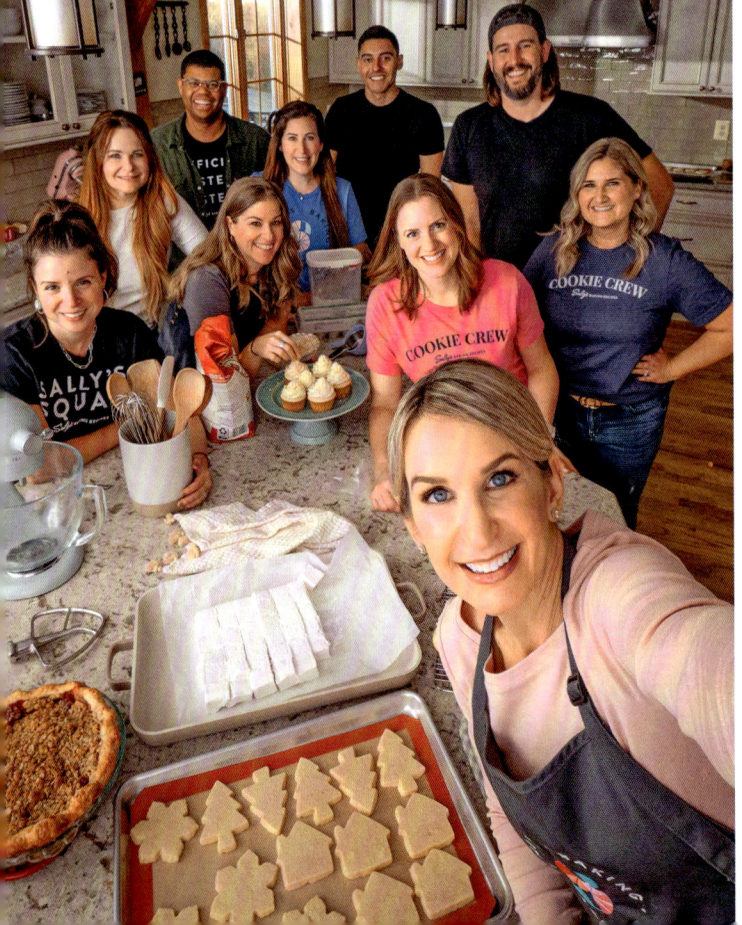

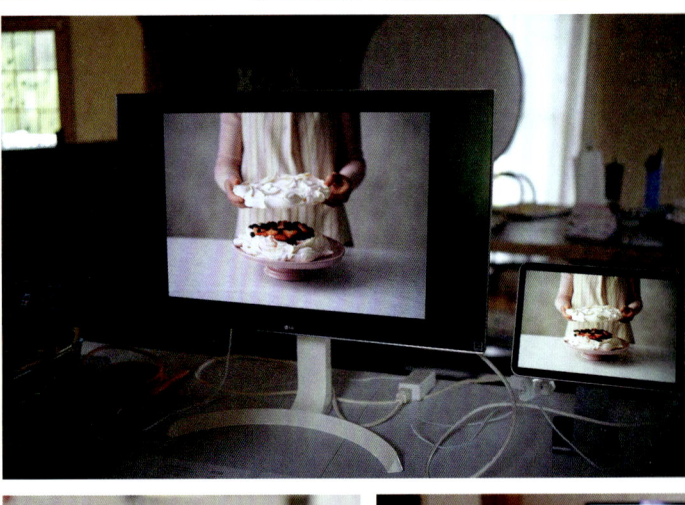

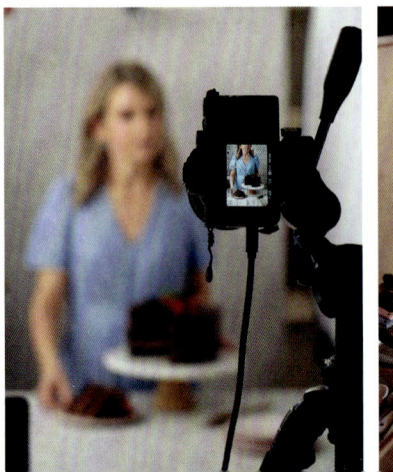

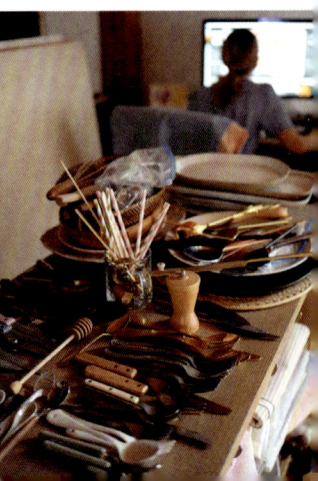

Index

CLARKSON POTTER/PUBLISHERS
An imprint of the Crown Publishing Group
A division of Penguin Random House LLC.
1745 Broadway
New York, NY 10019
clarksonpotter.com
penguinrandomhouse.com

CLARKSON POTTER is a trademark and
POTTER with colophon is a registered
trademark of Penguin Random House LLC.

Portraits of the author on pages 8, 78–79,
130, and 278 by Stronz Vanderploeg.
How-to and process photographs on pages
4, 26, 28, 32, 35, 43, 44, 51, 60, 75, 82–83,
87, 88, 95, 104, 106, 108, 110, 117, 121, 122, 126,
132–133, 134–135, 137, 138, 140, 153, 155, 158,
170–171, 179, 183, 184, 189, 192, 194, 199, 201,
204, 208, 214, 218, 227, 230, 240–241, 242, 244,
247, 249, 251, 252, 256, 259, 262, 268, 270, 272,
276–277, and 282 by Stronz Vanderploeg.

Library of Congress Cataloging-in-
Publication Data
LC record available at https://lccn.loc.
gov/2024032485
LC ebook record available at https://lccn.loc.
gov/2024032486

ISBN 978-0-593-58196-4
Ebook ISBN 978-0-593-58197-1

Manufactured in China

Editor: Susan Roxborough
Editorial assistants: Elaine Hennig and
    Darian Keels
Art Director/Designer: Marysarah Quinn
Production editor: Terry Deal
Production: Jessica Heim
Compositors: Merri Ann Morrell and
    Hannah Hunt
Food stylist: Diana Jeffra
Prop stylist: Giulietta Pinna
Photographers: Sally McKenney
    & Stronz Vanderploeg
Recipe developers: Sally McKenney
    & Beth Walk
Copy editor: Patricia Dailey
Proofreaders: Rachel Markowitz and
    Alissa Fitzgerald
Indexer: Elizabeth T. Parson
Publicist: Natalie Yera-Campbell
Marketer: Andrea Portanova

10 9 8 7 6 5 4 3

First Edition

The authorized representative in the EU for
product safety and compliance is Penguin
Random House Ireland, Morrison Chambers,
32 Nassau Street, Dublin D02 YH68, Ireland,
https://eu-contact.penguin.ie.